Nigel Cawthorne is the author of *Military Commanders* and *Vietnam – A War Lost and Won*. His writing has appeared in over a hundred and fifty newspapers, magazines and partworks – from the *Sun* to the *Financial Times*, and from *Flatbush Life* to *The New York Tribune*. He lives in Chatham, Kent.

Recent titles in the series

A Brief History of Roman Britain
Joan P. Alcock

A Brief History of the Private Life of Elizabeth II
Michael Paterson

A Brief History of France
Cecil Jenkins

A Brief History of Slavery
Jeremy Black

A Brief History of Sherlock Holmes
Nigel Cawthorne

A Brief Guide to Angels and Demons
Sarah Bartlett

A Brief History of How the Industrial Revolution Changed the World
Thomas Crump

A Brief History of King Arthur
Mike Ashley

A Brief History of the Universe
J. P. McEvoy

A Brief Guide to Secret Religions
David Barrett

His Finest Hour: A Brief Life of Winston Churchill
Christopher Catherwood

A Brief History of Witchcraft
Lois Martin

A BRIEF GUIDE TO

JAMES BOND

ROBINSON

RUNNING PRESS
PHILADELPHIA · LONDON

Constable & Robinson Ltd
55–56 Russell Square
London WC1B 4HP
www.constablerobinson.com

First published in the UK by Robinson,
an imprint of Constable & Robinson Ltd, 2012

A copy of the British Library Cataloguing in
Publication data is available from the British Library.

ISBN: 978-1-84901-507-3

1 3 5 7 9 10 8 6 4 2

First published in the United States in 2012 by Running Press Book Publishers,
A Member of the Perseus Books Group

US ISBN 978-0-7624-4628-5
US Library of Congress Control Number: 2011942358

9   8   7   6   5   4   3   2   1
Digit on the right indicates the number of this printing

Running Press Book Publishers
2300 Chestnut Street
Philadelphia, PA 19103-4371

Visit us on the web!
www.runningpress.com

Printed and bound in the UK

Contents

Introduction   vii

1. Ian Fleming   1
2. The Creation of James Bond   28
3. Bond, James Bond   47
4. Bond: The Books   69
5. Bond: The Films   97
6. M and Friends   160
7. Gimmicks, Guns and Gadgets   180
8. The Girls   202
9. The Villains   233
10. Never Say Never Again   263

Further Reading   285

Index   289

Introduction

In the 1950s, Britain was a dowdy place, still recovering from World War II. With Dwight D. Eisenhower in the White House, America was at its most conformist. Then along came a hero like no other. He was definitely on the side of the good guys, but he drank and smoked, and there is no indication that he ever went to church. Even in a foxhole, he was not a man who would say a prayer. The only vespers he knew were a cocktail he had named after his latest sexual conquest.

Bond bedded beautiful women who surrendered without a struggle. He drove fast cars and visited exotic places. He saw off a series of powerful villains and, whatever happened, James Bond could cope with the situation. For me, as a young lad, this was a revelation. Ian Fleming described his James Bond books as the 'pillow of fantasy of an adolescent mind'. They certainly were for me.

Although Bond had been through the war, he did not talk about it. I had already noted in my own family that those who talked about what they had done in the war had not done anything important. Those who remained silent, I discovered, had faced real danger and wanted to forget about it. But more importantly, Bond was part of the new generation – the generation of Elvis and soon the Beatles and John F. Kennedy.

Indeed, when Bond first came to the screen in 1962 with *Dr No*, he wore the same sharp suits as the Kennedys. What's more, JFK was a fan. Despite actor Sean Connery's strong Scottish accent, Bond's persona remained curiously transatlantic. In later movies, he is equally at home in the US and the UK. But who can forget the scene when Ursula Andress emerges from the sea? It is a seminal moment in cinema history.

While the Bond of the books is vulnerable, often injured, prey to nerves, even afraid, and kills sparingly, in the films he is fearless, barely even bleeds, suffers no psychological misgivings, and slaughters on an industrial scale. Yet the two Bonds are the same tough, resourceful, stylish, sardonic, well-brought-up man of-the-world that I, even in my late middle age, seek to emulate – not altogether successfully, it has to be said.

Fleming said that his James Bond books were autobiographical. There are indeed similarities between Fleming and the Bond of the novels – both went to Eton; both saw wartime service in the Royal Navy. Fleming had an inside knowledge of espionage, having served in Naval Intelligence, where he liaised with the Special Operations Executive and MI6, the same Special Intelligence Service that Bond worked for. He knew about the Soviet Union, visiting as a journalist to cover the Metro-Vickers spy trial in 1933 and returning in 1939. He also knew about armed assaults, at command level, from his time with 30 Assault Unit during World War II. He even carried a Beretta. But Fleming never had a licence to kill – let alone the ability to perform James Bond's death-defying feats.

While Fleming did share Bond's love of drinking, fast cars and women, the James Bond of the novels and the films was not Ian Fleming of Goldeneye, his Jamaican home. Bond was a fantasy born out of Britain's post-war austerity, but he went on to become a fantasy the whole word shares.

During Ian Fleming's lifetime, his books sold over thirty million copies. All are still in print and more Bond books have been written by other authors since Fleming's death in 1964. The Bond films are the highest grossing franchise in Hollywood's history. It is estimated that half the population of the world has seen at least one Bond movie as the legendary Cold War warrior now takes on the villains of the post-Cold War world.

Now that another Bond movie has just come to the screen it is, perhaps, a good time to go back and take a good hard look at the character and his creator, and see what Bond tells us about ourselves.

While writing this, I am, of course, sipping a dry martini, shaken, not stirred.

Nigel Cawthorne
Bloomsbury, 2011

1. Ian Fleming

Of his James Bond books, Ian Fleming once said: 'Everything I write has a precedent in truth.' So for the truth about James Bond we should first look at the life of Ian Fleming, the wellspring of 007's creation.

Like James Bond, Fleming was born to a Scottish family. His grandfather, Robert Fleming, was from a poor background in Dundee. As a clerk working in a textile company, he seized the opportunity to represent his firm in the United States. In the aftermath of the Civil War, America was desperately short of capital, so Robert Fleming set up a pioneering investment trust that took the savings of thrifty Dundonians and invested them in American railroads with yields twice that of the stock markets in Edinburgh or London. He was in his twenties when he made his first big railroad deal in 1873.

As a wealthy banker, Robert Fleming crossed the Atlantic more than a hundred times. He married and moved to England, where he bought a large house in London's Grosvenor Square, later demolished to make way for the US embassy, and a run-down estate at Nettlebed in Oxfordshire. He had the seventeenth-century mansion there knocked down to make way for a massive red-brick palazzo with forty-four bedrooms and a dozen bathrooms, but he retained the house's name: Joyce Grove. This was home to family gatherings until Robert died in 1933. Among the frequent visitors was Queen Mary, wife of George V and a friend of Ian's grandmother Katie.

Ian Fleming's father Valentine was born in 1883; his aunts Dorothy and Kathleen in 1885 and 1887; and his uncle Philip in 1889. Valentine and Philip were sent to Eton and Oxford. With a second in history, Valentine read for the Bar but never practised. He missed a rowing blue due to a troublesome boil and listed as his recreations in *Who's Who* 'deerstalking, salmon fishing, fox-hunting...'. After working in his father's bank in the City, Valentine became the Conservative MP for South Oxfordshire in 1910. He was also an officer in the Oxfordshire Yeomanry and used to train his men in the grounds of Joyce Grove.

At the age of twenty-four, Valentine Fleming married Evelyn St Croix Rose at St Paul's church, Knightsbridge. Of mixed Celtic–Huguenot stock, the bride was a society beauty and was later painted several times by Augustus John. The couple moved into Mayfair. They had four boys. The eldest, Peter, excelled at school and went on to become a noted writer and soldier. The second son, Ian, lived in his brother's shadow for most of his life.

Born in 1908, Ian Lancaster Fleming took his middle name from John of Gaunt, who his mother claimed ancestry from. At the outbreak of World War I, he was sent to boarding school. His father wrote; his mother didn't. Then, just eight days before Ian's ninth birthday, his father was killed in action in France. Winston Churchill wrote his obituary in *The Times*.

Fleming did not enjoy his prep school. He followed his older brother to Eton, where he excelled in athletics and rebelled, suffering beatings as a result. A moody child, he made no secret of preferring his own company. He read widely and made his literary debut at Eton, publishing a short story in his own, one-off magazine *The Wyvern*, which also included contributions from his mother's friends, Edwin Lutyens and Vita Sackville-West and her lover Augustus John. The magazine showed some sympathy for Fascism. During the General Strike, Ian helped man the signal box at Leighton Buzzard. Soon after this, he had sex for the first time, on the floor of a box in the Royalty Kinema in Windsor, an experience retold from the woman's point of view in *The Spy Who Loved Me*. To avoid Ian being expelled, his mother decided to send him to the Royal Military College at Sandhurst. But first, he was shipped out to a finishing school for young gentlemen in Kitzbühel in the Austrian Tyrol, where he brushed up his German and spent time skiing, rock climbing and charming young women. By then, his mother, a wealthy widow, had moved into a house in Cheyne Walk that had once belong to the painter Turner. Here she gave birth to a daughter by Augustus John.

In the Sandhurst entrance examination, Ian came sixth in the country. His tutor, Colonel William Trevor, wrote: 'He is an exceptionally nice fellow – manly and sensible beyond his years . . . He ought to make an excellent soldier, provided always that the ladies don't ruin him.'

Among Fleming's intake at Sandhurst was Ayub Khan, who later became president of Pakistan. There Fleming enjoyed shooting, but not the interminable square-bashing and horse riding. He was also taught map reading, tactics and constitutional history. And it was here that he fell in love for the first time: with Peggy Barnard, the pretty daughter of a former Indian Army colonel. He took his amour on fast drives down country lanes, to flashy restaurants and tea dances – though she was not the last woman to complain of his lack of skill on the dance floor. With a private income and a dress uniform, he was a popular escort for debutantes, though he disliked the debs' balls, preferring the informality of jazz clubs. He would stay up all night at the Kit Kat or the Embassy and return to Sandhurst only just in time to make morning parade.

During a fit of jealousy, Fleming had sex with a prostitute in Soho and caught gonorrhoea. His mother booked him into a nursing home for residential treatment. While there, he sent his letter of resignation to Sandhurst and his mother then sent him back to Kitzbühel. There he was in the charge of a former British diplomat and spy, Forbes Dennis, and his American wife, a successful novelist who, as Phyllis Bottome, would publish a novel about a womanizing British Secret Service officer named Mark Chalmers, who bore a striking resemblance to James Bond. Her book, *The Life Line*, was published in 1946, seven years before the first Bond book came out.

Dennis and his wife, devotees of the psychologist Alfred Adler, ran the school where Fleming was to receive intensive tutoring for the Foreign Office entrance exams. Meanwhile he was encouraged to take an interest in European literature and translated a German play into English, which his mother then had printed and bound. In the evening, students entertained each other with tall tales. In Fleming's group, there were two other students who went on to become writers. Ian committed some of his impromptu stories to paper. He also slept with local girls, while writing poems to the sweetheart he had left at home. A collection was printed under the title *The Black Daffodil*, but later he became so embarrassed by his juvenilia that he rounded up every copy and burned them all.

During his time on the Continent, Fleming spoke for the first time of his ambition to write thrillers. He had some thrills of his own. With a passion for fast cars, he once topped a hundred miles an hour on the open road near Joyce Grove. Then in Austria the front of his Standard Tourer was sliced off by a train at a level crossing.

In 1928, Fleming enrolled at Munich University at a time when Hitler was active in the city. He was also sent for psycho-analysis, but refused to say a word. During the vacations he holidayed with the family in Scotland, Ireland and Corsica. Peter's friend Rupert Hart-Davis, who went on to become a publisher, would often come along. Also on hand were a circle of actresses – Peggy Ashcroft, Joyce Grenfell and Celia Johnson, who later became Peter's wife. Ian spent his time playing bridge or swimming as many as five or six times a day.

He moved on to the University of Geneva, where he studied psychology and social anthropology in French. He also learnt Russian. Meanwhile, Percy Muir, a bookseller in Bond Street, sent him titles that might interest him, including the French Surrealist magazine *Transition*. Ian also translated into English a treatise on the Swiss physician Paracelsus by Carl Jung. In his spare time, he played golf, drove a Buick sports car and hung around cafés where he was feared for his caustic wit, though many dismissed him as a playboy. While he could discuss Goethe and Schiller, and recite passages from Thomas Mann, his preferred reading was Georges Simenon. In his summer holiday in 1930, he worked for the League of Nations, which left him sceptical about the usefulness of international bodies. Meanwhile, he developed a passion for Picasso prints and tracked down and bought Mussolini's passport.

Returning to London, Fleming passed his Foreign Office examinations, but was not offered a post. His mother then persuaded him to write to her friend Sir Roderick Jones, head of Reuters, asking for a job. Despite an elementary spelling mistake in the letter, he was taken on to join a coterie of high-flying journalists at the agency. But he still lived at home. When Monique Panchaud, his unofficial fiancée, turned up from Switzerland, his mother cold-shouldered her. Male friends also got short shrift at Mrs Fleming's establishment, while lovers had to be entertained in a workmate's flat. Otherwise life, for Fleming, was not unpleasant. He swam in the International Sportsmen's Club and his correspondence issued from the St James's Club.

Through Sir Roderick, Fleming mixed in high social circles, appearing as a character in a number of novels, including *Public Faces* by Harold Nicolson. Alaric Jacob portrayed him as a well-bred chancer with a Romanian baroness as a mistress, who otherwise had little time for women. According to Jacob, he 'knew all about Stein and Rilke . . . played bridge beautifully and skied like a ghost'.

Fortunately, his employers found him 'accurate, painstaking and methodical'. He also had an instinct for business. In the summer of 1932, he was sent back to Munich, not to cover the antics of Hitler, but to report on the Alpine motor trials where he would navigate for British rally driver Donald Healey. Then in early March 1933 Fleming returned to Switzerland, ostensibly for a skiing holiday with his fiancée, but actually to monitor

German broadcasts concerning the election that was about to bring Hitler untrammelled power.

Through contacts, Fleming broke the story of the Metro-Vickers case: six British engineers working for the company in Russia had been charged with wrecking a large Soviet hydro-electric project. He was then sent to cover the trial, flying to Berlin then taking the train via Warsaw to Moscow. Staying at the National Hotel with the rest of the press corps, he began to file colour pieces. During the trial itself, he dropped his copy from an upstairs window in the court building to a messenger who rushed it to the censor, then to the telegraph office. He also indulged a Bondian taste for vodka and caviar, but complained bad Beluga gave him a tapeworm. Others dismissed it as hypochondria. Fleming was frequently absent from work with migraines caused by a plate that had been placed in his nose following a football accident at Eton. He also suffered from black melancholia.

After being fined in an Oxford court for driving an unlicensed car, Fleming skipped the hearing because he was attending the World Economic Conference. His mother then forced him to break off his engagement, threatening to withdraw her financial support. This brought the threat of a breach-of-promise suit in a Swiss court from his ex-fiancée's parents. Meanwhile, he consoled himself with an older woman, the wife of a merchant banker, the flighty granddaughter of an earl and a number of actresses and entertainers, including a bubble girl named Storm who 'leapt around the stage with very little on'. They made love in the back of his mother's Daimler, leaving the car strewn with black boa feathers.

After being sent to Berlin to cover a plebiscite over rearmament and to interview propaganda minister Joseph Goebbels, Fleming quit Reuters to go into merchant banking. But his time at the news agency had taught him, he said, 'to write fast and, above all, to be accurate'. His change of direction had been precipitated by the death of his grandfather, Robert, who had left Evelyn's children nothing in his will. Fleming's mother now planned to marry again.

With his older brother already an established travel writer, it was now time for Ian to stand on his own two feet – with a little help from family connections in the City, of course.

Fleming showed no aptitude for banking, but he enjoyed the lifestyle with its golfing trips to Gleneagles – via a private train with carriages set aside for gambling and dancing – and visits to the casinos of Le Touquet and Deauville by private plane. He became fascinated by baccarat, a game recently introduced to society by the Prince of Wales, but always played for fairly low stakes. He took up with the daughter of an earl – and this time, Mother approved. But his new girlfriend was shocked at the bad blood between Fleming and his mother, and found Ian 'schizophrenic'.

'He was tough and quite cruel,' she said, 'but at the same time he could be very sentimental. He was an emotional character who was good at suppressing his feelings.'

After a year and a half, Fleming quit banking to become a stockbroker, after taking a short holiday driving around the Continent with the wife of a friend. Though Fleming showed no aptitude for stockbroking either, it brought him more rich and influential friends, and he could lunch his clients at White's or the Savoy. His boss was Lancelot 'Lancy' Hugh Smith, cultivator of royalty and one-time lover of novelist Jean Rhys. Fleming maintained his position, as always, by buttering up older men. Smith had been in intelligence during World War I and his brother was deputy director of Naval Intelligence.

With little else to do, Fleming was put to work on the firm's monthly investment newsletter. He was also employed to write a short history of the company, which was later consigned to the waste-paper bin. Colleagues complained that he was supercilious and did little for the firm. He had, for example, adopted the affectation of smoking custom-made Morland cigarettes blended from three choice Turkish tobaccos.

The company soon sent Fleming on a meet-the-client trip to the United States. Before leaving, he asked a friend at the publisher Chatto & Windus – whose magazine *Night and Day*

Ian had invested in – for contacts among the Greenwich Village set. As a result, he was given a letter of introduction to Bennett Cerf, the proprietor of Random House.

One evening, when staying at the St Regis with a colleague, Fleming excused himself from dinner with a client on the grounds that he was ill. Checking on his health later, the colleague found Fleming in bed with a glass of whiskey and an attractive blonde. Moving on to the Mayflower in Washington, he dined with an old friend from Reuters. The conversation turned to President Roosevelt's foreign policy and the friend got the distinct impression that Ian was snooping for the intelligence services.

Fleming used any money he made from stockbroking to buy antiquarian books, specifically those concerning technical or intellectual progress since 1800. In charge of this enterprise was his old friend Peter Muir, who was also using the book trade to smuggle money out of Germany for Jews who intended leaving the country. Fleming stored his collection in black buckram boxes adorned with the Fleming family crest.

Through Muir, Fleming became a member of the Left Book Club, a pacifist and anti-Fascist group started by the publisher Victor Gollancz. But they quit after less than a year because of the club's increasingly Marxist leanings. Fleming remained a committed anti-Fascist, though. He mixed with people who opposed appeasement, those close to Churchill and others who were secretly charting the rise of German militarism. He was also the treasurer of a committee that arranged a tour of Britain for the psychologist Alfred Adler.

Fleming's mother bought a country home near Joyce Grove, and here she converted the stable, which had once been home to Cromwell's troops, into a library for Peter, making a home for the peripatetic author. Meanwhile Ian had the run of Turner's house as a bachelor pad. Then Peter married the actress Celia Johnson. Mother did not approve – she had wanted him to take a wife from the aristocracy – but Ian talked her round. Then she quit her new house and moved back to

Cheyne Walk. To get away from her, Ian moved into a flat in a converted school in Pimlico, having bought the lease from Oswald Mosley, head of the British Union of Fascists, whose wife, Diana Mitford was a friend of the family. The place was decorated by Rosie Reiss, a young refugee Peter Muir had helped to escape from Germany. The flat was full of avant-garde novels, copies of the *Paris Review* and the Surrealist photographs of Man Ray. Also on display were a framed copy of his father's obituary, Mussolini's passport and silver trophies Ian had won at Eton amid an autobiographic diorama of his life so far. Underneath was a quote, in German, from the eighteenth-century German Romantic poet Novalis: 'We are about to wake up when we dream that we dream.' To complete the household, he had an Irish maid called Mary.

Female guests were entertained with sausages and champagne, and either seduced or repelled by his collection of French pornography. His other visitors were upper-class male friends, including at least one Fascist sympathizer. Another was John Fox-Strangways, whose name Fleming appropriated for that of the Secret Service station chief in the Caribbean in *Live and Let Die* and *Dr No*; he also got a namecheck in *Diamonds are Forever* and *The Man with the Golden Gun*. This circle of friends came to play bridge, a game Fleming did not excel at. At weekends, they played golf. He called them the *Cercle* – short for *Le Cercle gastronomique et des jeux hazard*.

After breaking off his engagement, Fleming boasted that he was going to be 'quite bloody minded about women from now on', claiming to be 'without any scruples at all'. Women found him, if good-looking, vain and supercilious – 'a man with sex on the brain'. Nevertheless, he managed to surround himself with the type of fresh-faced *ingénues* who would be the model for his Bond girls. The brother of one of them turned up on his doorstep with a horsewhip.

Embarrassed at being a stockbroker and still feeling that he was playing second fiddle to his brother Peter, Fleming began to talk again about writing a thriller whose villain would snort

Benzedrine, as he did himself. His model at the time was Geoffrey Household's *The Third Hour*. Household's typical hero is an Englishman with a highly developed sense of honour. Another favourite was *Three Weeks* by Elinor Glyn, the story of a torrid affair where the woman makes the running. However, no one thought that he would get round to writing a novel himself, believing that he needed the discipline of office life to get anything done.

During a visit to the International Surrealist Exhibition in London in 1936, Fleming suffered appendicitis. After an appendectomy, paid for by his mother, he convalesced with friends on Capri in Fascist Italy, where he had a brief affair with a Hungarian countess. Another girlfriend gave him a cigarette case that looked as if it was made of gunmetal – like James Bond's. In fact, it was made of oxidized gold.

As part of the country house set, Fleming rubbed shoulders with a mixture of people – those who were helping Jews who were fleeing Germany, appeasers, politicians, diplomats and spies. And on his regular trips through Germany and Austria he kept his eyes and ears open for information. Although Fleming stood up for democracy against what he called the 'younger and more exciting creeds, such as Fascism and Communism', on his one visit to the House of Commons, he found the debate there hollow and infantile.

In the social round, Ian met Ann Charteris, a friend of Somerset Maugham and Evelyn Waugh. Her marriage to Lord O'Neill had broken down and she was having an affair with Esmond Harmsworth, son of the newspaper proprietor Lord Rothermere. Her friends called Fleming 'Glamour Boy', but Ann found his moody good looks appealing and soon went to bed with him.

He declined an offer to take a trip around the Balkans with her in May 1939. Instead, he intended to return to Moscow; with war looming, he wanted to get more involved in intelligence work. Already his brother Peter was working part-time for Military Intelligence. With Peter's help, he was taken on by

The Times to cover a British trade mission to the Soviet Union, where he bedded a young lady from Odessa. He brought back Russian condoms made from artificial latex so that industrial analysts could judge the state of Soviet manufacturing. Otherwise, an article he wrote on the state of the Soviet Union's armed forces was rejected by *The Times*. Instead, he sent it to a friend at the Foreign Office. They called him in. Soon after, Fleming made another trip to the Continent, where he had a one-night stand with the actress Diana Napier in a wagon-lit, a scene revisited in *From Russia with Love*.

This freelance spying had done him no harm. Back in London, he was taken to lunch in the Carlton Grill by Admiral John Godfrey, director of Naval Intelligence. After a brief trial, Fleming was taken on as Godfrey's deputy and given a commission in the Royal Naval Volunteer Reserve. He appeared for dinner at the O'Neills' in his naval uniform on 4 September, the first day of the war, only to be teased by his friends. However, for once in his life, what he was doing was deadly serious. At Room 39 in the Admiralty and in Operational Intelligence Centre deep below Whitehall, he worked plotting German shipping movements from the intercepted signals being decoded at Bletchley Park. Fleming's Section 17 formulated strategy and briefed Winston Churchill, initially when he was First Lord of the Admiralty and, later, as prime minister. Commander Fleming occupied a desk outside Admiral Godfrey's green baize door and liaised with the other secret services, often via meetings at White's. It seems that Fleming had, at last, found his métier. He worked long hours, starting at six in the morning – two and a half hours before his boss – and stretching long into the night. Part of his job was to liaise with the heavily censored press. As a result he got to know Lord Kemsley, owner of the *Sunday Times*.

He also got to know the Australian pilot Sydney Cotton who undertook photo-reconnaissance work for the department. Cotton was an amateur inventor who came up with novel solutions for technical problems, along the lines of Q. Together they encouraged the use of radar, then in its infancy.

Peter Fleming was now working for Military Intelligence's dirty tricks department MI(R). With his old journalist colleague Sefton Delmer, Ian began dreaming up dirty tricks too – producing Reichsmark coins with propaganda on the rear, forging German banknotes to sabotage the currency, making black propaganda broadcasts, spreading morale-sapping rumours and devising a plot to entrap German secret agents after two SIS – Secret Intelligence Service – men had been grabbed in the Netherlands. Fleming also set a up scheme to buy up German shipping docked in Spanish ports so that it could not be used by the enemy. And he oversaw a plan to scuttle barges full of cement at the narrowest point of the Danube to deny Germany petrol from the Romanian oilfields. The plan went wrong, but the department's agent Merlin Minshall escaped, in true James Bond style, on a high-speed Air Sea Rescue launch, then over the border to Trieste. However, the botched operation delivered the Nazis a propaganda coup and the Foreign Office was furious.

If Minshall was a prototype Bond, there were others who could have served as a model too. The rugged Michael Mason, an accomplished boxer, was also involved in the Danube barge affair. When two Nazi agents were sent to assassinate him he killed them both. Then there was Commander Alexander 'Sandy' Glen, an alumnus of Fettes like Bond who, while naval attaché in Belgrade, seduced the wife of a Belgian diplomat; and Commander Wilfred 'Biffy' Dunderdale, the immaculately dressed SIS station chief in Paris. Wearing Cartier cuff-links and handmade suits, he drove a bulletproof Rolls-Royce. Dunderdale had pulled off the biggest intelligence coups of the war. He had learnt of the Polish progress towards breaking the German Enigma code and sent plans of the 'bombe' used to decipher the code and two Polish copies of the Enigma machine to London.

Meanwhile, Fleming's brother Peter made his first foray into light fiction with *The Flying Visit*, which concerns Hitler's unplanned arrival in England after his plane had been shot down while the *Führer* was observing a bombing raid. When Hitler's deputy Rudolf Hess mysteriously turned up in Scotland in May 1941, Peter appeared chillingly prescient. Peter had also seen action in Norway – even reported killed in action at one point – before taking a post parallel to Ian's as assistant to the director of Military Intelligence. Together they spent Whitsun weekend in Southend after intelligence had been received that the Germans were planning a raid.

Ian then became a field agent himself. When SIS pulled out of Paris, he flew in, sustaining his two-week secondment with cash that SIS kept in the offices of Rolls-Royce in Paris. It was here that Fleming made his first contact with the Deuxième Bureau, which features regularly in the Bond novels. As the Germans closed in on Paris, Fleming headed to Tours, temporary home to the French Ministry of Marine. His mission was to find out from Navy Minister François Darlan what would happen to the French Navy in the event of an armistice.

Next Fleming went to Bordeaux, where he arranged shipping to carry fleeing Britons and other refugees to England. While SIS agents and British diplomatic staff headed home, Fleming moved on to Lisbon. From there, he was to fly to Madrid to liaise with the British naval attaché. However, the only airline flying that route was the German airline, Lufthansa, and they refused to take him. Fleming insisted. As a commercial airline, they were obliged to take him anywhere they flew to, provided he could pay for the ticket.

Fleming returned to Room 39 with his reputation enhanced. But now that German U-boats were sailing from ports along the west coast of France, Naval Intelligence had no more time for dirty tricks. However, Fleming would keep in touch with clandestine operations as liaison officer with the newly formed Special Operations Executive, whose job, Churchill said, was to 'set Europe ablaze'. He also liaised with Robert Bruce Lockhart, who later headed the Political Warfare Executive; and Fitzroy Maclean, who fought alongside Tito in Yugoslavia; the Free French and the Norwegians who sent agents via the 'Shetland bus' service across the North Sea into Scandinavia.

Fleming also took an interest in gadgets. With gunsmith Robert Churchill, he developed a gas pistol disguised as a fountain pen. Bomb-maker and dirty-tricks expert Lord Suffolk taught him how to kill a man by biting the back of his neck, and Charles Fraser-Smith at the Ministry of Supply showed him shoelaces that acted as saws, shaving brushes with secret compartments and hollowed-out golf balls. These would make their appearance in *Diamonds are Forever*, where they are used to carry uncut stones. Fraser-Smith was the model for Major Boothroyd, the departmental armourer in *Dr No*, a character that was developed into Q in the films. Fleming also liaised with William 'Wild Bill' Donovan – the World War I Medal-of-Honor winner who was to set up the US Office of Strategic Services, which later became the CIA – when he made a fact-finding trip to England.

Friends were found jobs at Bletchley Park, the Operational Intelligence Centre, where enemy submarines were tracked, or the 'secret navy' that landed agents in occupied Europe. But although Bletchley Park had cracked the codes used by the German army, air force and intelligence service – the *Abwehr* – it had not broken those used by the German Navy, or *Kriegsmarine*. So Fleming devised Operation Ruthless. A captured Heinkel would be ditched in the Channel. When its crew were picked up by a German vessel, they would kill the boat's crew and steal its code books. Fleming pencilled in his own name as one of the German-speaking Heinkel crew, but he was not allowed to go on the mission. Naval Intelligence could not risk his capture – he knew too much. Ian assembled the team in Dover but, in the end, the operation was cancelled either because there were no suitable German vessels plying the Channel or because the crew would probably have drowned before they could get out of the ditched plane.

Disappointed, Ian continued his social round in London, bedding women and dining out with friends who now included Prince Bernhard of the Netherlands and Martha Huysmans, the daughter of the Belgian prime minister. On three occasions he was lucky to escape death during the Blitz when the place he was dining was hit by a bomb. Fleming and his set rarely retreated to the air-raid shelter. Then came the news that his younger brother Michael was missing in action, then a PoW though wounded, then dead.

Ian was sent back to Lisbon and Madrid on Operation Golden Eye, a sabotage operation to prevent the Germans from entering Spain and threatening Gibraltar. 'Wild Bill' Donovan was making a trip around British facilities in the Mediterranean at the time and it was vital to convince him that Britain would not capitulate.

In May 1941, Ian and Admiral Godfrey flew to the US to see Donovan again and co-ordinate intelligence matters between the two countries. On the way, they stopped at Bermuda where Ian lost money to some Portuguese businessmen at the tables. As he was leaving the casino, he turned to Godfrey and said: 'What if those men had been German secret service agents, and suppose we had cleaned them out of their money? Now that would have been exciting.'

The scene would be recalled in *Casino Royale*. However, there may have been some other origins for the tale. Ralph Izzard, another member of Naval Intelligence, told Ian about the time he played roulette with expatriate Nazis in Lisbon while en route to South America on a wartime mission. Then there was Dusko Popov, the Yugoslav playboy and MI5 double agent in the *Abwehr* that many people think James Bond is based on, who passed messages by the numbers he bet on in the Casino in Estoril. Once Popov was gambling in Lisbon when he was annoyed by a Lithuanian who would call '*Banque ouverte*' every time he held the bank, indicating there was no upper limit. Popov pulled out $30,000, which belonged to MI5. The Lithuanian blanched and declined the bet. Popov put the money back in his pocket and walked away. This incident became part of the Popov legend. Fleming would have known about it and it was possibly the inspiration behind some of Bond's gambling antics. Popov was also a legendary womanizer. His disinformation operation was called 'Tricycle' because of his fondness for taking two women to bed at the same time and he had a celebrated affair with French actress Simone Simon. In August 1941, Popov discovered that the Japanese were preparing to attack Pearl Harbor. He informed the FBI. But bureau chief J. Edgar Hoover discovered that Popov had taken a woman with him from New York to Florida and threatened to have him arrested under the Mann Act if he did not leave the US immediately.

When asked whether he was the inspiration for James Bond, Popov was dismissive. 'I doubt whether a flesh-and-blood Bond would last forty-eight hours as a spy,' he said.

In Washington, Fleming and Godfrey were given a curt tour of the FBI facilities – and the brush-off by Hoover, who was notoriously anti-British. Moving on to New York, they met William Stephenson, whose British Security Coordination Office in Rockefeller Center ran all British intelligence in the western hemisphere. A decorated fighter-pilot in World War I and European lightweight amateur boxing champion, Stephenson was a millionaire by the time he was thirty, having invented a way to transmit photographs by radio. Fleming was fascinated by Stephenson's operation in New York and his secret Station M in Canada which produced technical gadgets and forged documents.

Fleming joined Stephenson on a mission. The Japanese Consulate was on the floor below Stephenson's office and a cipher clerk there was sending coded messages back to Tokyo by shortwave radio. His movements were studied by Stephenson, who had duplicate keys prepared. At three in the morning, they broke into the consulate, microfilmed the code books and returned them to the safe. In *Casino Royale*, Bond said that he earned his double-O number after killing a cipher expert in the Rockefeller Center.

Stephenson lent another element to the mix. According to Fleming, Stephenson mixed the largest dry martinis in America and served them in quart glasses. In a letter to the *Sunday Times* in 1962, Fleming said: 'James Bond is a highly romanticized version of a true spy. The real thing is . . . William Stephenson.'

Stephenson even had a plan to get his hands on three million dollars in gold, which belonged to the Vichy government and was held on the Caribbean island of Martinique. his may have helped inspire *Goldfinger*. The plan never came to fruition.

Godfrey dined with President Roosevelt, presenting the final arguments that the Americans set up a centralized intelligence agency under Donovan. His job done, he left Ian in Washington to help draw up proposals for this new agency. To express his gratitude, Donovan gave Fleming a .38 Police Positive Colt, inscribed: 'For Special Services.'

On his way back to England, Fleming stopped off in Tangiers, where he and the local Golden Eye representative got drunk and broke into a bullring where they marked out a twenty-foot V for victory.

Ian then attempted to get himself posted to Moscow, but was blocked by the head of the Military Mission there. Instead, he began working with the Political Warfare Executive (PWE). He made broadcasts in German, telling the *Kriegsmarine* their U-boats leaked. He also supplied debriefs of captured U-boat crew to Sefton Delmer, now head of PWE, who used details in his black propaganda broadcasts put out on bogus German radio stations the PWE had set up. Also on the staff were Robert Harling, who Fleming knew from publishing circles before the war, and the thriller-writer Dennis Wheatley. Ever the gentleman, Ian also took captured German naval officers out for drinks in the hope of pumping them for information.

Fleming and his various girlfriends made the best of the privations of the war. Although he complained that the Savoy was now making martinis out of bathtub gin and sherry, he could still get his Morland Specials – with three bands to denote his rank as commander – upping his order to four hundred a week. He went to great lengths to obtain other luxuries. His mistress, Ann O'Neill, said that Ian could stand anything except discomfort.

Fleming had thought the war was as good as over when the United States entered in December 1941. He became rapidly disillusioned. When Singapore fell two months later, he blamed it on the fact that the British Army no longer shot deserters. Then he began to complain about Donovan – and even Stephenson. Fleming wanted more action. He had noticed that during the German invasion of Crete a special intelligence unit had gone in with the frontline troops to seize documents before the defenders could destroy them. He asked divisional directors in the Admiralty what materials they would have wanted in such circumstances. Soon he had a shopping list. A unit of what Fleming called 'Red Indians' was set up, operating out of Room 30 at the Admiralty. Unfortunately, the first action it took part in was the disastrous raid on Dieppe in August 1942. Fleming was allowed to go along as an observer, though he was not allowed to land. Again, he was considered too valuable to risk capture. He took delight in seeing the casino on the front being destroyed by naval shell fire. His ship was also hit by a shell and was forced to return to England. Ian wrote up the raid for the department's Weekly Intelligence Report, putting as favourable gloss on it as possible under the circumstances.

Ian and Godfrey headed off to the US to liaise with the now full-fledged OSS, though on the eve of their departure Godfrey was sacked as director of Naval Intelligence. In New York, Ian was introduced to Walter Winchell, king of gossip journalists, before moving on to Jamaica for an Anglo-American naval conference. He travelled by train to Miami, along the line taken by James Bond with Solitaire in *Live and Let Die*. In Jamaica, Fleming lodged with his old school friend Ivar Bryce in a house where Ian's hero Lord Nelson had stayed as a young man. On his flight back to Washington, Ian announced: 'When we have won this blasted war, I am going to live in Jamaica . . . and swim in the sea and write books.'

Back in London, Fleming heard from his Golden Eye operation that miniature submarines had tried to attack British aircraft carriers in the harbour at Gibraltar. They had been delivered to

Algeciras Bay by a tanker and deployed through a trapdoor in the bottom: the idea would be used in *Thunderball*.

Back in England, Fleming oversaw the training of his new intelligence force, now known as 30 Advanced Unit, which accompanied the Anglo-American landings in Algeria and Morocco that November. During the operation, Admiral Darlan was murdered. He had been set up by the SIS.

Fleming was involved in Operation Mincemeat – the inspiration behind the book and film *The Man Who Never Was* – where a body was washed up on the shores of Spain carrying documents indicating that the next Allied landings would be in Greece and Sardinia, rather than Sicily where they actually took place. He also maintained his contacts in the City and crossed the Atlantic twice more, to attend summits between Churchill and Roosevelt. On one occasion he met his brother Peter, who had been posted to India and was making a pitch to run all deception operations in the Pacific.

During the Quebec Conference of August 1943, Fleming visited Stephenson's Camp X in Canada, where SOE and OSS agents were taught the rudiments of their craft. It seems that Ian was not allowed to participate, but Camp X seems to be where James Bond learnt his stuff.

Next Fleming went to the Churchill–Roosevelt conference in Cairo. On the flight, he travelled with Joan Bright, a woman he had got a job for at SIS; he had been seeing her for about a year, and amused her with his stories.

In the run-up to D-Day, Fleming liaised with Lieutenant Alan Schneider of US Naval Intelligence. Schneider was also drafted in to help when Ian got more involved than he intended with an attractive captain in the US Women's Army Corps. Ian explained: 'Women are like pets, like dogs; men are the only real human beings you could be friends with.' However, when a long-term girlfriend he had treated abominably was killed in an air raid, Ian was visibly shaken and carried her bracelet on his key ring from then on.

At the time, Fleming was running a special committee

channelling information from Bletchley Park to the naval side of Operation Overlord, the D-Day landings. He also went to visit 30AU in North Africa and took a shooting trip to the Atlas Mountains with the British minister Duff Cooper. Fleming's 'Red Indians' had now swelled to three hundred men. There was a core of trained intelligence officers with a large force of Royal Marines to protect them. When they were returned to England in preparation for the Normandy landings, Fleming spent his time compiling lists of German equipment to be captured. Then a week before D-Day, he held a dinner at the Gargoyle club for the unit's officers and their wives and girlfriends.

In Normandy, the now-renamed 30 Assault Unit fought hard and produced results. However, they had a bad reputation when it came to drink and women, prompting Admiral Cunningham to dub them 30 Indecent Assault Unit. They did not take it too kindly when their well-tailored commander crossed the Channel to tell them off and deliberately put Fleming in the way of German fire. Nor was Fleming popular with General Patton, who was in overall command of that sector. He did not like sailors. After Patton had inspected the vast V-2 installations the Allies had uncovered, Fleming was invited to have lunch him. He ducked out. Instead he went for a picnic with Robert Harling, who asked him what he was going to do after the war. Ian's reply was that he would write 'the spy story to end all spy stories'.

After the liberation of Paris, 30AU returned to England for further training, ready for the invasion of Germany. Ian was visiting Ann at the home of her other lover Esmond Harmsworth, now Lord Rothermere, when a telegram arrived telling her that her husband, Lord O'Neill, had been killed in Italy. Ian was sympathetic and thoughtfully handled the practicalities concerning the children.

Fleming volunteered to review the intelligence infrastructure of the newly created Pacific Fleet. He headed for Cairo, then Ceylon (now Sri Lanka). In Colombo, he met a Wren named Clare Blanshard and told her that he never intended to spend another winter in England. He then travelled on to Australia, and returned to England by way of Pearl Harbor.

By this time, 30AU were entering Germany and Fleming was drawing up lists of new German inventions the unit was to capture. These included a jet-powered hydrofoil and 'Cleopatra', an amphibious device that blew up beach defences. Another item on the list was a one-man submarine. Admiral Ramsay, now in overall command, doubted that such a thing existed. When one was found beached near Ostend Ramsay was still sceptical, so the midget submarine was put on a tank transporter and sent round to him.

'The thing's a toy,' said Ramsay. But when he looked down the periscope, he could see the eye of a dead German who had been drowned when the mini-sub had foundered.

The men of 30AU captured not only a boat designed to run on hydrogen peroxide, but the torpedo experimental station at Eckernforder and the entire German Navy's Warfare Science Department. Fleming went personally to seize the German naval archives dating back to 1870 and stopped them being torched. He had them shipped back to London, along with an elderly admiral to edit them. Fleming's final signal to his unit was: 'Find immediately the twelve top German naval commanders and make each one write ten thousand words on why Germany lost the war.'

At a party celebrating the closing down of Sefton Delmer's black-propaganda radio stations, Ian was spotted doodling on Admiralty blotting paper. Asked what he was doing, he said he was designing the house he would live in on Jamaica. It was now common knowledge that he intended to write a book. It would be just like making salad dressing, he said. All you needed were the right ingredients in the right quantities.

Indeed, some of the essential ingredients were already in place. One evening in a pub in Westminster in 1943, C.H. Forster from the Ministry of Aircraft Production had been introduced to Lieutenant-Commander Fleming. During their discussion Forster said that Fleming had asked him what his call-up number was. Forster replied that he had been a 'Bevin Boy', conscripted to work in the mines, and had been given DMZ 7 – his lucky number – by the Ministry of Labour.

'This caused Fleming some thought,' said Forster. 'Another gentleman nearby agreed that it could not be a War Department number. That would have had eight digits, such as 10,000,007, which a telephone operation would describe as one treble oh treble oh double oh seven.'

Fleming liked the sound of this and asked if he could use it for a book he was writing.

'I agreed that he could,' said Forster, 'especially as 007 had no traceable value, but sounded impressive and secretive. I also asked how he invented names of this characters.'

'That's easy,' said Fleming. 'I take the first couple of names from my house at school and swap their Christian names.'

'In my case, they were James Aitken and Harry Bond,' said Forster. 'So you would have Harry Aitken and James Bond. Fleming's face lit up. James Bond 007 was born.'

During a stroll in Hyde Park in 1945, Fleming's long-term lover Ann O'Neill told him that she was going to marry Lord Rothermere. Ian was unperturbed. He would live just around the corner from their London house in a new flat in Montagu Square. There were other women, of course, but the affair continued while Ian maintained Lord Rothermere as a friend.

After the war, Lord Kemsley offered Fleming a generous salary to be the foreign manager of his newspaper group. He would have been made foreign editor, but did not want the responsibility of writing the occasional think piece. Kemsley allowed him two months' holiday a year to work on his putative novel. By the end of 1945, Fleming was on his way to Jamaica to start building his new house. It would be called Goldeneye after the wartime operation. The site Ivar Bryce found for him was on the north coast just outside the town of Oracabessa – 'Golden Head' in Spanish. There he would swim among the brightly coloured fishes and spear a lobster for his dinner.

The newly knighted Sir William Stephenson also moved to the island. At the time, he and William Donovan, along with other former spooks, were running a front company that bartered goods in developing countries. Stephenson also introduced Fleming to Lord Beaverbrook, the owner of the *Daily Express* and another resident. Ian was also friendly with Thomas and Marion Leiter, who lent their surname to James Bond's CIA sidekick.

Ian continued his womanizing ways and Marion Leiter chastised him for his treatment of her friend Millicent Rogers.

'Mr Fleming,' she said, 'I consider you a cad.'

'You're quite right,' he replied. 'Shall we have a drink on it?'

Travelling back to England on the *Queen Mary* the following spring, Fleming was introduced to Winston Churchill, who made it plain that he would rather have been meeting Peter than Ian.

Many found Fleming's love of gadgetry faintly ludicrous. Back in his office at the *Sunday Times*, he had a large map of the world installed with flashing lights indicating the presence of Kemsley's eighty or so correspondents. Many of the correspondents he took on were spies, or former spies. Reports sent back were often not for publication and were passed on to the intelligence services. Fleming even ran one Far East correspondent, a hard-drinking Australian, as a double agent for the SIS, after the KGB had approached him. Otherwise, reporters were told to inject more 'brightness and champagne' into their stories to cheer up a Britain that was now undergoing a period of austerity after the war.

When Ann took off to New York on the *Queen Elizabeth* with her new husband, Ian grew jealous. Learning that Rothermere was travelling on to Canada, Ian flew over to New York and spent four nights in the Plaza Hotel with her. During the trip, he suffered pains in the chest. He consulted a doctor and was told to cut down on his smoking and drinking: at the time, he was getting through seventy cigarettes and a bottle of gin a day. On another occasion he was seen to be bruised and hinted at a sadomasochistic element to the relationship. In her letters, Ann admitted to enjoying being whipped by him.

On Jamaica, Goldeneye began to take shape. A concrete construction, it was initially compared to a district commissioner's residence. Noël Coward, later a neighbour, once referred to it as the 'Golden eye, nose and throat clinic'. Fleming took on staff, including a housekeeper who would stay on at Goldeneye for the next seventeen years. When friends visited, they swam naked in the warm sea. Ian was full of stories of diving on the reef there. Evenings were spent partying with other denizens of the upmarket resort the north shore of Jamaica had become, where everyone seemed to know about his relationship with Lady Rothermere. He wrote a piece about north-shore society for *Horizon* magazine, whose editor Cyril Connolly became a friend.

In London, when the Rothermeres moved house, Ian moved too to be near Ann, at the same time taking on a succession of pretty au pairs. He would spend his evenings at Boodle's or dining innocently with the Rothermeres. However, whenever Esmond was away at the office, Ian found himself in Ann's bedroom. Meanwhile he maintained a string of other female acquaintances, continuing the search for his perfect woman who, he said, was 'thirtyish, Jewish, a companion who would not need an education . . . would aim to please, have firm flesh and kind eyes'. But Ian and Ann still spent what time they could together and Ann even found an excuse to visit him in Jamaica. She was an amateur naturalist and Ian bought a *Field Guide to the Birds of the West Indies* to amuse her. It was written by an obscure American academic named James Bond.

After Ann left, Ian went shark hunting, dragging the carcasses of a cow and a donkey out to sea as bait. It was, he said, the most thrilling thing he had done in his life and was, perhaps, the inspiration for the climax of the novel *Live and Let Die*. The writers Rosamond Lehmann and Elsa Maxwell came to stay. Noël Coward rented Goldeneye when Ian was away and wrote a song about his stay. In London, Fleming mixed with literary luminaries such as Osbert and Edith Sitwell, T.S. Eliot, the biographer Peter Quennell, the academic Maurice Bowra and South African novelist, poet and librettist William Plomer, who later edited some of Fleming's novels.

In 1948, Ann fell pregnant with Ian's child. She miscarried but, with her husband around, Ian could not be on hand to console her. However, his thoughtful letters convinced Ann that she loved him. In reply, she urged him to write the book he was always talking about. At the time, he had dreamed up a crime story where the murder weapon was a frozen leg of lamb which was disposed of by being cooked and eaten. Roald Dahl, who knew Fleming from the war, used this plot for his 1952 story 'Lamb to the Slaughter'.

In the wake of the miscarriage, there was no hiding Ian's relationship with Ann. Rothermere contacted Lord Kemsley, who duly upbraided his foreign manager on his ungentlemanly behaviour. Nevertheless, the affair continued and Fleming and the Rothermeres went on mixing in the same social circles, though tensions ran high.

When Ian next visited Jamaica, Ann went with him, though to keep appearances she said she was staying with Noël Coward at his new house, Blue Harbour. They began to talk about marriage. When they returned to England, Ann received an ultimatum from Rothermere – she must stop seeing Ian or he would divorce her. She ignored this and, in the summer of 1949, they rented a cottage near Royal St George's golf club in Kent from thriller writer Eric Ambler. Here Ann surrounded them with her literary friends. However, while Ann remained a socialite, Ian preferred his own company.

Fleming began to show signs of ill health, perhaps brought on by the stress of living with Ann and in her milieu. Doctors again advised he cut down on his drinking. That Christmas he went alone to Jamaica where he began a study of the sea life. Ann threw herself into the social whirl on the Continent, writing that she missed Ian and whipping him.

At the *Sunday Times* he did not go to the pub with his colleagues, but rather lunched at his club with friends. With

Britain now coming off rationing, he introduced the food columnist of an American magazine to the readers of the *Daily Graphic*. He got his friend Stephen Potter's book *Gamesmanship* reviewed by the *Sunday Times*, but rejected Fitzroy Maclean's book *Eastern Approaches* for serialization. Fleming also became a director of Dropmore Press, a Kemsley subsidiary, and worked as a commissioning editor. One of the company's titles was *Book Handbook*, aimed at fellow bibliophiles.

The devaluation of the pound in 1949 hit Fleming's foreign news operation. It was also noted that his idea of foreign news came from lifestyle magazines such as *Life* and *Paris Match*, rather than *The New York Times* or *Le Monde*. Nevertheless, at the height of the Cold War, he strove to obtain a visa for a permanent correspondent in Moscow for the *Sunday Times*, the only newspaper in the Commonwealth to get one, then sent wine writer and connoisseur Cyril Ray. He also started a magazine on typography and design, set a literary competition for the *Spectator* and wrote a speech for Princess – soon to be Queen – Elizabeth to give to the American press. It was not used. Meanwhile he kept up his contacts with SIS.

Searching for a larger place where he could live with Ann, Ian took a flat in the block in Chelsea where T.S. Eliot lived. Every July he did two weeks' naval training, allowing him to retain his rank a commander in the Royal Naval Volunteer Reserve. Afterwards, in the summer of 1950, he went to stay with Ivar Bryce for the first time in the Green Mountains of Vermont where, later, *For Your Eyes Only* and *The Spy Who Loved Me* would be set. He was to return to Vermont nearly every summer.

Meanwhile, others in his family decamped to the Caribbean. Peter spent time in Barbados, while his mother moved to the Bahamas. The following spring Rosamond Lehmann arrived at Goldeneye. Having just finished a nine-year affair with Cecil Day Lewis, she was intent on bedding Ian. He had the same thing in mind, but Ann was there and he had to palm Rosamond off on Noël Coward, which must have been frustrating for both of them.

By the summer of 1951, while talk was of the defection of the

Cambridge spies, Guy Burgess and Donald Maclean, the Rothermeres agreed to a divorce. Ann was pregnant again and she and Ian decided to marry. Friends and family were aghast, believing Ian not to be the marrying type and that Ann had become pregnant to ensnare him.

They retired to Jamaica where they intended to marry and Ian, finally, began to write the thriller he had been talking about for so long. For three hours in the morning, he pounded his twenty-year-old Imperial portable typewriter. Then, around five, after an afternoon nap, he read through what he had written. It was a routine he would follow the next twelve years, whenever he was at Goldeneye.

2. The Creation of James Bond

Fleming's biographer John Pearson says that James Bond was born on 15 January 1952. However, Ann later said that Ian did not start writing the first Bond book, *Casino Royale*, until after dining with Noël Coward, who only arrived in Jamaica on 16 February. The book was finished on 18 March. This would mean that he finished the 62,000-word novel in just four weeks, at the astonishing speed of over two thousand words a day.

Fleming maintained that he wrote *Casino Royale* to take his mind off his forthcoming marriage, which annoyed Ann, particularly as the final words of the novel are: 'The bitch is dead now.' However, another motive may have been sibling rivalry. That year, Peter Fleming published *The Sixth Column*, a novel about the secret service with a Bond-style hero named Colonel Hackforth. The book was dedicated to Ian, but that must have rankled. After all, Ian had long been talking about writing a thriller and must have considered this his territory. With a child on the way, he also needed money; and he had to support a new wife who had previously been married to a wealthy press baron. He also needed some way to divert his energies. As Ann had already lost one child, she was not about to risk losing another by having sex. Still, she was on hand to give him the support he needed to get down to work. Ian and Ann married just six days after *Casino Royale* was finished. They celebrated at Noël Coward's house with dry martinis. Then they honeymooned in Nassau and New York.

Back in London, Fleming had to get used to living not only with Ann, but also with her two children from her first marriage, now teenagers, plus a parrot called Jackie. Yet although he was worried about how he was going to support this menagerie, along with an extravagant wife, he bought himself a wedding present – and a reward for finishing the novel: a gold-plated Royal typewriter which he had shipped over from New York. He joked that, in future, he would write on vellum provided by his 'personal goatherds in Morocco', studded with diamonds from Cartier. For ink, he would use his own blood. Clearly, he believed *Casino Royale* marked him out as a 'writer of distinction'. However, it was not until 12 May that he mentioned that he had written a book to his friend William Plomer, a literary adviser at Jonathan Cape, and promised to send him the manuscript. Two months later, Plomer had to remind him. Only then did he actually send it. Ian was still protesting that he was intending to make revisions on his return to Jamaica the following spring, when Plomer sent it to a fellow reader at Cape, who also like it. Jonathan Cape himself rejected it and was only persuaded to publish when Peter Fleming put in a good word for his brother.

At this time Kemsley made Fleming a director of a new imprint, Queen Anne Press, and relaunched the *Book Handbook* as the quarterly *Book Collector*. Now a publisher, Fleming gained a new cachet among Ann's literary friends as he published offerings from Evelyn Waugh and Cyril Connolly.

On 12 August 1952, Ann gave birth to their son, Caspar, by Caesarean section after a painful labour. Ian was seen to weep openly. While Ann was in hospital, Fleming started the final revision of *Casino Royale* on his gold typewriter, though afterwards reverted to his Imperial portable. He also wrote a piece about Jamaica for the *Spectator*, but an article he wrote on road safety was rejected by the *Sunday Times*. Later, through the good offices of Lord Kemsley, it was published in the *Daily Graphic* under the pen name Frank Gray.

With no agent, Fleming negotiated his own deal with Cape,

assigning the rights to a small company, Glidrose Productions, he and Ann had just taken over; but he retained the movie and serial rights himself. Friends helped him find a publisher in the US and author Paul Gallico put Fleming in touch with his agent in Hollywood.

Ian was repelled by the scar left by Ann's Caesarean and sex ceased. He also avoided her friends. Even so, they moved into a larger home. The following January, they flew to the US to research *Live and Let Die* in New York, travelling by train from Penn Station to Florida as in the book. In St Petersburg, he checked out the waterfront for a suitable site for Ourobouros Worm and Bait Shippers, Inc. Then they flew on to Jamaica, where Cabarita Island, near Oracabessa, became Mr Big's hideaway the Isle of Surprise. That had indeed been where the seventeenth-century pirate Henry Morgan had careened his ships, as it says in the book. The sections on voodoo were gleaned from Ann's friend Paddy Leigh Fermor's book *The Traveller's Tree*, which was written, in part, at Goldeneye. Fleming also witnessed the local version of a voodoo funeral in Jamaica.

Guests that winter included Graham Greene, novelist Angus Wilson, painter Lucian Freud and actress Katharine Hepburn. Meanwhile, news came from the nanny in London of Caspar's first tooth.

Back in London, at a party given by publisher Hamish Hamilton, Fleming met the pioneer of the aqualung Jacques Cousteau, who invited him to a dive in the Mediterranean, so he was away from England when *Casino Royale* was published on 13 April 1953. Ann stayed in Antibes with Somerset Maugham, who praised the book. For the rest of his life, Fleming kept a copy of the *Times Literary Supplement* containing a glowing review by Alan Ross, a literary friend of Ann's.

He could depend on reviews in the papers owned by Kemsley and Beaverbrook, though he received cool notices from Rothermere's publications. He was also helped by W.H. Smith, the leading chain of booksellers, which was owned by family friends. Fleming had designed his own book jacket and flyers, and constantly pushed Cape over publicity. This paid off and the first print run of 4,750 sold out. James Bond was on his way to becoming an international sensation, and soon Hollywood movie companies were showing an interest.

Fleming used the success of the second and third print runs to renegotiate his contract, upping the royalty. Then he went to New York to sign a deal with Macmillan, where the publisher's editor bowdlerized the book. Fleming did not care. He was more concerned with promotion. On the *Queen Elizabeth*, he corrected the proofs of *Live and Let Die*. These were circulated to film companies and attracted praise. His next book, he said, would be written specifically with a movie in mind. That winter, he sat down to write *Moonraker*.

Meanwhile, he took up treasure hunting, caving and gambling in casinos – all, ostensibly, to provide copy for Kemsley newspapers. He later took over the Atticus column in the *Sunday Times* and used it to attack Senator Joe McCarthy's Reds-under-the-bed scare. It was James Bond, not McCarthy, who was the ultimate Cold Warrior. Otherwise, Fleming used the column to puff his friends.

Fleming consulted old intelligence colleagues for information about the Nazi Werewolves, a guerrilla force who were supposed to fight on after the war, and V2-style rockets, both of which make an appearance in *Moonraker*. He also consulted a Harley Street psychiatrist about the character traits of megalomaniacs before creating the book's villain Hugo Drax.

As Fleming wrote *Moonraker* he began to think more deeply about James Bond, realizing already that he was doomed to continue writing a series of fantastic adventures concerning the same character. It did not matter how fantastic the stories were, he concluded, as long as the author believed in the fantasy.

Casino Royale was given a cool reception in the US and *Moonraker* failed to attract a movie offer. Nevertheless, *Live and Let Die* got good reviews in the UK, where Fleming had the press, apart from the Rothermere group, in the palm of his hand. And the book was banned in Ireland, which helped generate publicity.

Fleming's life fell into a pattern. He spent the first three months of the year in Jamaica writing a manuscript, then returned to London to prepare for publication the book he had written the year before. Meanwhile, the book he had written the year before that came out in the US. For the rest of the year, Fleming would use his position at the *Sunday Times* to research exotic locations. He paid great attention to detail, even driving the routes mentioned in the books to see how long the journey took. He had experts from the British Interplanetary Society look over the details of the rocketry in *Moonraker* as Arthur C. Clarke was away in the US at the time.

He visited De Beers in London to research *Diamonds are Forever*, then headed for Saratoga Springs in upstate New York where, by mistake, he happened upon a run-down mud bath, like the Acme Mud and Sulphur Baths Bond visits to pay off the jockey who then gets bumped off. A friend he met there had a Studillac – a Studebaker with a Cadillac engine – which Fleming also appropriated for the book.

On this trip, Fleming became a director of the North American Newspaper Alliance (NANA), a new features agency. He tied this to the foreign operation he ran at Kemsley, then negotiated a lucrative syndication deal with Beaverbrook's Express newspapers.

Back in London, Ian avoided Ann's friends – a group which now included James Pope-Hennessy and Cecil Beaton – fearing that they looked down on his thrillers. One night, it is said, he returned from his club to find them laughing at a reading from one of his sex scenes.

Leaving Ann in London, he took a train from New York to Los Angeles where he sold a movie option on *Casino Royale*. Curtis Brown, the agent he had taken on in New York, sold the TV rights and a hour-long version of the book appeared on CBS. Money was also offered for options on *Live and Let Die*, *Moonraker* and subsequent James Bond books, but Fleming turned them down.

During a visit to the LA Police Department, Fleming was briefed on the surveillance techniques that greeted Bond when he arrived at Las Vegas in *Diamonds are Forever*. He then flew to Las Vegas for more research. At the airport he delighted in the slot machine that gave two minutes of oxygen for 25 cents – which, again, Bond used in the book. With Ernie Cuneo, Bill Donovan's former liaison officer with Royal Naval Intelligence, he made a tour of all the casinos in Las Vegas. Placing small bets, he quit when he was $1 ahead, then drank a glass of champagne and moved on. By the end of the evening he could boast that he had beaten every casino in town – and Ernie Cuneo appeared as Ernest Cureo, Bond's cab driver and undercover Pinkerton man in Nevada.

While writing *Diamonds are Forever* in Jamaica in the winter of 1955, Fleming came across a local character called Red Grant, the name he later used for the assassin in *From Russia with Love*. Evelyn Waugh was also on hand to help him polish up the love scenes.

Live and Let Die sold poorly in the US despite an endorsement from Raymond Chandler, who Fleming had met at a party given by the poet Stephen Spender. Meanwhile, the $600 movie option on *Casino Royale* turned into $6,000 for the rights. With it, Fleming bought a Ford Thunderbird. He was so enamoured of the car, Ann began to call him Thunderbird.

James Bond spoofs began to appear, much to Fleming's delight. On the downside, Billy Woodward, who used to accompany Ian to the racing at Saratoga, was shot and killed by his wife, who mistook him for a prowler. *Diamonds are Forever* was dedicated to J.F.C.B (Ivar Bryce), 'E.L.C' (Ernie Cureo) 'and W.W. (Woodward) 'at Saratoga 1954 and '55'.

That September Fleming accompanied Scotland Yard's assistant commissioner to the Interpol Conference in Istanbul to get an insight into international crime. It also gave him an interesting setting for his next Bond adventure, *From Russia with Love*. There he was shown around by a hard-living, Oxford-educated Turk named Nazim Kalkavan. He became the model for Darko Karim, the Istanbul SIS station chief who assisted Bond. Fleming returned on the Simplon-Orient Express where Bond fought it out with Red Grant and bedded Tatiana Romanova.

Queen Anne Press was now in financial difficulties and Fleming bought the *Book Collector*, giving him the academic credibility he craved. The rest of the company was bought by Robert Maxwell, who had all the elements of a Bond villain, though Fleming remained a director until his death.

Through a friend from Eton, Fleming became a member of the Royal College of Art. That September, he and Ann visited Anthony Eden and his wife Clarissa at the prime minister's country retreat, Chequers, where they were told not to mention Burgess and Maclean. He then went back to the US where he arranged to sell NANA to a Canadian syndicate, taking a welcome profit. On his trip, he noted encouraging signs that the American public were at last taking notice of Bond, perhaps because Pocket Book's paperback edition of *Casino Royale* – published under the name *You Asked For It* – had the picture of a young woman *déshabillé* on the cover.

The American critics were a little kinder to *Moonraker* and Hollywood offered $1,000 for a nine-month movie option. Meanwhile, the UK's Rank Organization – who owned Pinewood Studios, Bond's eventual home – offered £5,000 and Fleming had to unmake the Hollywood deal. But Rank had no clear idea of what to do with James Bond and *Moonraker*. Fleming was well aware of the problem.

'The reason it breaks so badly in half as a book', he said, 'is because I had to more or less graft the first half of the book onto my film idea in order to bring it up to the necessary length.'

He proposed a short biography of Marthe Richard, a prostitute who had spied for France in World War I. During World War II, she spied for her country again, this time as a brothel keeper, and was awarded the *Légion d'honneur*. After the war, she became a politician and, as poacher turned gamekeeper, introduced the law that closed the brothels down. It was known as *La Loi de Marthe Richard*. *La Loi Marthe Richard* is mentioned in *Casino Royale* as the reason why the villain Le Chiffre has lost the Soviet money he had invested in brothels and needs to win it back at the tables. However, Curtis Brown persuaded Fleming that a biography of Marthe Richard was not a commercial idea.

Fleming was now seen as the heir to Eric Ambler and Ambler helped Ian with the business side of Bond, putting him in touch with accountants and lawyers who created trust funds and other tax shelters. By then, Bond books were appearing in foreign languages and Peter Janson-Smith, who dealt with foreign rights at Curtis Brown, set up independently as Fleming's agent.

On his way to Jamaica to work on *From Russia with Love*, Ian met Truman Capote, who amused him with tales about his recent trip to Russia. He came to stay at Goldeneye. Meanwhile one of Fleming's correspondents got the first interview with Burgess and Maclean in Moscow.

Without Ann again that winter, Ian met Blanche Blackwell, a wealthy divorcee who said she thought he was the rudest man she had ever met. Nevertheless, she was physically attracted to him and invited him to her house for drinks. Later, they swam together at Goldeneye. Although he mentioned Blanche in his letters to Ann, he wrote mainly about the time he spent with Noël Coward and other homosexual friends.

In Nassau to write a piece for the *Sunday Times*, Ian was invited to visit the flamingo sanctuary on the island of Inagua – which became Dr No's hideaway Crab Key. A naturalist from the Audubon Society briefed him on guano, the dung of the cormorant used for fertilizer that was the source of Dr No's wealth. They even travelled around the island on a strange swamp-buggy that could have inspired Dr No's monster.

Diamonds are Forever got good reviews. Fleming was particularly pleased with the one Raymond Chandler wrote for the *Sunday Times*. After Chandler's death in 1959, Fleming published their correspondence. However, his habit of using friends' names now became cause for complaint. A relative by marriage, Arthur 'Boofy' Gore, later the Earl of Arran, objected to his nickname appearing in *Diamonds are Forever*, particularly as Leiter says, 'Kidd's a pretty boy. His friends call him 'Boofy'. Probably shacks up with Wint. Some of these homos make the worst killers.'

Suffering from sciatica, Fleming went off to Enton Hall, a health farm which made an appearance in *Thunderball*. Then he took Ann to the next Interpol Conference in Vienna. They stayed with Antony and Rachel Terry, two old friends from his Naval Intelligence days who told him about Emma Wolff, an ugly NKVD agent with dyed red hair. Wolff was the model for Rosa Klebb in *From Russia with Love*. By the time they returned to London, Ian was suffering from kidney stones and had to take morphine to still the pain. He took consolation in the work of F. Scott Fitzgerald, who died at the age of forty-four. Ian was already forty-eight. He complained to Chandler that his muse was 'in a bad way' and his literary powers were stretched to their limits.

Fleming played bridge for money and gambled in the casinos in Nassau, basing his story 'Quantum of Solace' there. In the Bahamas he met former Harvard football star, John 'Shipwreck' Sims Kelly, who knew everyone from the Duke of Windsor to Ernest Hemingway and introduced Ian to Aristotle Onassis. Ian also spent time with Ivar Bryce, who now lived an international lifestyle. His home-from-home was Schloss Mittersill, a sports club for the super-rich near Kitzbühel which became the model for Piz Gloria, Ernst Blofeld's Alpine research facility in *On Her Majesty's Secret Service*. At this louche establishment, Fleming indulged his passion for women and black lingerie, and met the wife of Prince Alex Hohenlohe, former showgirl Patricia Wilder who was known universally as Honeychile. He used the name for the heroine of his next book, *Dr No*. Meanwhile, Ann began an affair with Labour Party leader Hugh Gaitskell.

In 1956, Fleming was commissioned to write the pilot for an American TV series starring secret agent Commander James Gunn. The villain would be a Dr No and a part was written for Ian's friend, Jamaican swimming champion Barrington Roper.

But Fleming's script was rejected. The Roper character reappeared in the book *Dr No*.

A gun enthusiast from Glasgow named Geoffrey Boothroyd wrote to Fleming, complaining that the .25 Beretta Bond used in the first four books was a 'ladies' gun'; he recommended a .38 Smith & Wesson Centennial Airweight, carried in a Berns Martin triple-draw holster. These sentiments appear in the mouth of Major Boothroyd, the departmental armourer in *Dr No*. Meanwhile, Ian began turning up the collar of his overcoat. He was being sucked into the role of James Bond.

Macmillan in the US were delighted with the manuscript for *From Russia with Love* and began promoting *Diamonds are Forever*. CIA chief Richard Helms picked up a copy of *Live and Let Die*. Impressed, he contacted Roger Hollis, head of MI5, and asked about Ian Fleming. Hollis claimed never to have heard of Fleming. However, he was soon to come to the attention of the security service. When Anthony Eden resigned due to 'ill health' after the Suez fiasco, he went to Goldeneye to recuperate. Blanche was on hand to help with the arrangements. When Ann heard about this, she assumed that Ian had been unfaithful, giving Blanche no further reason to resist. Unperturbed, Ian appropriated the storyline from his failed TV pilot and was getting on with *Dr No*.

When *From Russia with Love* came out, Fleming was in Tangiers interviewing a real-life spy about a diamond scam for the *Sunday Times*. His publishers were now claiming that Fleming had sold over a million copies in English, and he was translated into a dozen languages. However, several reviewers concluded that, after his murderous run-in with Rosa Klebb on the last page of the book, they might have seen the last of James Bond. He was, however, resurrected in *Dr No*.

Despite Fleming's misgivings, the *Daily Express* began publishing *Casino Royale* as a cartoon strip. Fleming published a non-fiction account of the diamond scam he had learnt about in Tangiers as *The Diamond Smugglers*. This trod on the toes of his brother-in-law Hugo Charteris, who covered the same ground in his book *Picnic at Porokorro*. By then Fleming's marriage had broken down to the point where he was seen lunging drunkenly at women at parties. Nevertheless, Rank made an offer for the film rights of *The Diamond Smugglers*.

Fleming planned another non-fiction book off the back of another proposed series for the *Sunday Times* called, tentatively, 'Round the World in Eight Adventures'. Meanwhile, he returned to Goldeneye – and Blanche – to write *Goldfinger*.

Back in England, Ian had begun playing golf with Blanche's brother, John Blackwell, who provided advice for the golf match Bond plays against Auric Goldfinger. They played at Sandwich where the short, tight sixth was known as 'The Maiden'. This became 'The Virgin' in the book, where Blackwell got a namecheck – but as a supplier of heroin. A more crucial namecheck went to Blackwell's cousin who was married to the modernist architect Erno Goldfinger. When the book was published, he threatened to sue. Ian suggested the publishers insert an erratum slip changing the name to 'Goldprick' throughout.

Now that James Bond was proving a hit with the public, the critics sharpened their knives and tore into *Dr No*. Everything from snobbery to sadism was cited. Chandler gave the book a good review in the *Sunday Times*, but then Fleming had commissioned him to interview Lucky Luciano on Capri, all expenses paid.

Ducking the controversy, which soon spread to the US, Fleming headed to the Seychelles for the first of his globe-trotting 'Eight Adventures'. Another short story, 'The Hildebrand Rarity', is set there and his article, along with a little lobbying on behalf of the islands, led the Seychelles to become one of the leading long-haul destinations.

Fleming was in Rome on his way home when he heard that an offer had been made on the movie rights for *Dr No*. He journeyed onward to Venice, where he intended to have a second honeymoon with Ann, travelling on board the Laguna Express, which appears in his short story 'Risico'. To help Ann get to know the city, Ian gave her a copy of Thomas Mann's *Death in Venice*.

Negotiations for the *Dr No* movie were put on hold when CBS proposed a thirteen-part James Bond series. This fell through. However, an omnibus edition of James Bond adventures, scheduled to come out with the TV series, survived.

Fleming was now fifty and feeling unwell. His doctors told him to cut down on cigarettes – he was still smoking sixty a day. He headed back Goldeneye alone to complete a book of five short Bond stories published as *For Your Eyes Only* in 1960. But after he mentioned Blanche in his letters, Ann joined him in Jamaica.

The critics rounded, once again, this time on *Goldfinger*, but it raced to the top of the bestsellers' list. Meanwhile, the *Sunday Times*, which had long been losing money, was sold to Lord Thomson. Fleming was retained for his editorial ideas and the occasional feature, and he began to spend more time working on the *Book Collector*.

Around this time Ivar Bryce set up a film studio on the Bahamas with one-time producer Kevin McClory to take advantage of tax breaks there and Fleming was called in to write a screenplay from a plot outline provided by Ernie Cuneo. This would become *Thunderball*. In the early Bond novels, the enemy had been SMERSH, a contraction of *Smert Shpionam* – Russian for 'Death to Spies' and the name of a Soviet intelligence agency founded in 1943. But Fleming was convinced that the Cold War would end while the film was in production, so SMERSH was replaced with SPECTRE as the villain of the piece. The acronym SPECTRE stood for the Special Executive for Counterintelligence, Terrorism, Revenge and Extortion. It was a fictional criminal organization made up of ex-members of SMERSH, the Mafia, the Gestapo and Peking's Black Tong.

Fleming completed a sixty-seven-page treatment before returning to London, where he was swamped with film offers. He went on to the Continent, travelling into East Germany with an old intelligence colleague. Then he travelled to Hong

Kong and Macao, ostensibly for the *Sunday Times* but actually researching exotic backgrounds for Bond books. Moving on to Tokyo, he was introduced by one of his correspondents, a hard-drinking Australian named Richard Hughes, to journalist Torao Saito, known as 'Tiger', who took him to a geisha house. This features in *You Only Live Twice*. Hughes became Dikko Henderson, Australia's man in Tokyo, and Saito Tiger Tanaka, head of the Japanese Secret Service. The book was also dedicated to 'Richard Hughes and Torao Saito, But for whom etc. . . . '

Fleming returned to Jamaica to write another Bond book – *Thunderball* – which was dedicated to 'Ernest Cuneo, Muse'. Ian was in Washington later that year where he dined with presidential hopeful John F. Kennedy, who was impressed with Fleming's ideas of how to handle Fidel Castro, the new dictator of Cuba. Kennedy listed *From Russia with Love* among his top ten books in *Life* magazine. Overnight, Fleming became the biggest-selling thriller writer in the US. It was later said that Kennedy was reading a Bond book the night before he was assassinated. So, it is said, was his assassin Lee Harvey Oswald.

In 1961 Fleming retired from his job at the *Sunday Times*, but continued to write his 'Eight Adventures' series – now called 'Thrilling Cities' – for the paper. In Hamburg, he enthused about the sex industry before moving on to Berlin where he crossed the Wall. In Switzerland, he dined with Charlie Chaplin, helping to secure the serialization rights to Chaplin's memoirs for the *Sunday Times*. Then in Naples, he had tea with Lucky Luciano. Returning to England, he crashed his Thunderbird into an ice-cream van.

In Beirut, Fleming discussed his old friend Kim Philby, a suspected Soviet spy, with the local SIS head. Soon after, Philby defected. Fleming moved on to Kuwait, where he had been commissioned to write a book, *State of Excitement*. After reading the manuscript, the Kuwait Oil Company expressed their disapproval and it was never published.

Next came *The Spy Who Loved Me*, written from the point

of view of the heroine, a young Canadian woman named Vivienne Michel. Fleming said it was the easiest thing he ever wrote. Again he toyed with the idea of killing off Bond, but decided not to.

Seeing an advance copy of the novel *Thunderball*, Kevin McClory claimed it was based on the film scripts he and others had been working on and sued for breach of copyright. Soon after this, at the age of fifty-three, Fleming had a heart attack. In hospital he wrote a bedtime story for his son Caspar, which became *Chitty Chitty Bang Bang*.

It was then that a Canadian producer based in London, Harry Saltzman, and an American émigré, Albert R. 'Cubby' Broccoli, teamed up. They signed a deal with United Artists for six Bond movies. The first was to have been *Thunderball*, but due to legal problems they went ahead with *Dr No* instead.

Convalescing in Provence, Fleming became a friend of artist Graham Sutherland. Once back in London, he suggested his friend David Niven to play James Bond. When it was suggested that Niven was too old and – as an established Hollywood star – too expensive, Fleming opted for Roger Moore, then playing *The Saint* on TV. Fleming objected to the choice of Sean Connery – 'that fucking truck driver,' he called him after Connery's role in the 1957 B-movie *Hell Drivers*. But he changed his mind when female friends assured him that Connery had 'it'. Otherwise Fleming limited his role in the film to finding locations. However, Fleming's old friend Reginald Maudling at the Colonial Office refused permission to use Government House in Jamaica as the governor was portrayed as an idiot in the book and his secretary a spy.

Ian recommended that the producers use Blanche's son Chris Blackwell as location manager for the movie. Blackwell also advised on authentic Jamaican music for the soundtrack and went on to found Island Records, which introduced Bob Marley to the world.

At the *Sunday Times*, Fleming had commissioned a series of articles on the Seven Deadly Sins. These were collected into a book with an introduction by Ian. He also wrote an introduction

James Bond

to a new edition of *All Night at Mr Stanyhurst's* by Hugh Edwards and the short story 'The Living Daylights' which appeared in the first edition of the *Sunday Times* colour supplement. In it, the female Russian assassin was based on his half-sister Amaryllis, his mother's daughter by Augustus John.

Back in Jamaica, he set to work on *On Her Majesty's Secret Service*, with Bond adopting the identity of Hilary Bray – the name of the man who had succeeded Fleming in the stockbroking firm in the City. The 'Rouge Dragon Pursuivant', the son of a friend at the College of Arms, while doing the genealogical research for the book, discovered that the Bonds of Peckham had the family motto 'The world is not enough', though the research is ascribed to the Griffon Or Pursuivant in the novel. The motto would become the title of a Bond movie. As it was, the Rouge Dragon was not amused to see the name of his heraldic office used in the manuscript, so Fleming changed it to the fanciful Sable Basilisk on the grounds that the mythical basilisk looks like a dragon and his friend lived in Basil Street.

The book contains the story of a man given a peerage for 'political and public services' – that in, charities and party funds, who wants to call himself Lord Bentley Royal after a village in Essex. However, it is explained to him that the word 'Royal' can only be used by the reigning family. The College of Arms mischievously pointed out that the title 'Lord Bentley Common' was available. The same story had been told about Lord Kemsley when he lived in Farnham *OHSS*; and it also drew on Fleming's visit to St Moritz the previous year.

Bond had made Fleming so famous that he was asked to comment on real-life intelligence matters such as the return of spy-plane pilot Gary Powers, who had been shot down over the Soviet Union two years earlier, in 1960. He also had a taste of danger when he visited the set of *Dr No* at Rolling River, with Ann, Peter Quennell and Stephen Spender, while the scene where Ursula Andress emerges from the sea was being filmed. In the scene, shots are fired. Fleming and his guest were found later cowering spreadeagled on the sand.

In the press, Fleming dismissed his Bond books as 'adolescent' with no social significance. However, when *The Spy Who Loved Me* was savaged by the critics, he defended it, saying that he was trying to examine Bond from the heroine's point of view, showing that he was no hero and little better than the criminals he came up against. Nevertheless, he contacted Cape and asked them not to reprint the book, or publish a paperback edition. The Soviets also took Fleming's creation seriously. An article in the government newspaper *Izvestia* condemned Bond as a tool of American propaganda.

While sitting for a portrait by engineer-turned-artist Amherst Villiers, Fleming was introduced to racing driver Graham Hill and listened with interest to their conversations about cars. But his life was slowing down. He worked just two days a week and spent most of his time playing bridge or golf. He presented the 'James Bond All Purpose Grand Challenge Vase' to the Old Etonian Golfing Society. It was a chamber pot.

To get away from the strains of his marriage, Fleming took a trip alone to Jamaica in July 1963, where he began work on 'Octopussy' – taking the name from a boat that Blanche had presented to Goldeneye. He wrote the introduction to the biography of Sir William Stephenson, *The Quiet Canadian*, then headed to Japan to research his next Bond book, *You Only Live Twice*, with Dick Hughes and Torao Saito.

In Tokyo, he visited the bar where Soviet spy Richard Sorge had picked up secrets from Nazi expatriates during World War II. He immersed himself in Japanese culture and was particularly interested in the girls who dived for pearls, traditionally naked. When Bond goes missing in the book, M writes his obituary for *The Times*. In it Fleming spoofed himself, saying: 'The inevitable publicity, particularly in the foreign Press, accorded some of these adventures, made him, much against his will, something of a public figure, with the inevitable result that a series of popular books came to be written around him by a personal friend and former colleague of James Bond. If the quality of these books, or their degree of veracity, had been any higher, the author would certainly have been prosecuted under the Official Secrets Act.'

Indeed, in 1959, when interest was first being shown in making a film of a James Bond novel, clearance was sought from the Foreign Office. A reply, signed by Frederick Hoyar-Millar, said that 'there are no security objections to any of the books about James Bond which have been published' and that 'there would be no objections to any film or television broadcast based on material in them'.

On Her Majesty's Secret Service was well received. At the same time Cyril Connolly's homosexual spoof *Bond Strikes Camp* came out in the *London Magazine*. With the defection of Kim Philby, it became increasingly clear that the world of espionage was gay, so Connolly has Bond dressed in drag, penetrating the 'Homintern' to unmask a traitor, who turns out to be M. Far from being displeased, Fleming was delighted by the parody, even making slight amendments to improve the manuscript before publication.

Ian visited Istanbul to watch the filming of *From Russia with Love*, returning to London in time to see the downfall of his friend, Defence Minister John Profumo, who had been caught sharing a young mistress with a Russian spy. Life, it seemed, was imitating fiction. He had lunch with Allen Dulles, who had recently retired as head of the CIA. After Dulles embarked on a career as an author and recommended the Bond books to a gathering of the American Booksellers' Association, Fleming dubbed him 008.

Oxford University set up a James Bond Club, while two editors of the *Harvard Lampoon* wrote a seventy-page spoof called *Alligator*. Then Fleming received the ultimate accolade – an appearance on the BBC radio programme *Desert Island Discs*.

He wrote the short story 'The Property of a Lady' for Sotheby's house magazine *The Ivory Hammer*. Meanwhile forty-four volumes from his book collection went on display at the exhibition 'Printing and the Mind of Man', by far the largest contribution from a private individual.

Fleming drove to Switzerland to interview Georges Simenon for the *Sunday Times*, then gave a terrified Blanche a high-speed tour of the haunts of his youth in his new Studebaker Avanti. Back in London, the court case over the rights in *Thunderball* began. In the end, McClory won the movie rights, while Fleming held on to the rights in the novel, which is now accredited as 'based on a screen treatment by Kevin McClory, Jack Whittingham, and Ian Fleming'. John Betjeman wrote to commiserate over the judgment. He put Fleming, he said, in the same class as Conan Doyle, P.G. Wodehouse, T.S. Eliot, Henry Moore and Evelyn Waugh.

Although Fleming was now in constant pain from angina, he took off for Jamaica again that winter to write *The Man with the Golden Gun*. The villain's name Scaramanga was taken from a contemporary at Eton. These days, Goldeneye was not as peaceful as it had been. A garage had opened nearby with a sound system which often blared out the reggae version of 'Three Blind Mice' that had been released on Chris Blackwell's Island label following its use on the soundtrack of *Dr No*.

Among the visitors that winter were Professor Northcote Parkinson, author of *Parkinson's Law*, and the real James Bond – the American ornithologist whose name Fleming may have appropriated. Fleming also agreed to write the guidebook *Ian Fleming's Jamaica* for André Deutsch, but in the end only contributed the introduction.

Despite his doctors' advice, Fleming refused to give up drinking and smoking. With acute pains in his chest, he was admitted to hospital suffering from pulmonary embolism – a blood clot in the lung. Although he recovered enough to return home, all those who saw him could tell that death was near.

On 11 August 1964, after lunch at the golf club and dinner at a hotel with a friend, Ian collapsed and was rushed to hospital. At 1.30 the following morning, he was pronounced dead. By then, he had written twelve novels and one book of short stories, selling over thirty million copies. Two films – *Dr No* and *From Russia with Love* – had already been made and two more

– *Goldfinger* and *Thunderball* – were in production. Another book of short stories, containing 'Octopussy', 'The Living Daylights' and 'The Property of a Lady' would be published in 1966. There would be more Bond books by other writers, more movies, and a Bond-related merchandise range from toys and games to clothes and toiletries. Further books and films are expected. Ian Fleming may be dead, but his creation seems fit enough to live for ever.

3. Bond, James Bond

Ian Fleming spent little time filling in the background of James Bond's life. Bond is essentially a man of action, a blunt instrument in the hands of M and Her Majesty's Government. However, in *You Only Live Twice*, when Bond goes missing, M writes his obituary for *The Times*.

According to M, James Bond's father was Andrew Bond, a Scot from Glencoe. Bond himself volunteers this in *On Her Majesty's Secret Service* when talking to the Griffon Or Pursuivant at the College of Arms. Griffon insists on looking up the ancestry of Bond's 'fine old English surname', which goes back as least to Norman le Bond in 1180. There are ten families in *Burke's General Armory*, but no Scottish branch. That does not mean there wasn't one. It is just that the Scots kept incomplete records – 'more useful with the sword than the pen,' Griffon opines. However, he does think that he can establish collateral lineage back to Sir Thomas Bond, baronet of Peckham. Bond insists he has no connection with Peckham. Undaunted, Griffon continues that Sir Thomas was the comptroller of the household of the Queen Mother, Henrietta Maria, and lent his name to London's Bond Street in 1686. Bond dismisses this, though he does concede, perhaps ironically, that he would adopt Thomas Bond's family motto: 'The world is not enough.'

Bond also tells Griffon that his mother was Swiss. M says her name was Monique Delacroix and that she was from the Canton de Vaud. John Pearson, author of *James Bond: The Authorised Biography* as well as *The Life of Ian Fleming*, says that James Bond was born in Wattenscheid near Essen in the Ruhr, where his father, an engineer with Metro-Vickers, was attached to the Allied Military Government dismantling Krupp's armament factories. His mother had intended to go back to England to give birth, but had been held up by a rail strike. However, Charlie Higson in *Danger Society: The Young Bond Dossier* says Bond was born in Zürich. This exotic background makes him a quintessential Englishman.

Curiously John Pearson, who was Fleming's assistant at the *Sunday Times* and fact-checked *The Spy Who Loved Me*, was commissioned to write *James Bond: The Authorised Biography* by Glidrose Productions, the company Fleming bought in 1952 to handle rights in *Casino Royale* and subsequent Bond novels. The company later changed its name to Ian Fleming Publications, which authorized the Higson 'Young Bond' series.

According to Pearson, Bond remained fiercely proud of his Scottish heritage and talked nostalgically about the family's stone house in the Highlands.

'I don't feel too comfortable in England,' he says, though this does not come across in Fleming's books. Indeed, Bond not only feels comfortable in England, he feels comfortable in America, the Caribbean, Turkey, Japan, and anywhere he goes.

Pearson fleshes out the Bond family. Followers of the MacDonalds, three Bond brothers were killed in the massacre in Glencoe in 1692. In the eighteenth century, the surviving family prospered, producing doctors, a lawyer and a missionary. They remained tough and wild, refusing to be softened up like Lowlanders. Bond's great-grandfather – another James Bond – won a VC with the Highland Infantry at the siege of Sevastopol during the Crimean War. And in 1973, when *The Authorised Biography* was first published, the head of the family was Bond's uncle Gregor Bond, a dour drunk of eighty-two.

M says that Bond's father was a foreign representative of the Vickers armaments company – a company that Fleming knew well from the Metro-Vickers trial – and that James' early education took place abroad. From his father he inherited a command of German and French, both languages Fleming mastered. His parents were killed in a climbing accident in the Aiguilles Rouges above Chamonix in France, an area Fleming often visited, when Bond was just eleven. Fleming's father had died when Ian was young and he may have wished his over-bearing mother dead too.

Bond went to live with his aunt, Miss Charmian Bond, near the Duck Inn in the village of Pett Bottom, near Canterbury, where Fleming had a weekend home. When he was twelve, he was sent to Eton – his father had put him down at birth. But after a term there was 'some alleged trouble with one of the boys' maids' and he was sent to Fettes College in Edinburgh, his father's old school. Like Fleming, Bond was a loner and athletic. He represented the school twice boxing as a light-weight and founded the first serious judo class in a British public school.

There then comes a little confusion about Bond's career. In *From Russia with Love*, the SMERSH file on Bond says that he has worked for the Secret Service since 1938. But Pearson's *Authorised Biography* gives his date of birth as 'Armistice Day, 11 November 1920', so he would have to have joined the SIS at the age of seventeen or eighteen. According to M's obituary, in 1941, at the age of nineteen, with the help of one of his father's colleagues from Vickers, Bond joined a branch of what subsequently became the Ministry of Defence. This would have meant he was born in 1921 or 1922. His duties were 'confidential' and, like Fleming, he joined the Royal Navy Volunteer Reserve – but in Bond's case the 'Special Branch of the RNVR' – as a lieutenant. M says that it is a measure of the satisfaction his services gave to his superiors that he ended the war with the rank of Commander. Fleming is giving himself a pat on the back there.

In the obituary, M says that he only 'became associated with certain aspects of the Ministry's work . . . about this time'. And it was M who accepted Bond's post-war application to continue working for the Ministry of Defence, presumably before the SIS was returned to the Foreign Office. At the time of his disappearance, Bond had risen to the rank of Principal Officer in the Civil Service. The SMERSH file implies that he got his double-O licence by December 1950. There were thought to be only two other spies in the SIS with the double-O licence to kill on active service. M notes that Bond was awarded a CMG – Companion of the Order of St Michael and St George – in 1954. SMERSH have it down as 1953. In *The Man with the Golden Gun*, Bond is offered a KCMG – a knighthood in the same order. He declines it on the grounds that he does not want to pay more in hotels and restaurants. Bond likes being plain James Bond, no middle name, no hyphen and no title. He cherishes his privacy and does not want to become a public person in the snobbish world of England.

The obituary mentions that he was briefly married in 1962 to Teresa, the only daughter of Marc-Ange Draco of Marseilles. Bond's wife Tracy was killed by Blofeld shortly after their wedding, which occurs at the end of *On Her Majesty's Secret Service*. M says that this was reported in the press at the time. What Bond got up to professionally was, of course, secret, but M praises his bravery and his ability to escape more or less unscathed from his adventures, though there was 'an impetuous strain in his nature . . . that brought him in conflict with higher authority'. This foolhardy streak amounted to what M called 'the Nelson touch'.

M also remarks that Bond's last mission was of supreme importance to the state. But in the book, Bond had been sent to Tokyo to ingratiate himself with the Japanese Secret Service, then involved himself in a personal vendetta against Blofeld. According to M, Bond left no living relative.

At the end of the obituary, Bond's secretary Mary Goodnight adds a few simple words that the junior staff in the department felt summed up his philosophy as an epitaph: 'I shall not waste my days in trying to prolong them. I shall use my time.' This was also Fleming's motto.

Like Fleming, Bond was a man who like to swim, play golf and gamble. To keep in shape, Bond did twenty slow press-ups, followed by straight leg-lifts until his stomach muscles screamed. Then he touched his toes twenty times and did arm and chest exercises combined with deep breathing until he was dizzy. Afterwards he would have one of his frequent hot showers, followed by a cold one. This was at a time when few people in Britain had a shower; most preferred a bath. While in training in *Dr No*, Bond gets up at seven, swims a quarter of a mile, takes breakfast, does an hour's sunbathing, runs a mile, swims again, eats lunch, sleeps, sunbathes, swims a mile, has a hot bath and massage, eats dinner and is asleep by nine, exhausted no doubt.

According to SMERSH his height was 183 centimetres – six foot – and he weighed 76 kilos – 168 pounds or twelve stone. He had a slim build, though Pearson says the men in his family were 'big-boned'. The SMERSH file said his eyes were blue, though elsewhere they are grey-blue. His eyes were wide and level under straight, rather long, black brows. His hair was black, parted to the left with an unruly black comma that fell down over the right eyebrow. His noise was longish and straight, his upper lip short, his mouth wide and finely drawn but cruel. This cruel mouth is referred to several times throughout the books. The line of his jaw was straight and firm. The skin of his face was dark, usually suntanned, clean-shaven, showing off a white three-inch scar down the right cheek. There was another scar on his left shoulder and his right hand showed signs of plastic surgery.

This description of Bond recalls Fleming himself, though Fleming said that Bond was considerably more handsome. In *Casino Royale*, the heroine Vesper Lynd compares him to American songwriter, singer and actor Hoagy Carmichael. The comparison is made again in *Moonraker*.

Bond, SMERSH noted, was an all-round athlete, expert shot with a pistol, a boxer and a knife-thrower, and spoke French and German. He did not use disguises and was thought not to take bribes.

The SMERSH file contained a number of photographs. They invariably showed Bond in a dark suit. Generally he favoured a dark blue serge, tropical worsted or alpaca, depending on the climate. Usually these would be accompanied by a heavy white silk shirt and a thin black knitted silk tie and black moccasin shoes. In informal situations, Bond wore dark blue trousers, a short-sleeved Sea Island cotton shirt in white or dark blue, and black casual shoes or sandals. On the golf course he occasionally wore a black windcheater. For the really casual look, in *Dr No* he fits himself out with cheap black canvas jeans, a dark blue shirt and rope-soled shoes – even leather sandals and shorts. He wears nylon underwear and, in bed, long silk pyjama coats in place of two-piece pyjamas, though he usually sleeps naked.

He sometimes carries an attaché case provided by Q. Otherwise Bond had few accessories. They were unostentatious, but expensive, and included a Rolex Oyster Perpetual on an expanding metal bracelet which, he notes in *On Her Majesty's Secret Service*, could double as a knuckleduster; a gunmetal cigarette case; and a black oxidized Ronson lighter, like one that Fleming himself owned.

SMERSH also noted that Bond smokes heavily; he admits to sixty a day according to Bond's medical report at the beginning of *Thunderball*. Like Fleming, he favoured custom-made Morland cigarettes with three gold bands, containing Balkan tobacco with a higher nicotine content than cheaper brands. However, when he runs out of Morlands abroad he smokes Chesterfields in the US and Royal Blend in the Caribbean. In *Goldfinger* he even accepts a Parliament offered by Junius Du Pont. Bond's second choice was Player's, Domino's brand in *Thunderball* – she spins a romantic story around the sailor's picture on the packet when she and Bond first meet. This must have had an effect on him because in the next novel, *The Spy Who Loved Me*, he is smoking Senior Service.

He drank, SMERSH said, but not to excess. Some may disagree. A medical report in *Thunderball* says: 'When not engaged upon strenuous duty, the officer's average daily consumption of alcohol is in the region of half a bottle of spirits of between sixty and seventy proof.'

However, in the books we do see him on strenuous duty, especially when it comes to drinking. In *The Man with the Golden Gun*, he drinks a pink gin, insisting on Beefeater's gin, which is between 80 and 94 proof, depending where it is made. In his famous dry Martini, Bond has Gordon's gin, which is currently 37.5 per cent by volume or 65 degrees proof in the UK, or 75 proof in the US. However, the original recipe was given in *Casino Royale*, published in 1953 when it was much stronger, closer to 90 proof. It does not say which vodka is used – and Bond drinks a lot of vodka, often neat. Again, in *Casino Royale* he recommends a vodka made of grain rather then potatoes – Stolichnaya perhaps, which is between 80 and 100 proof. The final ingredient, Kina Lillet, is a fortified wine. The cocktail was known as the Vesper. Bond said he named it for Vesper Lynd, the heroine of the book. In fact, Fleming and his friend Ivar Bryce invented the cocktail and called it Vesper in honour of an old colonel they knew who called drinks served at six in the evening 'Vespers'. The heroine of *Casino Royale* was called Vesper after the cocktail, not the other way around.

The recipe called for three measures of Gordon's, one of vodka and half a measure of Kina Lillet, now known as Lillet Blanc. That's well over the recommended daily intake of alcohol right there. Bond drinks other cocktails, including Americanos, Negronis, straight vodka Martinis and Felix Leiter's medium-dry Martinis, using Martini Rossi and over-proof American gin. *Thunderball* begins with Bond nursing two double bourbons in the lounge of Miami Airport; he then orders another double, deciding to get drunk that night as he does so. Bond also downs whisky, brandy, raki, ouzo and schnapps, all well over 70 proof. And he drinks copious amounts of champagne and other wines, plus beer – Miller High Life in the US, Red Stripe in Jamaica. Today we would say he had a drink problem. Even the medical officer in *Thunderball* thinks so. Bond's tongue, he notes, is furred. His blood pressure is a little raised at 160/90 and the liver is not palpable. However, 'when pressed, the officer admits to frequent occipital headaches and there is spasm in the trapezius muscles and so-called "fibrositis" nodules can be felt'. He recommends that Bond spend two or three weeks on a more 'abstemious regime'. Then in *On Her Majesty's Secret Service*, Secret Service chemists spot an excess of uric acid in the ink he used for a secret message, noting: 'This is often due to a super-abundance of alcohol in the blood-stream.' On the other hand, Pearson records that Bond's great-uncle Huw drank himself to death in his mid-thirties, a fate Bond escaped. The *Authorised Biography* purports to have been written when Bond was still alive at fifty-two.

Bond's other vice, SMERSH notes, is women. However, in *The James Bond Dossier*, the author Kingsley Amis points out that Bond beds almost exactly one girl per excursion abroad, an average he exceeds just once, by one.

'This is surely not at all in advance of what any reasonably personable, reasonably well-off bachelor would reckon to acquire on a foreign holiday or a trip for his firm,' Amis wrote in 1965. Today, it would hardly be thought promiscuous. However, in *Casino Royale*, Bond reflects: 'Women are for recreation. On the job, they got in the way and fogged things up with sex and hurt feelings and all the emotional baggage they carried around. One had to look out for them and take care of them.' These are the words of a confirmed womanizer.

The SMERSH file says Bond 'is invariably armed with a .25 Beretta automatic carried in a holster under his left arm'. Fleming himself had been issued with a .25 ACP Beretta during World War II and assumed it was the standard-issue secret agent's weapon. However, in the next book, *Dr No*, the Beretta is replaced by a Walther PPK. Bond is careful with his gun, shooting only when he has to, outside the practice range. However, his great-uncle Ian was sent down from university for shooting up his law books one night with a .45 revolver.

The SMERSH file also says that he had been known to carry

a knife strapped to his left forearm, had used steel-capped shoes, which are in evidence in *Live and Let Die*, and knew the basic holds of judo. Also he fought with tenacity and had a high tolerance to pain. Pearson concurs, saying that there is a lot of granite in Bond. He has 'the family determination and toughness mixed with a solid dose of Calvinism'. This Calvinism certainly does not show through in his attitude to the pleasures of the flesh – eating, drinking and sex. Nevertheless, Pearson says: 'The Bonds, as true Scotsmen, believed in guilt, great care with money and the need for every man to prove himself.' Bond certainly shows no guilt when it comes to seducing women, though he often expresses a desire to settle down and have kids. Though he did not like killing, he knew how to do it and forget about it. Only at the beginning of *Goldfinger*, where Bond reflects on the murder of a Mexican bandit, does he feel regret, which he calls a 'death-watch beetle in the soul'. When he gambles, he appears positively reckless when it comes to money. On the other hand, it is the department's money – or the CIA's – he is playing with, not his own. Besides, he always wins. However, there can be little doubt that Bond feels the need to prove himself, over and over again.

Pearson puts the Bond family down as melancholics. Bond certainly is. It suits his lone-wolf lifestyle.

Just as Fleming looked up to his lost father, so did Bond. At Fettes, Andrew Bond had been a prize-winning scholar and captain of games. He was in his early twenties when World War I broke out and he joined the Royal Engineers. Curiously, Pearson has him surviving the Somme, then losing an arm – and gaining a DSO and a lifelong admiration of the Turks – at Gallipoli. However, the First Battle of the Somme occurred after the end of the Dardanelles Campaign.

One would have thought the loss of an arm would have quelled his passion for mountain climbing. Nevertheless, Andrew Bond was mountaineering in Switzerland in late 1918 when he spotted through a telescope Monique Delacroix, his future wife, at the tail end of a team of climbers halfway up the

Aiguilles Rouge above Geneva. These are another Aiguilles Rouge – 'Red Peaks' – not the ones above Chamonix where they died. She was nineteen and engaged to a fifty-seven-year-old banker. Fleming's Swiss former fiancée was called Monique, also from Vaud, and his mother's middle name was Ste Croix.

The Delacroixs were not impressed with Monique's one-armed suitor, so the couple eloped. Monique was then disowned by her family. She quickly gave birth to Henry, James's elder brother. But there was tension in the marriage. When Andrew was offered his old job back at Metro-Vickers in Birmingham, Monique protested. So, instead, he joined the Allied High Command in Germany, where James was born soon after.

The Bonds lived like royalty in the Weimar Republic. They had a big house in Wattenscheid with servants, nannies, dogs and horses. Summer holidays were spent travelling down the Rhine or on the Baltic coast. Christmas and Hogmanay were spent in Glencoe where the young James was terrified of his grandfather Archie Bond and his broad Scots accent. Also on hand were the drink-addled Uncle Gregor, wealthy but miserly Ian and Aunt Charmian who had been married just three weeks when her husband was killed at the Third Battle of Ypres in 1917, leaving her a widow in Kent.

The young James idolized his mother, but she despaired of him. Pearson says that still, at the age of fifty-two, Bond kept a miniature of her beside him. However, he does not seem to have taken it with him on assignment. Nor do we see his Scottish housekeeper May dusting it in his Chelsea flat.

Alienated from his parents, James also fought with his older brother and soon found he could beat him in a stand-up fight. He also found consolation in food and grew fat. Even though he slimmed down in adolescence, he continued to relish eating.

The Bond family moved on to Egypt, where his father worked on the Aswan dam. Meanwhile, his mother took lovers. James would give the slip to his French governess and run with a street gang in Cairo; his dark skin helped him fit in. He became its leader, naturally. One day, he saw the Rolls-Royce belonging to an Armenian contractor who had visited the house pull up outside a hotel. His mother got out. She refused to acknowledge the street urchin who called out to her. Next day, when he asked her about it, she denied being at the hotel, insisting that she had been at home the whole time. It was, Bond said, his first insight into the female heart.

The family moved on to France. James's father was promoted. Money came easily and went even more easily. Servants too would come and go; as would his mother's lovers. James learnt to enjoy French food and he fell in love for the first time, with twelve-year-old daughter of the local butcher. But she was interested in an older boy who had a bike.

Pearson sends Andrew Bond off to work for Metro-Vickers in Russia. The family travelled in a first-class sleeper on the Moscow Express from Paris. Though James was only ten, this was the start of his lifelong love of caviar. He also formed an enduring image of the Soviet Union as a land of shortage and secret policemen, starving peasants and cowed citizens. This was reinforced when six of his father's work colleagues were arrested and put on trial for sabotage. So, as a child, James had experience of a Stalinist purge first hand. But amid the fear, James was left with one clear memory – of a limousine pulling up at the company compound in Perlovska. Out of it stepped a dapper young Englishman in a checked suit, unconcerned to the point of ennui. It was the Reuters correspondent sent from London to cover the trial. His name was Ian Fleming.

Thanks to Andrew Bond's efforts with officialdom, all but two of the engineers were acquitted. The Metro-Vickers mission was withdrawn and the family headed for England. They settled in an ugly Victorian house overlooking Wimbledon Common. Young James was not used to hearing English spoken. He and his mother usually spoke French. He felt more like an outsider than ever. Sent to King's College School across the Common, James became withdrawn while his older brother Henry flourished – like Ian and Peter, perhaps.

In July 1932, their mother had a nervous breakdown and

tried to stab the family's devoted Russian maid. Monique was sent to a sanatorium in Sunningdale. She rallied. The doctors advised a change of scenery, so Andrew decided to let bygones be bygones and reunite Monique with her parents. While they headed off to Switzerland, the boys were sent to Glencoe for the summer. Three weeks later, Aunt Charmian arrived bringing bad news. Their parents have been killed in a climbing accident. Henry wept, but James surprised everyone with his self-control. He said that, when his father saw them off at King's Cross, he knew they would never see him again – his father's parting words were: 'Look after yourself, laddie. If you don't, there's no one else that will.'

Later Bond managed to piece together what happened to his parents. It seems Monique's father blamed Andrew for his daughter's breakdown. During a row, Monique fled the house. Andrew followed her as far as Chamonix, where she had abandoned the car. With no climbing equipment, she set off up the Aiguilles Rouges in a pink dress. Andrew caught up with her on a narrow ledge at dusk. People in the valley saw the two of them edging towards each other. Suddenly, they plunged to their death. Bond believed that she could not face either leaving him or returning to him. They were buried in the village cemetery below the mountain.

The boys went to live with Aunt Charmian at Pett Bottom. The following year, James joined his brother Henry at Eton. Pearson relates how the moody and self-contained Bond found himself in the shadow of his brother. A friend at school named 'Burglar' Brinton took him to stay with his father in Paris. There Bond began playing bridge and canasta for money. It was Brinton's father who introduced him to Morland Specials. He also lent them a car – a large Hispano Suiza – to take them to Monte Carlo. The chauffeur was supposed to drive, but the two boys took turns, introducing Bond to the thrill of driving a powerful car across the continent. Brinton's father also introduced the boys to the casino at Monte Carlo, where Bond won 500 francs at roulette.

After the holidays, Bond found it hard to settle back at Eton. He proved difficult. Then came the 'alleged trouble with one of the boys' maids'. Apparently, Bond told Pearson that the girl in question was not a housemaid, but Burglar's illegitimate half-sister who was staying with her father at the Dorchester. Bond, who looked older than his fifteen years, borrowed a motorbike and a fiver and rode up to London to take this beautiful seventeen-year-old French girl out for dinner. Henry heard about it and reported him, and James was expelled.

After Fettes, Bond went to Geneva University to be near his grandparents. He studied psychology and law, and read widely. In Fleming's books, however, Bond reads little more than books on golf, card-sharping and the occasional thriller by Fleming's friends Eric Ambler and Raymond Chandler – though it has to be said, in *The Man with the Golden Gun*, he has John F. Kennedy's *Profiles in Courage* in his suitcase.

Despite the city's puritanical mores, Bond felt at home in Geneva. His landlady on the Quai Gustave Ador was supposed to keep an eye on him. But he charmed her and was soon in a position to do whatever he pleased. There were girls, of course, and it was in Geneva that he fell in love with winter sports. When mocked by a skiing instructor for his lack of style, Bond challenged the man to a race down the dangerous Aiguille du Midi run at Chamonix, risking his life. He gained the reputation of being the wildest skier at the university and took a bobsleigh down the Cresta Run, a feat he revisited in *On Her Majesty's Secret Service*. And he climbed. In *From Russia with Love*, Bond was flying over the Alps when he recalled being a young man in his teens with a rope round his waist, bracing himself against the top of a rock chimney on the Aiguilles Rouges as his two companions from the University of Geneva inched up the smooth rock towards him.

In Geneva, Bond met a Russian anarchist and was intrigued by his critique of society, but refused his offer to play Russian roulette with a rusty .32 Smith & Wesson. He was understandably indignant when a psychiatrist told him he had a death wish.

At the end of term he went to Paris with Brinton. There, he recalled, after reading an advertisement in the *Continental Daily Mail*, he visited Harry's Bar. It was one of the most memorable evenings of Bond's life, culminating in the loss, almost simultaneously, of his virginity and his notecase. Pearson says that this happened in an upmarket brothel called the Elysée on the Place Vendôme where a girl called Alys from Martinique introduced him to the pleasure that would feature so largely in his subsequent adventures. At the same time, she stole his notecase containing his passport, 1,000 francs and pictures of his parents. Outraged and slightly drunk, he decked the doorman and called for the manager. This turned out to be Marthe de Brandt, who seems to be a younger version of prostitute-turned-madam-cum-spy Marthe Richard. She slapped Alys and sacked her, returned Bond's possessions and took him as her lover. The teenage Bond became a toy boy. She gave him a crash course in the arts of love and indulged him lavishly, even buying him his prized Bentley with the Amherst-Villiers supercharger that appears in Fleming's books. In her hands, Bond lost all modesty when it came to sex. When he suspected she was seeing a former lover, she invited the man to her apartment and made him watch while she and Bond made love.

Another of Marthe's former lovers was a man named Maddox. Officially the British military attaché in Paris, he was head of the SIS in France. It was 1937. War was looming. Someone had been leaking details of co-operation between the French and British high commands to the German newspapers. Maddox suspected Marthe. He took Bond to dinner and showed him pictures of Marthe in compromising positions with the German military attaché. At Maddox's behest, Bond agreed to kill Marthe. On the eve of her thirtieth birthday, on a weekend in the countryside, Bond staged a car crash. He went through the windscreen, giving him the distinctive three-inch scar on his right cheek. But Marthe was dead. This murder did not count towards his double-O rating. A few days later, Maddox discovered that Marthe was not to blame. There had been a German spy in the British embassy all along.

Maddox took care of everything. He installed Bond in a nursing home and got the Bentley fixed. Once Bond was back on his feet, Maddox inducted him into the Secret Service. Bond was then given a crash course in card-sharping by an American named Steffi Esposito which would stand him in good stead throughout his career. They tried out what he learnt at Casino Royale in Royale-les-Eaux on the French coast where Bond used his new-found skills to win at baccarat. He was then sent to Monte Carlo with René Mathis from the Deuxième Bureau, whom he worked with again in *Casino Royale, From Russia with Love* and *Thunderball,* and the film *Quantum of Solace.* Their assignment was to stop a team of Romanians who were breaking the bank at the casino: it seems they were using special glasses to read normally invisible signs marked on the back of the cards. After seducing the leader's mistress, Bond got her to switch the glasses. Using the villain's glasses himself, Bond taught them a lesson at the tables. The Romanians were forced to return all the money they had won and were deported from France.

Bond was instructed to return to Geneva University and use it as a cover for spying activities that would take him routinely into Germany, Italy and Spain. One night in Berlin, Bond found that instead of the contact he had taken as his mistress, in his bed was a male assassin. In the ensuing struggle, Bond killed him, gashing his throat open with a broken perfume bottle. He then escaped through the window and high-tailed it back to Switzerland.

According to Pearson, Bond made some youthful errors. Sent to deliver money to the Secret Service's network in Istanbul, he handed a briefcase containing £20,000 to the wrong man. Pearson says that Bond met the man again when he was in Istanbul in *From Russia with Love.* Outside the action of the book or the film, Bond discovered that the man had used the money to open a restaurant. As a result, Bond and his guest ate for free.

Bond travelled to Moscow to help a scientist to defect, but the man died after falling from an eighth-storey window. This reminded Bond of the death of his parents and he resorted to drink and sleeping pills – as he does in *You Only Live Twice* after his wife Tracy has been killed by Blofeld at the end of *On Her Majesty's Secret Service*. To recuperate, he took a break in Kitzbühel where he renewed his acquaintance with Ian Fleming. Fleming helped Bond pull out of his depression by introducing him to a lot of girls. Somehow Fleming also knew about Bond's work for the Secret Service. While he was there, Bond learnt to ski under the tutelage of Hannes Oberhausen, the man Major Smythe has murdered in the short story 'Octopussy'.

'He was something of a father to me at a time when I happened to need one,' Bond tells Smythe.

However, Pearson reckons that Fleming got this wrong in the story. Bond already knew how to ski, though Oberhausen might have helped him refine his style. Pearson also says that Oberhausen, who had been close to death many times in the mountains, taught Bond to live for the moment without looking back, with no regrets or remorse. It was a lesson well learnt.

On the other hand, in *On Her Majesty's Secret Service*, after Bond has escaped from Blofeld's Alpine lair, M says to Bond: 'Didn't know you could ski.' So presumably it was not in his service record. Bond, self-effacing as ever, says that he only just managed to stay upright and he 'wouldn't like to try it again'. In the movies, Bond – or at least his stunt double – is an expert skier.

Bond then moved to Paris where he was taught unarmed combat and how to shoot. Twice a week he would play bridge for money with Maddox at the fashionable Club Février. The routine was supposed to tough him up. But he was not entirely without feeling. In *Casino Royale*, when he hears 'La Vie en Rose', it brings seduction to mind. The song would continue to haunt him in *Diamonds are Forever*.

After a holiday with a married woman, Bond was ordered back to London where he went to work for Fleming at Naval

Intelligence. He was sent to observe the shipping coming out of Wilhelmshaven. After secondment into the Navy, he was trained as an agent at William Stephenson's camp in Canada. Alongside standard weapons training and more unarmed combat instruction, Bond was trained as a frogman, specializing in underwater combat. Then Fleming commissioned Bond to assassinate the Japanese code-breaker intercepting British intelligence traffic in New York's Rockefeller Center – a murder Bond admits to in *Casino Royale*.

Bond worked in occupied France, then countered the one-man submarines attacking Allied shipping in Alexandria harbour. Then he was sent to Stockholm to kill a Norwegian double agent, a man he knew. Again he admits to this in *Casino Royale*. This second murder earned Bond his double-O status. He smuggled Jewish scientists out of Switzerland, fought behind the lines in Italy, co-ordinated the French Resistance in the run-up to D-Day and thwarted the left-behind Nazi Werewolves in the Ardennes, as mentioned in *Dr No* and alluded to in other stories.

When Admiral Sir Miles Messervy – M – took over SIS after the war, he was unsure whether to keep Bond on. During a probationary period, Bond was sent to Washington to liaise with what was left of the OSS. He worked with 'Wild Bill' Donovan and Allen Dulles in the formation of the CIA, while spending most of his time bedding politicians' wives in Georgetown. This led to a scandal. M disapproved and Bond was sacked. He found it difficult to find another job. The rent due, he decided to try making money by gambling at his wartime club Blades, resisting the momentary temptation to reverse his fortunes by employing the card-sharping techniques he had been taught. Then he bumped into Maddox, who took him back to Paris. Employed as a 'security director' for French bankers, he travelled widely in Francophone Africa. But Bond fell for Maddox's wife and Maddox had him set up to be killed in Algeria. Bond foiled the plot and resigned. He played around in Kenya for a while, then travelled to the Seychelles where he became involved in the search for a rare fish related in 'The Hildebrand Rarity'. After the millionaire fish-hunter from the story was dead, Bond lived with his widow. Then Fleming turned up in the islands. He said things had changed at MI6 and persuaded Bond to return to London.

Fleming arranged for Bond to met M for lunch at Blades. Over steak-and-kidney pie and a carafe of the Algerian 'Infuriator of the Fleet' red wine M inflicted on Bond too in *On Her Majesty's Secret Service* and *The Man with the Golden Gun*, M offered Bond his old job back. This time he would be in the double-O section recently reformed to counter SMERSH's assassination squad. Bond had misgivings. He had had enough of killing, but Fleming persuaded him to take the job.

Bond soon found it was good to be back. Although he was a loner, he needed to be part of an organization. It gave his life context. First he had to undergo three months' intensive training in unarmed combat, weaponry, gadgets and the latest in intelligence techniques. Passed fit for duty, he selected a .32 Beretta as his personal weapon and underwent a three-day interrogation session where faceless inquisitors tried to break him. There it was discovered that his 'pain threshold' and 'co-efficient of resistance' were extraordinarily high. Then he went before a number of Civil Service boards before he was finally taken on as a Principal Officer attached to the Ministry of Defence. He was given his official pass to the offices of Universal Export near Regent's Park, where he had his own office and a shared secretary. His salary was £1,500 a year. He had another £1,000, tax free, of his own. On assignment he could spend as much as he liked and, according to Fleming in *Moonraker*, for the remaining months of the year he could live very well on an annual £2,000 net.

Bond had little to do with other members of the Service, though he occasionally lunched with M's Chief of Staff, Bill Tanner. He found a flat off the King's Road in Chelsea and Aunt Charmian found him his Scottish housekeeper, May, who had previously worked for Uncle Gregor. Bond's domestic arrangements were paid for by an inheritance from his great-uncle Ian, who had died recently.

Bond was given his 007 code name – the post had been vacant for some time – and sent to Jamaica after the station chief had been sending bizarre reports about a Cuban assassin named Gomez who had taken over the labour unions and the sect of the Goddess Kull. In Kingston, Bond discovered that those summoned to visit the Goddess Kull were found dead; others were terrorized.

Investigating Gomez's beach house, Bond saw a beautiful girl naked, oiling herself on the terrace. Later, when swimming, he rescued her from a shark. Bond then disguised himself as Kull's next victim, a wealthy businessman named Da Silva, and attended an exotic ritual when he is ordered to make love to the goddess, who is lying naked on the altar. It was the woman he had just rescued. But before he could be killed, Bond killed Gomez and his henchmen. The spell of Kull has been broken and Bond spent several days making love to the now defrocked goddess around Montego Bay. This pattern of killing the villain and bedding his girl was set to continue. Da Silva showed his gratitude at the beginning of *Casino Royale* by sending Bond ten million francs to play the tables.

According to Pearson, Bond's next assignment was to blow up a ship carrying arms to the EOKA terrorists on Cyprus. He spent the evening drinking with the ship's captain; he liked the man, but showed no emotion when the ship went down with all hands. After a brief holiday with Aunt Charmian in the South of France, Bond was recalled to be briefed about Le Chiffre in preparation for Fleming's first novel *Casino Royale*.

Later Pearson has Bond confront the SMERSH agent who left him alive at the end of *Casino Royale* and kill him. In revenge, SMERSH makes several attempts to kill Bond. In one, the wife of a Conservative MP Bond was having an affair with is injured. M strips Bond of his double-O status and his Beretta, and posts him back to the Caribbean. But before he goes, Fleming gets in touch. He invites Bond to join him at Blades where he is having lunch with M the following day. Over lunch, Fleming persuades M that the only way to save Bond's life is to convince SMERSH that he doesn't really exist by turning him into a fictional character. This was a tactic borrowed from Sefton Delmer and 'black propaganda'. When the Soviets discovered the truth, they tried to have him killed again in *From Russia with Love*. But they botched it. After that, they have their own reasons for letting Bond remain a figure of fiction. Then M decides that the Bond books provide indispensable publicity for the department. At least, that was the story as Pearson told it.

In real life, Fleming did not have just one Bond to base his stories on, but several. There was Fleming himself, of course, who lent the character many of his personal tastes and traits – though Bond, he admitted, had more guts. There were numerous candidates for the prototype Bond among Fleming's colleagues in Naval Intelligence; and Peter Fleming knew an SIS officer named Rodney Bond, who had saved his life during a clandestine operation in Greece.

Bond may also have borrowed something from Peter, who was involved in a number of wartime escapades with SOE. In the 1930s, in Kitzbühel, Fleming met mountaineer, artist and spy Conrad O'Brien-Ffrench, who was setting up network Z of journalists and businessmen, which provided invaluable information on the Nazis' preparations for war. Then there was Patrick Dalzel-Job, a member of 30AU, who dived, skied, piloted mini-submarines and parachuted behind enemy lines. He kept a compass in a button of his jacket and carried a pipe with a hidden compartment containing maps. Like Bond, he was a daredevil with a rebellious streak. However, Dalzel-Job dismissed the claim that he was Bond. 'I only ever loved one woman, and I'm not a drinking man,' he said.

There is a James Bond in the Agatha Christie short story 'The Rajah's Emerald' published in 1934, which Fleming is known to have read. There is also a St James-Bond Church in Toronto, which Fleming could conceivably have seen on his visit to Canada. Then there was the eponymous ornithologist

James Bond, who once visited Fleming at Goldeneye. A Canadian TV crew was there at the same time and Fleming introduced the author of *A Field Guide to the Birds of the West Indies* as 'the real James Bond'. In *Dr No* it is ostensibly an interest in birds that leads Bond to the villain's lair on Crab Key, while in the film *Die Another Day* Bond, in the person of Pierce Brosnan, claims to be an ornithologist and is seen holding a copy of the other Bond's *Field Guide*. Fleming himself said: 'I wanted the simplest, dullest, plainest-sounding name I could find – brief, unromantic, Anglo-Saxon and yet very masculine.' The reason was that he wanted his protagonist to be 'unobtrusive. Exotic things would happen to and around him, but he would be a neutral figure – an anonymous blunt instrument wielded by a government department.'

His code name, 007, was simpler in origin, according to Fleming.

'When I was in the Admiralty during the war,' he said, 'all the top-secret signals had the double-O prefix. Although this was later changed for security reasons, it stuck in my mind and I decided to borrow it for Bond.'

It was only natural that Fleming should give Bond a code number. At Naval Intelligence Fleming himself was 17F. On another occasion Fleming said that he had taken 007 from the zip code 20007, which covers Georgetown in Washington, DC, where many CIA agents lived. Then there is Forster's explanation, given above.

Bondologists have come up with other explanations. During World War I, Naval Intelligence had intercepted the Zimmermann telegram from the German foreign secretary urging Mexico to attack the US. This helped bring America into the war. The telegram had been encrypted in the German diplomatic code prefixed 007. So the number 007 was associated with British intelligence's greatest achievement, it is said. However, the number group appears nowhere in the telegram and the code identification number is 13042.

Another theory is that 007 originated with the sixteenth-century English mathematician, scientist, occultist, numerologist and, possibly, spy, Dr John Dee. Several authors mention that, in his coded messages to Queen Elizabeth, Dee was identified as 007. The two 0s looked like two eyes sheltered by an elongated 7, which was generally regarded as a mystical number. Fleming had been introduced to the works of John Dee by Aleister Crowley.

The truth is, the real James Bond is to be found in Ian Fleming's books.

4. Bond: The Books

Ian Fleming wrote twelve Bond novels and two books of short stories. The first novel, *Casino Royale*, introduces us to James Bond late at night, in a casino – a place where he would spend much of his professional life.

Casino Royale (1953)

Fleming's first draft read: 'Scent and smoke and sweat hit the taste buds with an acid thwack at three o'clock in the morning.' Then he tried: 'Scent and smoke and sweat combine together and hit the taste buds with an acid shock at three o'clock in the morning.' Finally, he came up with: 'The scent and smoke and sweat of a casino are nauseating at three in the morning . . .' And he was up and running. '. . . Then the soul-erosion produced by high gambling – a compost of greed and fear and nervous tension – becomes unbearable and the senses awake and revolt from it . . .'

We are in the sophisticated, high-voltage world of the casino and James Bond is watching his quarry, the Soviet agent Le Chiffre. Within the first few pages we are told that Bond is a secret agent, working for M who occupies a 'deadly' office building near Regent's Park. The action switches to the office, where M, head of the British Secret Service, has received a memorandum outlining the situation. Le Chiffre works for SMERSH. We are told that the murderous organization's name is a contraction of *Smert Shpionam*, or 'Death to Spies'. He is the undercover paymaster of a trade union in Alsace, but has diverted Soviet funds into a private venture: a chain of brothels. However, he has been caught out by the Marthe Richard law, curtailing prostitution. SMERSH will kill him if they find out he has stolen their money, so he intends to win it back at the gaming tables of the fictional town of Royale-les-Eaux. As Bond has already proved adept at gambling, defeating the Romanian team in Monte Carlo, he was despatched to stop him.

The Deuxième Bureau sends René Mathis to help him, while Section S send the beautiful Vesper Lynd. Bond does not approve of women agents, but falls for her anyway. Felix Leiter from the CIA also turns up. Soon we are introduced to Bond's 1930 4.5-litre Bentley, his passion for scrambled eggs, his fondness for champagne and dry Martinis and his eye for pretty women. We also share his danger when two Bulgars blow themselves up while trying to bomb 007 – an incident Fleming said was based on the attempted assassination of Franz von Papen, the German ambassador to Turkey, by the NKVD in 1942. There too the bomb went off prematurely, killing the Bulgarian assassin while von Papen was only slightly injured.

Bond confronts Le Chiffre at the baccarat table. Bond is soon cleaned out, but Leiter slips him another thirty-two million (old) francs. A gunman sticks a pistol disguised in a malacca cane in Bond's back and whispers that he must withdraw his bet. Bond launches himself backwards and breaks the cane, disarming him. Bond then pretends he was merely overcome by the atmosphere and resumes his place at the table. This time he beats Le Chiffre, who leaves the table without a word.

After Bond and Vesper celebrate, she is kidnapped by Le Chiffre and his men. Bond pursues them. There is a car chase. Bond is captured after running across a bed of spikes laid across the road. To recover Bond's winnings, Le Chiffre tortures him by sitting him on seatless chair and beating his genitals with a carpet-beater. Bond won't relent, even though he is certain he is going to die. At the last moment, a SMERSH assassin arrives and kills Le Chiffre. He lets Bond live as he has no orders to kill him. However, he cuts an inverted M in his hand: this is the Cyrillic letter 'Ш' for шпион or *shpion*, meaning spy.

Bond spends three weeks in hospital recovering and considering whether to resign from the Secret Service. Then he drives off down the coast to convalesce with Vesper. A man called Adolph Gettler turns up, wearing a black eyepatch. Knowing that he is an assassin from SMERSH, Vesper kills herself, admitting in her suicide note that she had been a double agent all along. Bond rebukes himself for playing 'Red Indians' when 'the real enemy had been working quietly, coldly, without heroics, right there at his elbow'. He decides to stay in the service to fight SMERSH. He then receives a call warning him that Vesper is a double agent. He replies: 'The bitch is dead now.'

Casino Royal was published in hardback in the UK by Jonathan Cape in April 1953. It came out in paperback in the US as *You Asked For It* in 1955, then reverted to the title *Casino Royale* in the US in 1960.

Live and Let Die (1954)

James Bond reappears flying into Idlewild Airport (renamed JFK in 1963) at the beginning of *Live and Let Die*, which Fleming had originally entitled 'The Undertaker's Wind'. This became the title of Chapter 17, where Bond's sidekick from the Cayman Islands, Quarrel, explains that the 'Undertaker's Wind' blows the bad air from Jamaica from six at night until six in the morning. It is followed by the 'Doctor's Wind' that blows sweet air in from the sea.

Whisked through immigration courtesy of the FBI, Bond is taken to the St Regis hotel, where he meets up with Felix Leiter again. Back in London, Bond had been summoned by M, who explained that seventeenth-century gold coins, possibly part of a haul taken by Henry Morgan, the pirate, had been turning up in Florida and Harlem. M believes that the money is being used to sponsor Soviet espionage in the US. The man responsible is a Haitian named Mr Big. He was bringing the coins into St Petersburg on the Gulf coast of Florida from a small island off the north coast of Jamaica on his yacht, the *Secatur*. He covered his activities by posing as the head of a voodoo cult that believe he is Baron Samedi, a leader of the 'living dead'. Mr Big is also a Soviet agent.

Leiter and the FBI do their best to Americanize Bond, dressing him in American clothes and teaching him the rudiments of the language. Meanwhile Bond mugs up on voodoo, reading *The Traveller's Tree* by Ann Fleming's friend Patrick Leigh Fermor, a book that had been recommended by M. During breakfast, a parcel is delivered. Bond hears it ticking and dives behind a chair. It explodes.

Bond and Leiter go up to Harlem to investigate and end up watching a stripper from a booth in one of Mr Big's nightclubs. At the climax of her act, the lights go out. Bond and Leiter are grabbed as their booth disappears downward on a hydraulic lift. They put up a fight, but Leiter is badly beaten while Bond – 'the Limey' – is taken away to see Mr Big.

Bond is interrogated with the help of a beautiful white woman named Solitaire, who Mr Big intends to marry. She is supposed to be psychic. Bond denies that he has come to the US to assassinate Mr Big. Surprisingly, Solitaire confirms that he is speaking the truth. Mr Big then orders his bodyguard Tee-Hee to break the little finger on Bond's left hand, but decides not to kill Bond. On his way out Bond takes his revenge on Tee-Hee, kicking him down a flight of stairs with a steel-capped shoe and taking his gun. He shoots several more black men while making his escape. Mr Big is sure to be after Bond now. So to get out of New York in one piece, Bond is instructed to take the train – the Silver Phantom – from Pennsylvania Station to St Petersburg. But before he leaves, he gets a phone call from Solitaire, begging him to take her with him. When she threatens to kill herself, he relents and tells her to meet him on the train, giving her his Pullman car number.

On the train, she tells him that Mr Big has alerted a man named The Robber to look out for him in Florida. She also explains more about voodoo and zombies, and confirms that

Mr Big is working for Moscow. They kiss and she undresses, but Bond's broken finger hurts too much for him to make love to her. It also prevents him shooting the person who tries to break into their compartment.

They slip off the train at Jacksonville and take the next train to St Petersburg. There they meet up with Felix Leiter again, who tells them that, after Jacksonville, their compartment was machine-gunned and blown up. While Bond and Leiter go to investigate Ourobouros Inc. Worm and Bait factory on the wharf where the *Secatur* frequently docks, Solitaire is kidnapped. That night Felix returns to the Ourobouros, only to be returned to Bond half-dead after an encounter with a shark: on his body is a note saying, 'He disagreed with something that ate him.'

Discovering that the Ourobouros warehouse sell sharks, Bond heads back there. Breaking in, he finds that the gold coins are being transported under the mud at the bottom of tanks containing poisonous tropical fish. He is caught by The Robber, who tries to push Bond into the shark tank where Leiter had been mauled. But Bond throws The Robber in instead.

Bond heads for Jamaica where he meets John Strangways, head of SIS in the Caribbean, and is introduced to Quarrel. The best swimmer and fisherman in the Caribbean, he gives Bond training in scuba diving and Bond swims through shark- and barracuda-infested water out to Mr Big's island. There he puts a limpet mine with a time fuse on the hull of the *Secatur*. He finds the entrance to the underwater cave where Captain Morgan's treasure was hidden, then goes after Solitaire. But Mr Big is waiting for him.

Bond and Solitaire are tied together and dragged through the water behind Mr Big's yacht. His aim is to drag them across a shallow coral reef that will tear the flesh from their bodies. Their blood in the water would then attract the sharks and barracuda, that would devour them. Just seconds before they reach the reef, the limpet mine explodes; Mr Big is blown into the water and is eaten by the sharks and barracuda. Bond and Solitaire return to

Jamaica where M cables, granting him two weeks' 'passionate leave'.

The novel has been criticized for its racism. Indeed Fleming calls Mr Big and his African-American henchmen 'negroes'. He even uses the chapter title 'Nigger Heaven'. While Fleming showed no personal animosity towards black people, counting them among his friends in Jamaica, he was a man of his time and he was writing in 1953, an unenlightened era. But times were changing. Even the unswervingly Edwardian M says: '. . . the negro races are just beginning to throw up geniuses in all the professions – scientists, doctors, writers. It's about time they turned out a great criminal.'

Moonraker (1955)

The next novel *Moonraker* finds Bond back in England, where the multimillionaire Sir Hugo Drax is posing as a super-patriot. At his own expense, Drax is building a rocket that could carry a nuclear warhead to almost any capital city in Europe – the ultimate deterrent to anyone who tries to drop an atomic bomb on London. It is called the Moonraker. But M has a problem. Drax cheats at cards – and he has to be stopped.

Bond goes to Blades, where he and M play Drax at bridge. Bond puts Drax at ease by staging a show of getting drunk. However, he adds Benzedrine to his champagne to keep alert. Bond notices that Drax deals the cards over a shiny cigarette case he leaves on the table so that he can read them. Even though he is losing, Bond ups the stakes, then by sleight of hand substitutes a deck he has stacked earlier. Drax loses £15,000 and warns Bond to spend the money quickly.

When a security officer working on the Moonraker project is murdered, Bond is assigned to replace him at the rocket site which is on the Kent coast between Dover and Deal, near where Fleming had a country cottage. There Bond meets the attractive Gala Brand, a Special Branch agent working undercover as Drax's assistant. Bond catches Drax's henchman Krebs snooping in his room. Then, when Bond and Gala take a walk under the cliffs, they are almost killed in a rock fall.

Gala discovers that the trajectory co-ordinates she has been given for the rocket are not the same as those in a notebook she purloins from Drax's pocket. But she is caught and locked in a London flat that contains a homing beacon for the missile. When Gala does not turn up for a dinner date, Bond goes after Drax, who is taking Gala, bound in the back of his car, to Kent. Bond gives chase. But after an accident that writes off his Bentley, Bond is captured too.

It turns out that Drax, rather than being a British patriot, is in fact an ex-Nazi, hell-bent on extracting his revenge for the fall of the Third Reich. With the help of the Soviets, who have supplied a nuclear warhead, Drax is going to destroy London with Moonraker.

Bond and Gala are imprisoned in the silo under the rocket where no trace will be left of them once the engines have been ignited. But they manage to escape and change the rocket's gyros back to their original settings, so that it will fall harmlessly into the middle of the North Sea. Believing London is about to be destroyed, Drax is making his escape in Soviet submarine when he is hit by the nuclear warhead as the submarine sails through the original target area.

After being debriefed by M, Bond intends to take Gala off for a holiday on the Continent in his new Bentley. But she has other plans: she is to marry someone else the following day. It is the only time in any of the novels that Bond does not get the girl.

Diamonds are Forever (1956)

Bond has no such trouble in *Diamonds are Forever*, which begins with two men from the diamond mines in Sierra Leone waiting for a helicopter to land at night. They hand the pilot a package.

After a two-week holiday in France – apparently alone – Bond is assigned to infiltrate a smuggling ring that has been running diamonds stolen from mines in Africa to the United States. Posing as gentleman burglar Peter Franks, Bond meets Tiffany Case, half-naked in her hotel room, who offers to pay him £5,000 to carry diamonds hidden in golf balls from London to

New York. She, in turn, takes her instructions by telephone from a mysterious figure known only as ABC.

Washington believes that the diamonds are being run for the Spangled Mob, a gang run by mobsters Jack and Seraffimo Spang. After Bond delivers the diamonds, he is told that he can collect his money by betting on a rigged horse race at Saratoga. Pinkerton agent Felix Leiter, who left the CIA after losing an arm and a leg in *Live and Let Die*, then fixes the race so that the arranged horse does not win. Consequently, Bond is sent to Las Vegas where he is to be paid off in a crooked blackjack game in the Tiara Hotel, which is owned by the Spang twins.

The dealer at the blackjack table is Tiffany Case. Bond takes his money, but then moves to the roulette table and walks out with $200,000. Las Vegas Pinkerton man and cab driver Ernie Cureo tells Bond that, as well as the Tiara Hotel, Seraffimo Spang also owns an old Western ghost town called Spectreville. (Despite its determinedly British spelling, it has no connection to SPECTRE, which does not appear until *Thunderball*.) Spang has turned it into a private vacation retreat, complete with a nineteenth-century railroad train called the Cannonball. But hoodlums are on their tail and, after a car chase, Bond is captured and taken out to Spectreville, where he is unmasked as an agent and given a 'Brooklyn stomping'. With Tiffany's help, he escapes and together they flee down the railway line on a handcart. The Cannonball comes after them, but they switch it on to a branch line. Bond shoots Spang as the Cannonball crashes into a rock at the end of the line.

Tiffany and Bond then take a romantic cruise from New York back to London on the *Queen Elizabeth*. But two of Spang's henchmen, Wint and Kidd, are on the liner. They grab Tiffany – they have orders to kill her. Bond rescues her and kills the two henchmen, making it look like a murder-suicide.

The mysterious ABC turns out to be Jack Spang, who Bond had come across when he was working under the pseudonym Rufus B. Saye in London's Hatton Garden. He turns up on the helicopter in West Africa to close down the pipeline – by shooting the two men from the diamond mines. Bond turns up with a detachment of soldiers and a Bofors gun and blows Spang and the helicopter out of the sky.

From Russia with Love (1957)

Bond and Tiffany lived together for a few months, though she was out of his life by the time we meet Bond in *From Russia with Love*. The book begins with SMERSH assassin Donovan 'Red' Grant, a British defector, lying naked beside the swimming pool of his villa in the Crimea, being massaged by a topless girl. The phone rings and he is ordered to Moscow where a top-level meeting of SMERSH is being held. They identify James Bond as the man who has thwarted them – in France in *Casino Royale*, in England in *Moonraker* and in the US in *Live and Let Die* – and sign his death warrant. Its execution is put in the hands of Colonel Rosa Klebb. Women, it is decided, are Bond's weakness. So the beautiful Corporal Tatiana Romanova is employed as bait.

Tatiana is terrified when she is summoned to Klebb's apartment one evening. She is treated to French champagne and Swiss chocolates, and asked about her sex life. She is told that she must fall in love with an English spy and is shown Bond's picture. Rosa Klebb then disappears into the bedroom and returns in a see-through nightgown. Tatiana flees.

When Red Grant turns up in Klebb's office, he is told to strip naked. She examines him, then suddenly punches him in the solar plexus with a knuckleduster. When he does not flinch, he is told that he is to kill an English spy. It is decided that the assassination must take place in France, or nearby, as the French press would make the most of the story.

In London, Bond is ruing the loss of Tiffany, who has left him and gone back to America. He is bored when he is summoned by M. A message has come from Darko Kerim, head of Station T in Istanbul, saying that a Soviet cipher clerk named Tatiana Romanov has seen Bond's picture in his file, fallen in love with him and wishes to defect. She says that she will bring a Spektor cipher machine, which the British are desperate to get their hands on – on the condition that Bond comes out to Istanbul to collect her.

Bond flies to Istanbul where he forms an instant friendship with Darko Kerim, who takes him through an underground tunnel he uses to spy on the Soviet Consulate. Here Bond first glimpses Tatiana and is smitten. That evening, Kerim takes Bond for dinner with some gypsies. Two gypsy girls have a cat-fight, tearing off each other's clothes. The camp is attacked by Bulgarian hit men and in the ensuing gunfight, Bond saves Kerim's life. They then go and kill the man who ordered the attack. Returning to his hotel room, Bond finds Tatiana in his bed, naked except for silk stockings and a black velvet ribbon around her neck. She insists that, instead of flying back to London, they take the Orient Express. Then they make love. Meanwhile, behind a two-way mirror, two men from SMERSH are filming them.

The following day, Tatiana arrives at the station with the Spektor machine and chides Bond for being more interested in the machine than in her. For a moment he feels a pang of guilt, but there is little time for such feelings. On the train are three Soviet agents. With trickery and bribery, Kerim gets two of them taken off the train at the Greek border. But the remaining Soviet agent stabs Kerim, who uses his dying strength to stab and kill his assassin.

At Trieste, a man purporting to come from the Secret Service gets on. He introduces himself as Captain Norman Nash. Tatiana does not trust him, but collapses, drugged. Bond is tricked into handing over his Beretta. Nash shoots at him with a gun concealed in a copy of *War and Peace*. The bullet ricochets off Bond's Rolex. Nash then introduces himself as the chief executioner of SMERSH – Red Grant. He looks at his watch. They have twenty minutes before they reach the Simplon Tunnel where he has been ordered to kill Bond – so he has plenty of time to explain the plot and reveal that he has to report to Rosa Klebb in the Ritz Hotel in Paris. That done, he pulls the trigger and Bond falls. But the bullet has hit his cigarette case, not his heart. As Grant goes to kill Tatiana, Bond grabs one of the knives Q has hidden in his attaché case and stabs Grant, finishing him off with his own book-gun.

In the Paris Ritz Bond keeps Grant's appointment with Klebb. She tries to kill him, finally slashing him with a poisoned blade concealed in her shoe.

Dr No (1958)

In *Dr No*, we learn from the eminent neurologist Sir James Molony that Klebb used tetrodotoxin from the Japanese fugu fish to poison Bond. This paralyses the muscles, leaving the victim conscious but unable to breathe; he will die of asphyxiation. Fortunately Mathis from the Deuxième Bureaux was on hand to give Bond artificial respiration and the doctor summoned had been in South America and was familiar with curare, which has similar properties. Bond is now physically fit but needs a holiday. Fortunately an opportunity for a little rest and relaxation at the department's expense has presented itself.

The Secret Service's man in Jamaica John Strangways and his number two, Mary Trueblood, have been killed by some mysterious Chigroes – half black, half Chinese – and their bodies disposed of in a reservoir. But M thinks they may have run off together and sends Bond to investigate as a holiday assignment. First he is forced to replace his Beretta .25 with a Walther PPK. In Jamaica, he learns that Strangways was investigating the activities of Dr Julius No, a reclusive German-Chinese who lives on an island called Crab Key where several unexplained deaths have been attributed to a dragon said to live there. No makes money by exporting guano (seabird dung that is used as fertilizer).

Bond soon realizes that he is being watched. His room has been searched. A basket of fruit arrives, purportedly a present from the governor. Bond examines the fruit and discovers that it has been poisoned. Later, he awakes to find a deadly centipede crawling across him in bed. After he kills it with his shoe, he is violently sick.

Believing Dr No to be responsible, Bond sails out to Crab Key with his old friend Quarrel. On the beach, he sees a beautiful young woman, naked except for a belt carrying a hunting knife around her waist. When he surprises her, she covers her pudendum with one hand. But instead of covering her breasts with her other arm she covers her nose, which has been broken. Her name is Honeychile Rider. She explains that she comes out to the island to hunt for shells, which she sells for a living.

A gunboat appears. As they make their way inland they are pursued by the 'dragon' – which turns out to be a tractor armed with a flame-thrower, painted to look like a mythical beast. Quarrel is incinerated, Bond and Honeychile captured. Dr No's back story is that he stole money from the Tongs, who cut his hands off, and shot him. He was saved because he is one of those rare individuals who have their heart on the right side of their body. In place of hands, he is now equipped with two steel pincers.

He tells Bond that he is employed by the Soviets to sabotage US missile tests, using radio signals from Crab Key to throw them off course. No is also interested in the ability of the human body to withstand and survive pain and stress. He forces Bond to crawl and climb through an obstacle course inside the ventilation system of his lair. Bond is kept under regular observation and encounters electric shocks, burns and poisonous spiders along the way. The course ends in an inlet where a giant squid is trapped. Bond uses his ingenuity and physical toughness, along with objects that he had the foresight to steal to use as weapons, to defeat the squid.

Bond then kills Dr No by taking over the guano-loading machine at the docks and burying him alive in bird droppings. Meanwhile Honeychile has undergone her own ordeal. She had been pegged out naked at night to be eaten by crabs, but she knew the crabs would leave her alone if she lay perfectly still. When they disappeared into their holes in the morning, she had wriggled free.

Bond and Honey escape from Dr No's complex on the tractor-dragon and are rescued by the Navy. Then Bond telegrams

M requesting more sick leave, and spends the time making love to Honey.

Goldfinger (1959)

Despite this pleasant interlude, by the beginning of *Goldfinger*, Honeychile is forgotten. However, according to Pearson's *Authorised Biography*, Bond is still with Honeychile years later when he is in his fifties. She is wealthy by then and he is planning to resign from the Secret Service and marry her, but in the end cannot help accepting one further assignment.

Goldfinger begins with Bond in reflective mood. In the departure lounge of Miami Airport, he has two double bourbons and is thinking about the Mexican drug dealer he has just killed. After a third double, he bumps into Mr Du Pont – Bond had sat next to Du Pont and his wife at the game against Le Chiffre in *Casino Royale*. Over more drinks, Du Pont explains that he had been playing two-handed canasta against the multimillionaire Auric Goldfinger; he suspects Goldfinger of cheating, and employs Bond to investigate. Bond discovers that Goldfinger's 'companion', Jill Masterton, has been using binoculars to observe Du Pont's hand. She then radios the cards to a receiver in the hearing aid Goldfinger is wearing. Bond uses the radio link to threaten to expose Goldfinger unless he pays Du Pont back the money he has cheated him out of, along with a fee for himself. For good measure, he makes Goldfinger book a compartment on the train to New York – complete with caviar and champagne – for Jill and himself.

Back in London, the Bank of England has approached the Secret Service to investigate the smuggling of gold between England to India. Goldfinger is suspected. M is interested because he believes that Goldfinger acts as the banker of SMERSH's foreign operations. Bond is assigned to investigate. Goldfinger is back in England now and Bond gets involved in a high-stakes game of golf with him. Goldfinger cheats by switching balls, but Bond beats him at his own game and wins the match.

Goldfinger invites Bond to dinner in his home in Kent, where he sees armour plating being riveted on to Goldfinger's Rolls-Royce. He also meets Goldfinger's Korean 'handyman' Oddjob, who gives an impressive display of karate. And he demonstrates his metal-brimmed bowler hat which is a lethal weapon.

Having fitted a radio beacon to Goldfinger's Rolls-Royce, Bond follows him across France and sees him making a dead-letter drop with a gold bar, before he heads on to Switzerland. Bond also notes that a girl in a Triumph TR3 was shadowing Goldfinger. He deliberately runs into her car to delay her. But she insists that he give her a lift to Geneva. Once he has dropped her off, Bond tracks Goldfinger to a small factory on the road to Lausanne. There he sees men stripping the armour plating off Goldfinger's Rolls. It is, in fact, gold and is being melted down to be made into the frames of seats for an Indian airline so that it can be smuggled to the subcontinent.

Bond returns to the factory that night to collect evidence and again bumps into the girl with the Triumph. She has a rifle and has come to kill Goldfinger. It turns out that she is Tilly Masterson and Goldfinger has killed her sister Jill. When Jill had returned to Miami after her trip to New York with Bond, Goldfinger had her painted all over with gold. This clogged her pores and she died. Bond suffers pangs of guilt, figuring Goldfinger had killed her because Bond had taken her away with him. He too swore revenge. But before they can take their vengeance, Tilly and Bond are captured. Bond is tortured, strapped spreadeagled to the platform of a circular saw. As the saw approaches, he holds his breath until he passes out. When he comes round, he discovers that he and Tilly have been drugged and flown to the US: here Goldfinger forces them to work for him. He intends to rob Fort Knox. To pull this off, he assembles an army of mobsters from across the US. These include the Spangled Mob, last seen in *Diamonds are Forever*, and Pussy Galore with her lesbian gang, the Cement Mixers.

Goldfinger's plan is to add a nerve agent to the water supply to knock out the armoured division guarding the bullion depository. Using an atomic warhead he had bought, he will break into the vault, then take the gold out of the country on a Soviet cruiser that is making a goodwill visit to the US naval base at Norfolk, Virginia.

On a reconnaissance flight over Fort Knox, Bond hides a note in the lavatory offering the cleaner $5,000 reward to contact Felix Leiter at Pinkerton's with details of the plan. Leiter turns up with the army and foils the robbery. But Tilly is killed with Oddjob's bowler, while Goldfinger and his crew escape.

After a red-carpet reception in Washington, Bond heads back to the UK. But at Idlewild, he is drugged and taken aboard a Stratocruiser stolen from BOAC – British Overseas Airways Corporation, which was amalgamated with British European Airways to form British Airways in 1974. It is also taking Goldfinger and what remains of his bullion to Moscow. Using a knife concealed in the heel of his shoe, Bond breaks a window. The cabin depressurizes and Oddjob is sucked out. In a struggle, Bond strangles Goldfinger. He ordered the pilot to ditch the plane near a weather ship. On board, Bond finally beds Pussy Galore.

For Your Eyes Only (1960)

Bond makes his next appearance in the collection of short stories, *For Your Eyes Only*. The first story is 'From a View to a Kill', which begins with the murder of a NATO despatch rider in France. Bond, who is in Paris at the time, is tracked by local agent Mary Ann Russell and sent to investigate, taking the place of another despatch rider on the run. The assassin comes after him, but Bond is ready and kills him instead. He then discovers the enemy's secret lair in the forest, but the men there get the better of him, until he is saved by Mary Ann Russell.

The story 'For Your Eyes Only' begins with the murder of the Havelocks, a Jamaican couple who have refused to sell their estate to a former Gestapo officer named von Hammerstein who is the chief of counterintelligence for the Cuban Secret Service. They are killed by two Cuban hit men under the

direction of Major Gonzales. But the Havelocks are close friends
of M, who had been best man at their wedding in 1925. Von
Hammerstein is currently at an estate he is renting at Echo Lake
in Vermont. Bond volunteers to sneak over the Canadian border
and kill him. But when Bond arrives at the estate, he finds that
the Havelocks' daughter, Judy is there on a revenge mission.
Judy shoots von Hammerstein in the back with a bow and arrow
as he dives into a lake. In the shoot-out that follows, Bond kills
Major Gonzales and the two Cuban gunmen. He then takes
Judy off to a motel.

For the story 'Quantum of Solace' the scene shifts to the
Bahamas, where Bond is having dinner with the governor and a
boring Canadian couple. After they have left, Bond remarks
that he'd always thought that if he were to marry he would
marry an air hostess. Whereupon, the governor tells a tale. A
rather innocent colleague of his in the Colonial Service named
Philip Masters fell for a pretty young air hostess named Rhoda
Llewellyn who had taken an interest in him on a flight to
London. They married. He was then posted to Bermuda. But
she found colonial life boring and began a long, extremely indis-
creet affair with the eldest son of a rich Bermudian family. As a
result Masters had a nervous breakdown. While recovering he
was sent to Washington to negotiate fishing rights. The governor's wife had a talk with Masters's wife and her affair came to
an end. When Masters returned, he divided their home in two
and refused to have anything to do with his wife in private,
although in public they put on a brave face as a happy couple.

The governor has a theory that gives the story its title. He
says that he has seen couples repair relationships after flagrant
infidelities – even murders. But once the 'quantum of solace' –
the amount of basic humanity the couple feel for each other
– drops to zero, then it is time to get out.

Although Masters thought he had taken an apt revenge on
his unfaithful wife, he never recovered emotionally. After a
time Rhoda married a rich Canadian and went on to find
happiness again. Bond remarks that she hardly deserved her

good fortune, but the governor says Masters had always been a weak character. Perhaps 'Fate' had chosen Rhoda as its instrument to teach him a lesson. The governor then reveals that the dinner companions Bond found so boring were Rhoda and her Canadian husband.

This dinner party plainly took place on Bond's night off. He neither killed anyone, won a bundle at a casino nor bedded some tortured beauty.

The action returns in the story 'Risico'. Bond is sent to investigate a smuggling operation based in Italy, which is flooding Britain with drugs. M puts Bond in touch with a CIA informant named Kristatos who tells Bond that a man named Enrico Colombo is behind the racket. When Bond sets out to investigate, he is captured and taken aboard Colombo's ship. Colombo explains that he is a relatively innocent cigarette smuggler and tells Bond that Kristatos is actually the one behind the drug smuggling operation, which is backed by the Soviets. Bond agrees to help Colombo eliminate Kristatos. They set off to Santa Maria, a small fishing port north of Ancona, where Kristatos's men are loading a shipment of drugs. Bond, Colombo and his men attack Kristatos's ship. Bond discovers Kristatos detonating a bomb to destroy the warehouse and kills him as he tries to escape. Then Colombo, out of gratitude, gives Bond the key to his mistress's hotel bedroom.

The story 'The Hildebrand Rarity' finds Bond diving in the Seychelles. Through his friend Fidele Barbey, Bond meets American millionaire Milton Krest. Bond and Barbey agree to help in the search for a rare fish with spiny fins named 'The Hildebrand Rarity' after the scientist who discovered it. But it transpires that Krest only wants to collect the fish to justify the tax-free status of his yacht, which he claims is used for scientific research. On board is Krest's English-born wife, Elizabeth. During the trip, Krest verbally abuses everyone around him and physically abuses his wife, whipping her with a stingray tail he calls the 'Corrector'. When they reach the atoll where the rare fish was last spotted, instead of trying to catch it with a net, Krest pours poison into the water, killing the local sea life. With the dead specimen of the Hildebrand Rarity, they head for home. Along the way, Krest gets very drunk, insults Bond and Barbey, and schedules another appointment for his wife with the 'Corrector'. He also threatens to get the crewmen to throw Bond overboard, after seeing him talk to his wife.

That night, Bond hears Krest choking and goes on deck to find Krest dead with the Hildebrand Rarity stuffed down his throat. Bond throws Krest into the sea, making it look as though, in his cups, Krest simply fell overboard. Once the formalities have been completed in the Seychelles, Mrs Krest invites James to accompany her to Mombasa, her next destination. Knowing that she probably killed her husband, Bond hesitates for a moment, then accepts her invitation.

Thunderball (1961)

At the beginning of *Thunderball,* Bond is in poor physical condition and M sends him to Shrublands health farm. There he meets Count Lippe, who is, curiously, a member of the Red Lightning Tong from Macao. Lippe tries to kill Bond by tampering with the spinal traction machine. Bond is saved by nurse Patricia Fearing; he then seduces her and gets his own back on Lippe by trapping him in a steam cabinet.

Bond is fit for action again, when a communiqué is received from SPECTRE, then headed by Ernst Stavro Blofeld. It says that SPECTRE has hijacked an RAF V bomber with two nuclear bombs on board and is demanding £100 million for details of its whereabouts. Otherwise it will destroy a piece of property worth more than £100 million, killing people and causing panic. Then SPECTRE will blow up a major city.

As a member of SPECTRE, Lippe had been despatched to Shrublands to keep an eye on Giuseppi Petacchi, a NATO observer seconded to the RAF. On board the V bomber, he murdered the crew and flew the plane to the Bahamas where he landed it in shallow water. Petacchi was expecting a reward.

Instead he was killed, along with Lippe, who was now considered unreliable after his run-in with Bond.

M suspects that the bombs have been taken to the Bahamas:
as the islands are close to the US coastline, the bombs could be
carried there easily on a motor launch. Bond is sent to investigate in what is designated Operation Thunderball. In Nassau,
he meets Dominetta 'Domino' Vitali. She is the mistress of
Emilio Largo, who is ostensibly in the Bahamas on a secretive
treasure hunting expedition. This piques Bond's interest.

Felix Leiter, who is back with the CIA, turns up. Bond discovers that Largo's yacht, the *Disco Volante*, has an underwater
compartment where the bombs could be transported. They also
find the submerged V bomber. Bond dives on it and recovers
Giuseppe Petacchi's dog tags. It transpires that Petacchi is the
brother of Dominetta Vitali.

After Bond has made love to Domino, he reveals the fate of
her brother. She agrees to take a Geiger counter on board the
Disco Volante to see if the bombs are there. Meanwhile, Bond
and Leiter board the US submarine *Manta* to follow the *Disco
Volante*. But Largo captures Domino with the Geiger counter
and tortures her.

As Largo's men begin to deploy one of the bombs, a team of
divers from the *Manta* attack. After saving Leiter's life, Bond
confronts Largo. He manages to thwart Largo's plan to plant
the bomb, but is trapped by Largo in a narrow passage in the
coral. Largo clamps an octopus over Bond's mask and is about
to kill him, when Domino arrives and fires a harpoon through
Largo's neck. Both Bond and Domino end up in hospital.
Though he can barely walk, Bond makes it to Domino's room
before collapsing.

The Spy Who Loved Me (1962)

The next of Bond's lovers we know about is a young French-
Canadian woman named Vivienne Michel. In a prologue to
most editions of *The Spy Who Loved Me*, Fleming says that he
found a manuscript written by Vivienne Michel on his desk one

morning. He was interested because it presented a view of James
Bond 'through the wrong end of the telescope so to speak'. After
clearing for any infringement of the Official Secrets Act,
Fleming says, he sponsored its publication.

In the first part of the book, entitled 'Me', Vivienne writes of
the loss of her parents and her childhood in Quebec. At the age
of sixteen, she was sent to a finishing school in England. After
two unsuccessful relationships, she returns to Quebec, then sets
off on a road trip down into the US on a motor scooter.

In part two, 'Them', she gets a job in The Dreamy Pines
Motor Court. When the motel was closing for the season, she
is asked to stay on to hand the keys over to the owner, Mr
Sanguinetti. She is alone at night when two men turn up
claiming they are from Sanguinetti's insurers and have come
to take an inventory. It turns out they are two gangsters
named Sluggsy Morant and Sol 'Horror' Horowitz. When
she tries to escape, they beat her, strip her naked and threaten
to rape her. She is fighting them off when the front door
buzzer sounds.

Part three is called 'Him'. The man at the front door is
English. It is Bond. His car has a flat tyre and he needs a room
for the night. When Sol and Horror try to turn him away, he
threatens to make trouble for the motel's owner. Viv goes to help
Bond get his bags from the car and informs him that the men
are armed. Bond arms himself and when he registers he tells
them he's with the police.

Bond then, uncharacteristically, starts running at the mouth.
He talks about Operation Thunderball and how he killed an
ex-Gestapo assassin working for SPECTRE who had been
hired by the Russians to kill a Soviet defector in Toronto. Then
he takes some Benzedrine to keep him awake in the night..

That night Sol and Horror set fire to the motel in what Bond
has already figured out is an insurance scam. They try to kill
him, but Bond has put a makeshift dummy in his bed, which
they shoot. He rescues the girl. Together they confront the
villains. Bond kills one of them. When Vivienne hits the other,

who is trying to escape, his car runs off the road into the lake. Bond and Vivienne then make love. It is unlike anything she has experienced before. Sluggsy then reappears and Bond finishes him off.

In the morning Bond has gone. The cops turn up, sent by Bond. The police captain has checked out Bond with Washington and warns Vivienne to keep away from men like him: 'They are not for you, whether they are called James Bond or Sluggsy Morant.' They are, he says, a 'different species'.

The Spy Who Loved Me was not well received and Fleming persuaded Jonathan Cape not to reprint the book, or publish a paperback version. Many critics do not consider it part of the James Bond canon.

On Her Majesty's Secret Service (1963)

There was no doubt that Ian Fleming was back on form with his next novel *On Her Majesty's Secret Service* and sales soared. James Bond was back in the centre of the action, pitted once more against SPECTRE and its mastermind Ernst Stavro Blofeld, who made a fleeting appearance in *Thunderball*.

At the beginning of *On Her Majesty's Secret Service*, Bond believes that Blofeld is dead. For a year, he has been pursuing Blofeld and SPECTRE and can find no trace of them. Frustrated, he is taking time to draft his letter of resignation from the Secret Service during a driving holiday in France. Returning to Royale-les-Eaux, he stops a young woman from drowning herself, only to be grabbed by two gangsters.

He first saw the girl as she raced past him in a Lancia Flaminia Zagato Spyder with the hood down. By chance they are both staying at the Hotel Splendide in Royale where he is told that she is La Comtesse Teresa di Vicenzo, though she calls herself Tracy. That night at the casino, she is humiliated when she cannot pay her losses. To help her out, Bond tosses chips over to her and apologizes for forgetting that he had agreed to play as her partner that night. Afterwards, they make love. In the morning, she tells him that he is a lousy lover and throws him out.

The two gangsters take Bond to meet Marc-Ange Draco, Tracy's father and head of the Union Corse – the Corsican equivalent of the Mafia. He offers Bond £1 million to marry his daughter. Bond refuses, but says he will see her again. He then asks Draco whether he knows anything about Blofeld. Draco knows that Blofeld is alive as he has recently recruited three members of the Union Corse for SPECTRE. He soon reports that Blofeld is in Switzerland.

For two months, the Secret Service can find no sign of Blofeld in Switzerland. Then the College of Arms reports that Blofeld has claimed the right to use the vacant title of Comte Balthazar de Bleuville. Impersonating Sir Hilary Bray from the College of Arms, Bond goes to visit Blofeld in his Alpine lair, Piz Gloria. He finally meets Blofeld and pretends to start work on his genealogy. Meanwhile he entertains himself with the other residents of the Piz Gloria – ten young English women who are being cured of various allergies under the aegis of Blofeld's partner in crime, Irma Bunt. In fact, the girls are being brainwashed to spread biological agents that will destroy the agriculture that post-World War II Britain is dependent on.

With this information, Bond makes his escape on skis and is fired at. This causes an avalanche. Bond narrowly escapes being buried. Nevertheless, Blofeld's men are still after him. He reaches the village of Samaden where the festivities for Christmas Eve are in full swing. Knowing that Bond is at Piz Gloria, Draco has sent Tracy there. She rescues him by disguising him in her parka. They make off in her car. A Mercedes follows, firing at them. Round a hidden bend, Bond jumps out and turns a sign so it directs the car following into a deep ravine.

Bond returns to England in time to have Christmas lunch with M at his home, Quarterdeck. According to an expert from the Ministry of Agriculture and Fisheries, fowl pest is already ravaging the country. Blofeld has to be stopped. Meanwhile Bond has decided to marry Tracy and visits Draco in Marseilles. To help out his future son-in-law, Draco volunteers to take care of Blofeld. With his men, they fly into Switzerland in a stolen army helicopter, identifying themselves on the radio as a Red Cross aircraft flying plasma to Italy. They land at Piz Gloria. As fighting breaks out, Blofeld heads for the bobsleigh run. Bond follows. Blofeld sets off down the run on a one-man sled with Bond close behind. Blofeld drops a grenade that blows Bond over the side of the run. He lands in soft snow. Then Blofeld's mountain-top lair blows up, but the man himself has escaped.

Bond then makes his way to Munich where Tracy is waiting. They marry in the British Consulate, but Bond refuses Draco's £1 million wedding present. As they head off down the auto-bahn to Kitzbühel for their honeymoon, Bond spots Blofeld in a Maserati that flashes past. A bullet takes out the windscreen of Tracy's Lancia. The car crashes. Tracy is killed; Bond survives.

You Only Live Twice (1964)

Uniquely, *You Only Live Twice* begins with an epigraph. It is a quotation from the seventeenth-century Japanese poet Basho and reads:

> You only live twice:
> Once when you are born,
> And once when you look death in the face.

As the book begins, Bond is partying with Japanese girls in a geisha house in Tokyo, apparently unaffected by the death of his wife. This is not the case. Only a month before, M feared that Bond was slowly going to pieces. He had bungled two assign-ments and nearly got himself killed. Sir James Molony advised that there was only one way to turn Bond around – send him on an impossible mission.

Bond is sent to Japan to get access to MAGIC 44, the decrypts of all Soviet radio transmissions that the Japanese normally share only with the Americans. In Japan, Bond meets Tiger Tanaka, head of Japan's Secret Service, and offers in exchange Blue Route, similar decrypts from China. But the Japanese already have Blue Route. Nevertheless Tanaka shows Bond an example of MAGIC 44, which concerns a direct threat to Britain. Bond sends this home, averting a major crisis.

When Tanaka and Bond get to know each other, Tanaka says he will give the British access to MAGIC 44, if Bond will complete a mission that has already killed Tanaka's best man. Dr Guntram Shatterhand, a Swiss botanist, has opened a garden in a remote Japanese castle and has stocked it with poisonous plants and insects, as well as deadly snakes and fish. The area is dotted with fumaroles, geysers of scalding mud that erupt hundreds of feet into the air at regular intervals. Although helium balloons with a skull and crossbones flying above the castle warn people to stay away, these only act as an advertisement. Every year, thousands of Japanese flock to the garden to commit suicide. If Bond kills Shatterhand, Tanaka will give the British MAGIC 44.

Bond agrees to take on the assignment, especially when he is shown photographs of Shatterhand and his companion. They are none other than Blofeld and Irma Bunt. During his extensive preparation for the mission, Bond is trained as a ninja and disguised as a Japanese. The plan is for Bond to attack the castle by climbing a cliff on the seaward side. To reach its foot, Bond needs the help of the Ama people of Kuro Island whose girls dive naked for fish. On Kuro Island, Bond meets the stunning Kissy Suzuki, who had been a Hollywood actress before returning to the simple life of a fisherwoman.

Kissy leads Bond through the straits to the cliff below the castle. He climbs it and hides in an outhouse. From there, he witnesses both the suicide and the murder of people entering the garden. He also sees Blofeld and Bunt, swathed in protective clothing, going for a walk. That night, Bond breaks into the castle, but is foiled by an oubliette – a trapdoor in a castle floor that hides the entrance to a dungeon. He pretends to be a Japanese beggar who is deaf and dumb, but Irma Bunt recognizes him by his scar.

Blofeld takes Bond to his 'Question Room' and seats him above a fumarole that he says is set to blow at 11.15. With a minute to go, Bond leaps from his seat. This proves that he is not deaf and dumb, but has understood what Blofeld was saying. Blofeld arms himself with a samurai sword ready to behead Bond. But Bond has spotted a stave leaning against a wall. He grabs it and strikes Bunt a fatal blow so that she cannot raise the alarm. Then he fights Blofeld, stave against sword. Using his ninja training, Bond defeats Blofeld, disarms him and strangles him. He then turns a big stone wheel that controls the fumarole and makes his way out on to the balcony. He grabs the mooring rope of one of the helium balloons and cuts it free with Blofeld's sword.

As Bond sails out over the straits, the pressure from the fumarole blows the top off the castle. Bond is hit on the head with a piece of debris and falls in the sea. When the news reaches London, M posts an obituary in *The Times*. But Bond is not dead. Kissy has seen him fall and rescues him. The blow to the head has left him with amnesia, though. Eventually Kissy becomes pregnant, but before she can tell him, he finds a square of newsprint they use as lavatory paper with the word 'Vladivostok' on it. This rekindles a vague recollection and he decides he must go there to find out what else he can recall. This inconclusive ending sets up the last of Fleming's Bond novels.

The Man with the Golden Gun (1965)

Months after James Bond disappeared in Japan, he reappears in London. He is now under the control of the KGB. He has been briefed by a Colonel Boris to talk his way through the security checks at SIS headquarters, then insists on seeing M. Although there are indications that Bond is now working for the KGB, M agrees to the meeting. Bond explains that he had been picked up by the police in Vladivostok and handed over to the KGB. They interrogated him, but he could not remember anything. However, Bond says, the Soviet interrogators convinced him of the need for peace. But first the warmongers must be eliminated, he says as he pulls a pistol from his pocket and sprays deadly cyanide at M. Instantly a sheet of armour-plated glass descends from the ceiling, blocking the jet. Bond is quickly subdued. It is clear that he has been brainwashed. Sir James Molony is called in, once again, to reverse the process.

Bond's deprogramming is successful, but now he has to prove himself again. He is assigned to kill Francisco 'Pistols' Scaramanga, a freelance assassin who is believed to have killed and maimed several British secret agents in the West Indies. Scaramanga is also known as 'The Man with the Golden Gun' because he uses a gold-plated, long-barrelled, single-action Colt .45. Bond is sent to Jamaica, where he meets up with Mary Goodnight, his former secretary who has now been posted to the Caribbean.

Operating under the name Mark Hazard, Bond meets Scaramanga in a Jamaican bordello. Bond introduces himself as a security man looking into fires in the cane fields. Scaramanga hires him to look after security at a meeting of stockholders in a tourist development near Negril which he has shares in. Also working undercover at the half-built resort is Felix Leiter, who has been recalled to duty by the CIA and is setting up bugs in Scaramanga's meeting room.

The stockholders are American gangsters and a KGB agent. Their aim is to undermine Western interests in the Caribbean sugar industry to boost the value of the Cuban sugar crop. Scaramanga knows that Bond is after him and proposes to dispose of his limey assistant when business is concluded. The US mobsters also want to move in casinos, which had recently been kicked out of Cuba by Fidel Castro, while the KGB man wants to sabotage Jamaica's bauxite industry. They are seeking protection money from the oil companies in the Caribbean and discuss smuggling girls and drugs into the US from Mexico.

After an evening of lewd entertainment, Scaramanga intends to take his party on a train ride to see the marina at Green Island Harbour, twenty miles away. On the trip, Bond is forced to show his hand when he sees a figure that appears to be Mary Goodnight tied across the tracks ahead. It turns out to be a dummy, but Bond is committed to a gunfight. He is saved by Leiter, who has smuggled himself aboard the train.

Bond and Leiter fling themselves into a swamp, while the driverless train crashes into a river. Leiter has broken his leg and is immobile. Bond, although wounded, sets off after Scaramanga, who has also escaped from the train crash. He finds Scaramanga sprawled among the mangrove roots, bleeding, crawling with insects and fending off a snake with a stiletto.

Scaramanga throws the knife at Bond. Bond dodges, but is loath to kill an unarmed man. Then Scaramanga pulls a Derringer, shoots Bond and grabs for the stiletto. As Bond falls he looses off five shots, killing Scaramanga. Bond thinks he has only suffered a flesh wound, but Scaramanga's bullet has been dipped in snake venom so even a slight wound would be fatal. Luckily a doctor recognizes the symptoms of a snakebite and administers anti-venom in time to save Bond.

Bond is offered a knighthood for his service, but refuses it. Instead, he accepts a better offer from Mary Goodnight, though he reflects that the love of Mary – or any other woman – would never be enough for him.

Octopussy and the Living Daylights (1966)

Fleming was already dead by the time *The Man with the Golden Gun* was published. But Bond did not die with him. The following year, *Octopussy and the Living Daylights*, a collection of short stories, was published. In 'Octopussy', James Bond turns up in Jamaica to interview Major Dexter Smythe, who admits to murdering Bond's old ski instructor Hans Oberhauser at the end of the war to conceal the fact that he has stolen Nazi gold. On his way to feed his pet octopus – the eponymous Octopussy – Smythe is killed by a poisonous scorpion fish in what Bond assumes is a suicide.

In 'The Living Daylights', Bond is sent to Berlin where British agent 272 is coming over the Wall from the East. Bond's assignment is to kill a KGB sniper called 'Trigger', who aims to kill the escaping agent. Bond spots that Trigger is a beautiful blonde he had seen earlier with a cello case. At the last moment, he alters his aim so that he hits the stock of her Kalashnikov and spoils her shot, rather than killing her as he has been ordered to. The local agent with him reports this insubordination and Bond resigns himself to being stripped of his double-O status.

In 'The Property of a Lady' Bond investigates suspected double agent Maria Freudenstein. In *The Man with the Golden Gun*, she appears as Maria Freudenstadt, so one of the names is possibly a proof-reader's error. She is about to auction an emerald sphere made by Fabergé, described by Sotheby's as the 'property of a lady'. Bond believes the head of the KGB in London will attend the auction to push up the price to pay her for her services as a double agent. Entering the bidding, Bond unmasks him and has him expelled as *persona non grata*.

Later editions of the *Octopussy* collection also include '007 in New York', in which Bond visits New York to warn a former Secret Service agent that her new boyfriend is working for the KGB.

5. Bond: The Films

The 007 in Ian Fleming's books is a man who does not like killing and occasionally suffers pangs of guilt. He gets nervous and sweats a lot, and is sometimes beset with bad dreams. None of this comes across in the Bond films – but then there is little interior life in English-language action movies. A number of actors have played Bond, each in their own way. However, no matter how different they may appear, the sophisticated womanizer, who is tough, cunning and determined and kills when he has to, is instantly recognizable throughout.

Casino Royale (1954)
Bond's first outing on the screen was in 1954, when CBS's Chrysler Climax Mystery Theater gave an hour-long episode over to *Casino Royale*. In it, 'Jimmy Bond' was an American, while Leiter was British. Le Chiffre was played by Peter Lorre. As TV shows then went out live, audiences coast-to-coast saw Lorre get up after Le Chiffre had been killed and walk off towards his dressing room.

Casino Royale (1966)
007's appearance in the 1966 version of *Casino Royale* was hardly more dignified. The feature film bears little relation to Fleming's book. Following the death of M, Sir James Bond, played by David Niven (Fleming's original choice for Bond), is called out of retirement to fight SMERSH. To confuse the

enemy, all agents – male and female – are to be called James
Bond, 007, including Bond's nephew, Jimmy Bond, played by
Woody Allen. Vesper Lynd, played by Ursula Andress, recruits
baccarat ace Evelyn Tremble, played by Peter Sellers, to defeat
SMERSH treasurer Le Chiffre, played by Orson Welles, at
Casino Royale. Tremble, as Bond, wins. Lynd is kidnapped.
Tremble is tortured, mentally not physically, and Le Chiffre is
killed by a SMERSH agent. There any similarity with the book
ceases. Ultimately, Jimmy Bond is exposed as Dr Noah, head of
SMERSH, and, implausibly, swallows a miniaturized atomic
bomb which goes off, destroying Casino Royale. This was
considered a spoof on the classic Bond movies produced by
Harry Saltzman and Albert R. 'Cubby' Broccoli. They had
acquired the film rights to Bond in 1961 through their company
Eon Productions, then signed a deal to produce five movies
with United Artists. Eon got a chance to produce their version
of *Casino Royale* forty years later in 2006.

Dr No (1962)

The first of the Bond movies was to have been *Thunderball*, but
the rights were enmeshed in legal wrangles with Kevin McClory
at the time. So Saltzman and Broccoli began with *Dr No*, starring Sean Connery. This follows the plot of the novel reasonably
closely, even down to Bond being forced by M to swap his
Beretta for a Walther PPK.

Arriving at Kingston airport, Bond is picked up by a chauffeur ostensibly sent by Government House. Unmasked, the
chauffeur commits suicide with a cyanide tablet. As Bond has
not been to Jamaica before – in the films, at least – he does not
know Quarrel, who is introduced, after a fight with Bond, by
Felix Leiter. And as Leiter has not appeared before – and does
not appear in the book – he has to introduce himself after
disarming Bond.

In the film, the last person to see Strangways alive is Professor
Dent, who conceals the fact that Strangways has picked up
some radioactive samples from Crab Key, where Dr No, in the

film, has a bauxite mine. But Dent is working for Dr No, who instructs him to kill Bond with a tarantula. It is the spider, not a poisonous centipede, that he puts in Bond's bed.

Another embellishment concerns Miss Taro, the secretary at Government House suspected of removing the files on Dr No and Crab Key. Bond asks her out. On his way to her house, an attempt is made on his life, but his pursuers are forced off a cliff. She is surprised when he turns up, but is instructed by a phone call to delay him and does so by making love to him. Afterwards, he has her arrested. Bond then makes up the bed so that it looks as if someone is in it. When Dent comes in and shoots what he thinks is the sleeping Bond, Bond, who is hidden behind the door, kills him.

Then Bond and Quarrel head out to Crab Key. But Honeychile Ryder turns up on the beach, not naked like Botticelli's *Venus* rising from the waves as in the book, but wearing a white bikini. The crew of the dragon, which incinerates Quarrel, wear radiation suits. Back at Dr No's lair, Bond and Ryder have to be decontaminated. Dr No, this time, has artificial hands covered in sinister black rubber gloves rather than pincers. During the obligatory scene where Dr No explains the plot, he mentions that he is working for SPECTRE, which is not mentioned in the book. However, SPECTRE first appears in the book *Thunderball*, which came out in 1961, the year before the film *Dr No*.

Bond is beaten and put in a holding cell. He escapes through the ventilation system, but is not observed or tortured this time. Emerging in the decontamination room, he disguises himself in a radiation suit and makes his way to the control centre where Dr No powers his attack on missiles taking off from Cape Canaveral with a nuclear reactor. Bond overloads it, causing panic. In a fight, Dr No ends up in the vat of water that cools the reactor. His artificial hands can't get a grip, so he can't climb out and he boils to death. Meanwhile, Bond finds Honeychile pinioned to the floor of a spillage basin, where she has been left to drown. Bond frees her. As Dr No's lair begins to blow up,

Bond and Honey seize a boat and make off. Leiter and the Navy turn up to rescue them, but Bond slips the tow cable so that he and Honey can make love unobserved.

From Russia with Love (1963)

Dr No had been a low-budget picture, but it had done so well at the box office that the budget for the next Bond movie, *From Russia with Love*, was doubled and more of it was shot on location in Europe, where *Dr No* had done particularly well. It also added two of the staples of a Bond movie – a title song and a pre-title scene. In a garden at night, James Bond is chasing and being chased by a blond assassin – Red Grant. Bond is caught and strangled by Grant. Then floodlights come on. A mask is pulled from the dead man's face. It is not Bond at all. The murder has merely been a SPECTRE training exercise. It was producer Harry Saltzman's idea to make it appear that Bond had been killed off before the movie had even begun.

Again SPECTRE is the villain here, though in the book it was SMERSH. Rosa Klebb has secretly defected from SMERSH to SPECTRE for a plan devised by chess grandmaster Kronsteen. In the book, Kronsteen works for SMERSH. The plot is to steal a Lektor machine – confusingly a Spektor machine in the book – and sell it back to the Soviets. Along the way they intend to take their revenge on Bond for killing SPECTRE agent Dr No. Klebb goes to SPECTRE island to recruit Grant, again by punching him with a knuckleduster in the solar plexus. She recruits Tatiana Romanova secretly in Istanbul by pretending she is still working for SMERSH.

Bond flies to Istanbul where the plot is reasonably faithful to that of the book, though Darko Kerim becomes Ali Kerim Bey, the underground route to the Soviet Consul goes through one of the underground Byzantine reservoirs, the gypsy girls in the cat-fight do not strip each other naked, scenes in Hagia Sophia on a ferry crossing the Bosporus are added, and Tatiana does not simply turn up at the railway station with the cryptographic machine. Instead when the Soviet Consulate is blown up, Bond grabs the machine and Tatiana. They make direct for the station where they are spotted, by accident, by Soviet agents and just one boards the train. However, as luck would have it, Red Grant is already on board.

After Kerim is killed, Bond arranges for Nash from Station Y to meet him at Zagreb. Grant finds Nash and kills him. Posing as Nash, Grant drugs Tatiana. He then disarms Bond and taunts him that SPECTRE has set Britain and the Soviet Union at each other's throats. He also reveals that Tatiana knows nothing of the plot. She thinks she is working for SMERSH. Bond tricks Grant into opening the attaché case provided by Q which, in the movie, has a tear-gas canister inside. In the ensuing struggle, when Grant is strangling Bond, Bond gets the knife from the attaché case, finishing him off with his own garrotte.

Bond and Tatiana then leave the train to avoid being arrested at the border and make their getaway in Grant's truck. Along the way, Bond destroys a pursuing helicopter. They then take a powerboat and head for Venice. Meanwhile Klebb and Kronsteen appear before the cat-stroking head of SPECTRE, who reminds them that he will not tolerate failure. Klebb finishes off Kronsteen with the poisoned blade in the toe of her shoe.

More SPECTRE agents are sent after Bond. Their bullets pierce the spare fuel drums on Bond's boat. He cuts the drums loose, then ignites them with a flare gun, incinerating his pursuers. But in Venice, Rosa Klebb appears as a maid, enters Bond's room and attempts to steal the Lektor. Klebb gets the drop on Bond, but the gun is knocked away by Tatiana. Klebb releases her poisoned toe-spike, but Bond pins her to the wall with a chair. Tatiana grabs the gun and kills Klebb. Afterwards, riding in a gondola, Bond throws the film of him and Tatiana making love in Istanbul overboard.

Goldfinger (1964)

Goldfinger's pre-title sequence borrows from Bond's musings at Miami airport in the book. But instead of killing just one Mexican drug dealer, he appears from the sea in a wetsuit and

blows up the factory. Then he strips off the wetsuit to reveal a
white dinner jacket, puts a red carnation in his buttonhole and
goes into a bar. This is said to borrow from an operation in
World War II where an agent, similarly attired, swam ashore to
join a Nazi party. In a back room, a dancer is having a bath.
When she emerges to kiss Bond, an assassin attacks. Bond spots
his reflection in her eyes. After a fight, he pushes him into the
bath and throws in an electric fire. Then he says: 'Shocking . . .
positively shocking.' This marks the beginning of the quipster
Bond who inhabits the films that follow.

The story begins with Leiter delivering a message from M
to Bond at a Miami hotel, telling him to keep an eye on Auric
Goldfinger. Bond foils Goldfinger's cheating at gin rummy,
not canasta, and beds his assistant Jill Masterson. Then he is
knocked out by Oddjob and awakes to find Masterson dead,
painted gold.

In London, Bond is briefed on Goldfinger's smuggling activities. Q issues him with an Aston Martin DB5 that has been
modified with all sorts of gadgets, including an ejector seat. As
in the book, Bond plays a game of golf with Goldfinger, but the
stake in the film is a bar of Nazi gold. Again Bond out-cheats
him and Goldfinger issues a warning by having Oddjob decapitate a statue with his metal-brimmed bowler.

Goldfinger flies his armour-plated Rolls direct to Geneva.
Bond follows. He is overtaken by Tilly Masterson, whose car he
disables with the DB5's gadgets. Again, Tilly is out to avenge
her sister. Her attempt to kill Goldfinger alerts the guards. After
a car chase, she is killed by Oddjob's hat as she tries to escape.
Bond finds himself strapped to the table, not with a circular saw
but a high-tech laser. He escapes certain death by mentioning
that he has overheard Goldfinger talking to a Communist
Chinese agent about 'Operation Grand Slam'.

Bond is drugged and flown to the US in a private jet piloted
by Pussy Galore. At Goldfinger's Kentucky stud farm, Bond
overhears a meeting between Goldfinger and the mobsters,
outlining the raid on Fort Knox. While having drinks with

Goldfinger, Bond learns that the villain is planning not to steal the gold from Fort Knox, but to irradiate it using an atomic bomb supplied by the Chinese, thus increasing the value of his own holdings.

Instead of having the nerve agent introduced to the water supply, it is to be spread by Pussy Galore's Flying Circus, a team of women pilots. But Bond manages to seduce Pussy. The operation against Fort Knox seems to be going to plan, but once Goldfinger's men have broken into the vault, the soldiers surrounding the depository wake up. They had only been playing dead as, after her brush with Bond, Pussy Galore had contacted the CIA, who substituted a harmless substance for the poison gas.

Bond is locked into the vault handcuffed to the atomic bomb. He breaks free but is set upon by Oddjob, whose bowler cuts some electric cables. Bond retrieves the hat and throws it at Oddjob. He misses and it gets stuck between the bars of the vault. When Oddjob tries to retrieve it, Bond applies the end of a severed cable to the bars and electrocutes him. He then tries to disarm the bomb as the seconds tick away. With just seven seconds to go, Leiter arrives to switch it off. Meanwhile, dressed in an army uniform, Goldfinger escapes. He reappears on a private jet taking Bond for dinner with the President at the White House. In a tussle, his gun goes off, shattering a window. As the cabin decompresses, Goldfinger is sucked out. Bond and the pilot, once again Pussy Galore, bale out. Leiter and the CIA search for Bond in a helicopter. But he is far too busy making love to Pussy to be rescued.

Thunderball (1965)

By 1964 *Thunderball* was the biggest selling of the Bond books but as a result of a lawsuit McClory held the film rights. So Eon made McClory co-producer of their movie on the proviso that he would not make his own version of *Thunderball* for ten years.

The film begins with a funeral. On the coffin there are the

initials 'JB', implying, again, that James Bond is dead. However, Bond is among the mourners. The funeral is for Colonel Jacques Bouvar, SPECTRE number six, who had killed two British agents. However, Bouvar is not dead either. He attends the funeral disguised as the deceased's widow. Bond sees through the disguise, follows him to a nearby château and kills him, then escapes by jetpack and the Aston Martin used in *Goldfinger*.

The story begins in a health farm. There is no explanation for this and Bond looks perfectly fit. He runs into Count Lippe and recognizes the mark of the Red Lightning Tong on his arm. He searches Lippe's room and is seen leaving by the man in the room next door, whose face is swathed in bandages. There is the spinal traction–steam cabinet duel between Bond and Lippe as in the book. Bond then finds the bandaged man dead.

The dead man is François Derval, a NATO observer on V bombers. In his place is a SPECTRE agent, who gases the rest of the crew and lands the bomber with its payload of two nuclear bombs in the shallow water off the Bahamas, where it is camouflaged. Derval is killed by Emilio Largo, SPECTRE number two, who then hides the bombs near his house, Palmyra.

This time the communiqué from SPECTRE arrives by tape. M plans to send Bond to Canada, but Bond spots a picture in the file that shows Derval with his sister, Domino, who is in the Bahamas. Bond tracks her there and rescues her when she traps her foot while diving. She turns out to be Largo's mistress.

At the casino, Bond beats Largo at baccarat and dances with Domino. Then he catches one of Largo's henchmen checking out his hotel room. Largo has the man thrown in to a pool of sharks.

Bond and Leiter meet up with Q, who turns up with an underwater infrared camera, a tracking beacon Bond must swallow, mini underwater breathing apparatus, a flare gun and a Geiger counter. Bond then dives under Largo's yacht, the *Disco Volante*, and takes photographs of the door to its underwater compartment. Largo has is men depth-charge Bond with hand grenades. He escapes, only to be picked up by SPECTRE agent

Fiona Volpe, who was François Derval's mistress and the killer who disposed of Count Lippe.

She contrives the capture of Bond's attractive assistant Paula Caplan, who kills herself rather than talk. Fiona and Largo's men then pursue Bond through the Junkanoo, the Bahamian carnival, which ends with Fiona being shot by her accomplices. Using a helicopter, Bond and Leiter find the V bomber. Bond dives on it and recovers Derval's dog tags and watch. After making love to Domino underwater, Bond uses these to convince her that her brother has been killed by Largo. She agrees to take a Geiger counter on board the *Disco Volante* to find out whether the atomic bombs are on board. Largo discovers this and tortures her.

Meanwhile, using information volunteered by Domino, Bond disguises himself as one of Largo's team of frogmen loading the atom bombs on the *Disco Volante* and discovers that Largo plans to bomb Miami. Bond is unmasked by Largo. A team of US frogmen land by parachute. There is an underwater battle and Largo tries to escape on the *Disco Volante*. With Leiter's help, Bond gets on board the yacht. In a final showdown, Largo gets the better of Bond, but Domino shoots Largo in the back. As the yacht careers towards the rocks, Bond and Domino jump overboard. The *Disco Volante* explodes at the same time as a US plane drops a life-raft then skyhooks Bond and Domino from the sea.

You Only Live Twice (1967)

The film of *You Only Live Twice* was the first to abandon the plot of the book and use only the characters and some of the locations. This is no suicide garden or medieval castle. The screenplay was by Roald Dahl, who worked in intelligence with William Stephenson and Ian Fleming during World War II before becoming a master of children's fiction and the short story with a twist in its tail.

The film begins with an American Jupiter spacecraft being swallowed up by an unidentified orbiter. The Americans suspect the Russians, but the British suspect that a third party is responsible. A pre-title sequence again ostensibly kills off Bond. He has just finished making love to a Chinese girl when she traps him in a fold-away bed which is machine-gunned. He is then given a very public burial at sea in Hong Kong harbour. Frogmen retrieve the corpse and take it to a submarine, where the shroud is cut open to reveal Bond alive, in naval uniform and wearing breathing apparatus, sealed in a plastic body bag. On board is M, who briefs Bond, and the submarine sets sail for Japan.

In Tokyo, Bond is contacted at a sumo wrestling match by an attractive agent named Aki. She takes him to see local MI6 agent Dikko Henderson, who claims he has evidence that the rogue spacecraft originated in Japan, but is killed before he can say more. Bond chases and kills his assassin. He then disguises himself as the killer and is driven to the source of the conspiracy, the head office of Osato Chemicals. Stealing documents from the safe, he sets off an alarm. In the ensuing gun battle, Bond is rescued by Aki in a sports car. But she refuses to answer Bond's questions, pulls to a halt and flees into a seemingly disused subway station. Bond gives chase and falls through a trapdoor. He then slides down a tube into the office of Tiger Tanaka, head of the Japanese Secret Service.

Together they examine the documents Bond has stolen. Among them is a manifest carrying quantities of liquid oxygen, a substance needed to power a space rocket. There is also a picture of a cargo ship, the *Ning-Po*, and a microdot containing a message saying that the tourist who had taken the picture had been liquidated for security reasons.

The following day, Bond returns to Osato Chemicals, posing as a representative of Empire Chemicals. When he leaves, the boss, Mr Osato, tells his assistant Helga Brandt to 'kill him'. Again Bond is rescued from a drive-by shooting outside the building by Aki in her sports car. The would-be killers give chase. Aki contacts Tanaka, who arranges for a helicopter equipped with a huge magnet to pick up the car pursuing them and dump it in Tokyo Bay.

Bond and Aki then head to Kobe docks to investigate the

Ning-Po. They are attacked by a dockside gang. Aki escapes, but Bond is captured. He awakes in Helga Brandt's cabin on board, where she interrogates him. But Bond uses his charm and bribery, he thinks, to turn her. However, when she is flying him to Tokyo in a light aircraft, she traps him in the back and bales out, leaving him to his fate. Bond struggles free and manages to crash-land the plane and escape before it blows up.

From surveillance photographs, Tanaka has deduced that the *Ning-Po* has delivered its cargo of liquid oxygen to an offshore island. Bond decides to take a look in a heavy-armed autogyro called Little Nellie, delivered personally by Q. He finds nothing on the island apart from a fishing village and a volcano, but is attacked by four helicopters. With the help of Little Nellie, he downs them. The question remains: what is so important on the island that it needs such defences?

To find out, Bond is to be disguised as a Japanese fisherman and to infiltrate the island undercover by marrying a local girl, Kissy Suzuki. But first he is trained in the martial arts with Tanaka's army of ninjas. His mission becomes more urgent. A Soviet spacecraft has also been hijacked, though the Americans still suspect the Soviet Union is responsible. Another American space mission is due for launch and the US threatens war if it goes missing.

Kissy mentions that a local woman had mysteriously died after rowing into a cave. She and Bond go to investigate. The cave is the vent of the island's volcano and is protected by phosgene gas, a man-made poison, again indicating that the island hides an important secret. Bond and Kissy climb the volcano. They see a helicopter disappear into the crater and discover that there is a secret rocket base hidden under the crater floor. Bond slips through the crater door while Kissy returns to alert Tanaka.

Bond finds and frees the captured astronauts. He steals a spacesuit and is about to board the spacecraft when Blofeld, head of SPECTRE, who is running this operation, spots him. For failing to kill Bond, Helga Brandt is dropped in a pool of piranhas that Blofeld keeps in his office.

Bond is taken to Blofeld. For the first time, we see the face of the cat-stroking SPECTRE number one. (Blofeld does not have the trademark white cat in the books. However, Goldfinger has a ginger cat which he gives to Oddjob for his supper.) Blofeld explains that he has been contracted to provoke a nuclear war between the US and the USSR, so that they will annihilate each other and allow a new power – presumably Red China – to emerge. Blofeld says he is going to kill Bond. As he has already escaped death once, Blofeld tells him: 'You only live twice.'

Bond asks for a last cigarette. He takes one from his case, which has a small rocket inside it, developed by Tanaka. He shoots the guard who operates the door in the crater floor and opens it himself. Tanaka's ninja army storm in. Battle is joined. Bond joins Tanaka and Kissy, then makes his way back to the control room where there is a button that will blow up the SPECTRE spacecraft. On the way he meets Blofeld's large Germanic bodyguard, Hans, and throws him into the piranha pool. Then he reaches the control room and blows up the SPECTRE spacecraft in the nick of time. The Americans stand down their nuclear strike force and the world is saved.

Blofeld escapes down a secret passage and activates the base's self-destruct system. Bond, Kissy, Tanaka and the surviving ninjas escape down the tunnel vent to the cave. Out at sea, inflatable lifeboats are dropped. Bond and Kissy are about to consummate their marriage, when their life-raft is picked up by the submarine with M on board.

On Her Majesty's Secret Service (1969)

Sean Connery announced that *You Only Live Twice* would be his last Bond movie. In his place Broccoli and Saltzman cast Australian actor George Lazenby, who had a bit part in the Italian–Spanish Bond spoof *Espionage in Tangiers* in 1965. He would star in the next Bond movie *On Her Majesty's Secret Service*. In the opening scene of *OHMSS*, he saves the heroine from the waves. Unlike in the book, he beats off the gangsters while she escapes. Lazenby says: 'This never happened to the other fella.'

After the title credits, Bond returns to the hotel, where he learns that the girl is the Comtesse Teresa di Vicenzo. That night in the casino, she is losing heavily. Bond rides to the rescue as she has no money. She invites him to her room, saying she hopes it will be worth it. There Bond is attacked by a large assailant, but beats him off. Back in Bond's room, Tracy pulls Bond's own gun on him. Nevertheless, she sleeps with him. In the morning, he finds she has left the money he paid in the casino and checked out. In the lobby of the hotel, Bond is picked up by two gangsters again carrying his own gun. They take him to see Draco who, again, offers him a million pounds to marry his daughter. Bond refuses, but agrees to continue seeing her if Draco finds out where Blofeld is.

Back in London, M relieves Bond of the mission to find Blofeld. Bond dictates his letter of resignation to Miss Moneypenny. M's only reactions is to say: 'Request granted.' However, Moneypenny has substituted a request for two weeks' leave. Bond attends Draco's birthday party. Tracy turns up and forces her father to tell Bond what he wants to know, otherwise she will never see him again. Draco tells Bond that he has traced a Swiss lawyer associated with Blofeld. Bond breaks into his office in Bern and copies a letter from Blofeld to the College of Arms asking for confirmation of his right to use the title Comte Balthazar de Bleuchamp – Bleuville, in the book – the French version of Blofeld. After Bond visits M at his home – annoying his boss, a butterfly collector, with his casual expertise in Lepidoptera – he is reassigned to the hunt for Blofeld.

Posing as Sir Hillary Bray from the College of Arms, Bond visits Blofeld's Alpine allergy clinic and meets the ten young women there. At dinner he wears a kilt and one of them, Ruby, writes her room number, 8, on his inner thigh. He visits her room and discovers that the girls are being brainwashed. The following night Bond returns to Ruby's room to find Irma Bunt in the bed. He is taken to Blofeld, who says that Bond has given himself away with several elementary mistakes. He then explains how he plans to hold the world to ransom, otherwise he will use the brainwashed girls he has sent around to world to spread biological agents that will destroy crops and livestock.

Bond makes a daredevil escape down the cable of the cable car, then flees on skis. Again he is rescued by Tracy, who lures their pursuers into a stock-car race on ice. Leaving the pursuers' car ablaze they escape, but run out of petrol and spend a night in a barn, where Bond proposes. In the morning, Blofeld turns up on skis, but Bond and Tracy have already gone. There is another ski chase. This time, Blofeld stops them by causing an avalanche. He rescues Tracy, but leaves Bond to die. However, Bond digs himself out. Back in London he learns that the United Nations has agreed to Blofeld's terms. Bond contacts Draco. With a squad of Draco's men on board helicopters, they rescue Tracy and blow up Blofeld's clinic. Blofeld escapes on a bobsled. Bond chases after him. After a prolonged tussle, Blofeld gets his neck caught in the fork of a tree which, miraculously, does not kill him.

Bond and Tracy marry. When they are heading off on their honeymoon, Blofeld and Irma Bunt drive by and shoot up their car, killing Tracy. Like the first four Eon films, *On Her Majesty's Secret Service* is relatively faithful to the book.

Diamonds are Forever (1971)

Sean Connery returned as Bond in *Diamonds are Forever*. The movie begins with him searching all over the world for Blofeld. He tracks him to a facility where he is making lookalikes of himself. Bond drowns a test subject, but is captured by Blofeld. After a tussle, he throws Blofeld into a pool of superheated mud.

The main story begins with Bond being briefed about diamonds, and showing off his connoisseurship of sherry – again to M's annoyance. There has been an increase in smuggling and the fear is that diamonds are being stockpiled to be dumped later on the market to depress prices. Meanwhile in South Africa, Mr Wint and Mr Kidd – Spang's 'torpedoes' in the book

– kill a dentist bringing the diamonds smuggled out of the mines and the helicopter pilot who is supposed to take them on the next leg of their journey. They then deliver the diamonds to a missionary who is to take them to Amsterdam. She turns up dead in a canal.

Bond is sent to Amsterdam posing as the smuggler Peter Franks. He meets Franks's contact Tiffany Case at her apartment. However, the real Franks turns up. Bond kills him and switches ID, so that Tiffany thinks that Franks has really killed Bond. The diamonds are smuggled to Los Angeles in Franks's corpse, which is cleared at LAX by Felix Leiter, posing as a customs official. The corpse is then taken to a funeral home in Nevada where it is cremated; the recovered diamonds are to be handed on to the next man in the chain, Shady Tree. When Bond picks up his $50,000 fee, he is struck over the head and wakes up inside a coffin that is being incinerated. At the last moment, the coffin is flung open and Bond is accused of passing on fakes. The smugglers demand that he hand over the real diamonds. Bond counters by accusing them of giving him fake money as they would hardly burn a genuine $50,000. When they give him real money, he says, he will give them the real diamonds. In the mean time, he relaxes in Las Vegas, where Shady Tree is killed by Wint and Kidd.

Bond is paid out on the craps tables at a casino owned by the reclusive millionaire Willard Whyte. Impressed by his winnings, a young lady named Plenty O'Toole invites herself up to his room. As she undresses, she is grabbed by the smugglers and thrown out of the window. Luckily, she lands in the hotel swimming pool. Bond spends the rest of the night with Tiffany Case, who ostensibly agrees to steal the diamonds and share them with Bond. Bond arranges for Tiffany to pick up the diamonds. They are hidden inside a stuffed toy at the Circus Circus Las Vegas casino, where she is under surveillance by Leiter and his men. She gives them the slip.

Bond catches up with her at her home when Plenty O'Toole has been drowned in Tiffany's pool. (In a deleted scene, Plenty returns to Bond's room to recover her clothes and takes a card from Tiffany's purse.) Realizing her life is in danger, Tiffany tells Bond that the diamonds are in a locker at the airport. Heading there, he sees a porter retrieve them and give them to Bert Saxby, the floor manager at Whyte's casino. Bond follows the diamonds to a research facility owned by Willard Whyte and discovers laser refraction specialist Professor Metz building a satellite. His cover blown, Bond escapes on a moon-buggy. He reunites with Tiffany and is involved in a spectacular car chase around Las Vegas.

They return to the bridal suite of Whyte's hotel. Bond then scales the building on the top of the elevator and, after a daredevil climb, breaks into Whyte's penthouse apartment. However, he is expected. He is confronted by two identical Blofelds who use an electronic voice box to imitate Willard Whyte on the phone. Bond kicks the villain's white cat: it flees into the arms of its master and Bond kills him with a shot through the forehead. But he has killed the wrong one. Blofeld had also cloned the cats.

Bond is allowed to leave, but is gassed in the elevator. Wint and Kidd then have him sealed in a pipeline that is under construction. He shorts out the machine that automatically welds the sections together and escapes. Q has developed an electronic voice box like the one Blofeld is using. Posing as Bert Saxby, Bond discovers where the real Willard Whyte is and rescues him. Together they work out that Blofeld is using the diamonds to build an orbiting laser. It has already been launched. The laser begins to destroy nuclear missiles in the US, USSR and China, while Blofeld proposes an auction for nuclear supremacy.

Whyte works out that Blofeld is using an oil rig off the coast of Baja, California as his control centre. Bond arrives and switches the cassette that controls the satellite for a music tape. Tiffany, who is being held hostage on the rig, in a misplaced effort to help him, switches them back. As Leiter and the CIA attack, Blofeld tries to escape in a mini-submarine. But Bond takes over the crane used to launch it and uses the mini-sub as a wrecking ball to destroy the control centre.

Bond and Tiffany then set off to England on an ocean liner. But Wint and Kidd are also on board. Posing as waiters, they try to assassinate the couple. But Bond gets the better of them and they end up overboard. The movie closes with Tiffany looking up at bright spot in the sky and asking how they are going to get the diamonds down again.

Live and Let Die (1973)

In *Live and Let Die*, Roger Moore – Ian Fleming's second choice – takes over as Bond. Again, the movie borrows characters and settings from the book, but abandons the plot. The film begins with the murder of the UK delegate to the United Nations. Another man is stabbed outside the Fillet of Soul restaurant in New Orleans and his body carried off in a coffin, accompanied by a jazz band. A third is killed on the Caribbean island of San Monique, in a voodoo ceremony by a priest brandishing a snake. All three are British and, by coincidence, the murdered agent at the UN had been sent there to keep an eye on San Monique's prime minister, Dr Kananga. Bond is sent to New York to investigate.

The CIA send a car to collect him from the airport. The driver is killed on the Franklin D. Roosevelt River Drive lending to a hair-rising fire. Leiter traces the killer's car to a voodoo shop, then to a Fillet of Soul restaurant in Harlem. Bond takes a seat, the booth revolves and he finds himself in Mr Big's lair where he meets the fortune-telling Solitaire. Mr Big orders his men to kill Bond, who turns to Solitaire and asks her to predict his future. She tells him to take a tarot card. It shows 'The Lovers'. Bond says: 'Us?'

Two of Mr Big's henchmen then take him outside. Bond knocks them unconscious, only to be stopped at gunpoint by another black man – who introduces himself as Harold Strutter of the CIA.

Bond follows Kananga to San Monique, where several attempts are made on his life. He meets Rosie Carver from the

CIA, who poses as Mrs James Bond. With the boatman Quarrel Jr, they set out to find the place where the MI6 man was killed. But Bond suspects Rosie is a double agent working for Kananga. When he threatens her, she takes off into the forest and is killed.

With the help of Quarrel and a boat-towed paraglider, Bond drops in on Solitaire. Again the tarot cards predict that they will become lovers – though, this time, Bond has stacked the deck. By losing her virginity, Solitaire believes that she has lost her powers to see into the future. Now that she is no good to Kananga, she has no choice but to go with Bond. Pursued by a helicopter, they seek cover under huge camouflage nets that are hiding poppy fields. To escape the island, Bond seizes a double-decker bus. After a car chase, they reach the pier where they are rescued by Quarrel.

Arriving in New Orleans, they are seized by a cab driver who delivers them to Mr Big's private aeroplane. But Bond takes over a two-seater with a trainee pilot – an old lady – on board and escapes, at the cost of the plane's wings. Bond and Leiter then go to investigate the Fillet of Soul restaurant in New Orleans. Strutter, who is outside, is stabbed and his body carried off in a coffin accompanied by a jazz band as before. While Leiter goes to take a phone call, the seat Bond is sitting on disappears into the floor and he arrives in another of Mr Big's lairs.

Mr Big reveals himself as Kananga, wearing a prosthetic mask. He is concerned about the loss of Solitaire's virginity. Ever the gentleman, Bond refuses to speak on the matter. Kananga also tells Bond about his plan to flood America with free heroin to drive out the competition, including the Mafia. Then, when he has the market to himself, the price will go up.

Bond is taken to a drugs laboratory in a crocodile farmer. Mr Big's one-armed henchman, Tee Hee Johnson, puts Bond in a small island in the middle of a pond of hungry alligators. He escapes by running across their backs to the shore. After luring the most savage into the drugs lab, he sets it on fire. Escaping on a speedboat, he sets off a chase that involves Kananga's men, the local sheriff J.W. Pepper and the Louisiana state police.

As Solitaire is now no good to Kananga, he decides to have her sacrificed in a voodoo ceremony. Bond rides to the rescue, killing the cult figure Baron Samedi by throwing him in a coffin full of snakes. Then he sets the poppy fields alight. However, while making their escape, Bond and Solitaire stumble into yet another of Kananga's lairs.

Kananga has Bond's shark pistol, which fires rounds filled with compressed air, blowing up the shark. Bond and Solitaire are tied to a hoist, and are about to be dropped into a pool full of sharks when Bond uses a magnetic watch provided by Q to attract one of the shark-pistol's rounds. With a tiny saw in the watch he then cuts through the ropes. In a tussle with Kananga, they end up in the water. Bond puts the shark round in Kananga's mouth. Hex swells up and explodes.

Leiter puts Bond and Solitaire on the train back to New York, while secretly Tee Hee Johnson gets loaded on in a sack. He attacks Bond, who bests him by cutting the control wire in his mechanical arm. This locks his pincers on to the window handle. Then Bond opens the window and throws him out. The film ends with Baron Samedi perched on the front of the speeding train, laughing.

The Man with the Golden Gun (1974)

While *Live and Let Die* retains much of Fleming's plot, *The Man with the Golden Gun* almost throws the book away. It is not set in Jamaica. The film begins with Scaramanga on an island we later learn is off the coast of China. He does indeed have three nipples, though the third nipple is not 'about two inches below his left breast' as in the book, but rather above.

A Mafia hit man arrives. He is instructed to kill Scaramanga by Scaramanga's manservant, a dwarf named Nick Nack. However, it transpires that this is an exercise for Scaramanga's entertainment. The assassin finds himself fired on by mannequins of a western gunslinger Al Capone and his gang, and James Bond. Scaramanga eventually kills the assassin in a hall of mirrors.

A gold bullet arrives in London – in the book Scaramanga uses gold-cored bullets, jacketed with silver. This one has '007' inscribed on it. Bond is asked what he knows about Scaramanga and reels off a brief biography mentioning that Scaramanga is an assassin who charges $1 million a hit and uses a gold-plated gun – hence, 'The Man With the Golden Gun'. The Secret Service assumes that Scaramanga has been hired to kill Bond, so Bond is taken off an assignment to find a scientist named Gibson who has discovered a new technique of harnessing the power of the sun that will be critical in solving the energy crisis.

Scaramanga's last victim is a British agent in Beirut. Bond retrieves the bullet which is being used as a lucky charm in a belly dancer's navel. This leads Bond to a gunsmith in Macao who makes the gold bullets. When Scaramanga's mistress collects his next consignment, Bond follows her to Hong Kong. He catches her in the shower and forces her to tell him where to find Scaramanga. She tells him to go to the Bottoms Up strip club. As Bond approaches, Scaramanga fires, hitting a man coming out of the club. It is Gibson. In the confusion, Nick Nack steals the 'Solex Agitator', the revolutionary device he has developed, from Gibson's pocket.

Bond is arrested by a Lieutenant Hip before the uniformed police arrive. But Hip is working for the Secret Service and takes him to their Hong Kong headquarters aboard the liner, the *Queen Elizabeth*, which capsized in Hong Kong harbour in 1972. On board are M and Q. Bond is now assigned to retrieve the Solex Agitator and kill Scaramanga. He travels to Bangkok to see the entrepreneur Hai Fat, who is thought to have hired Scaramanga. Reasoning that Hai Fat has never met Scaramanga in person, Bond breaks into Fat's heavily guarded compound and seizes on the invitation of a naked Chinese girl in the pool to take his shirt off, revealing a third nipple – a false one provided by Q. However, Fat has in fact met Scaramanga. Bond is captured and taken to his personal dojo where the students are to kill Bond. But he fights them off with the help of Hip and his two karate-trained nieces, then escapes in a boat chase around the canals of Bangkok. Meanwhile Scaramanga kills Hai Fat, now an unwanted business partner.

After dinner with local agent Mary Goodnight, she comes to his room. They are just about to make love when Scaramanga's mistress comes in. She reveals that she sent the bullet with '007' on it to London and agrees to get the Solex Agitator for Bond if he will kill Scaramanga. While Mary Goodnight hides in the closet, they make love.

Scaramanga's mistress agrees to hand over the Solex Agitator at a Thai boxing match. Bond sits next to her, and finds she is already dead. Scaramanga turns up and introduces himself. However, the Solex Agitator has fallen out of his mistress's purse. Bond grabs it and gives it to Hip, who passes it on to Goodnight. She then tries to put a radio beacon on Scaramanga's car and is locked in the trunk. Bond gives chase in a stolen car with Sheriff J.W. Pepper, a character borrowed from *Live and Let Die*, at his side. Scaramanga's car is transformed into a plane and he flies to his island lair with Goodnight.

Bond flies after him. Scaramanga welcomes him and shows him around the high-tech solar energy plant he intends to use to hold the world to ransom. But first, he proposes a duel. This ends in the strange 'funhouse' where Scaramanga killed the Mafia hit man at the beginning of the film. Climbing some scaffolding, Bond drops his gun, but finishes Scaramanga off by posing as his own mannequin. Meanwhile Goodnight has pushed the man operating the solar energy plant into a vat of liquid helium and the whole place is about to explode. So Bond must extract the Solex Agitator. Hampered by Goodnight, who backs on to the activation button, Bond does this at the last moment. They then escape on Scaramanga's junk and set sail for Hong Kong. Once again they are just about to make love, when the phone rings. It is M. When he asks for Goodnight, Bond says 'goodnight' and puts the phone down. They are then attacked by Nick Nack. Bond eventually cages him in a fish keep, strung from the mast.

The Spy Who Loved Me (1977)

Again *The Spy Who Loved Me* abandons any semblance to the book. There is no Vivienne Michel, no motel, no gangsters and it goes nowhere near New England.

The film begins at sea. Two nuclear submarines – one British, one Soviet – disappear. M calls for Bond. He is making love to a woman in the Austrian Alps. He dons ski gear. As he leaves the cabin, he is pursued by men who try to kill him. He kills one of them, then skis over the edge of a cliff – only to fall to safety thanks to a Union Jack parachute.

Soviet spymaster General Gogol calls agent Triple X, Major Anya Amasova, to investigate the missing submarine. He also informs her that her lover has been killed in Austria in an operation involving British intelligence.

Two scientists who have developed a sophisticated device that can track submarines underwater report to Karl Stromberg, a wealthy shipping magnate. He is having dinner with an attractive young woman in his underwater headquarters, Atlantis, which can rise above the waves when required. He congratulates the two men on their achievement, but tells them that someone has been trying to sell their secrets. They eye each other suspiciously. Stromberg then asks the young woman to leave. She gets in the elevator and Stromberg presses a button. The floor retracts. She falls into a pool with a shark in it and is torn to pieces while the three men watch on a video screen. The two scientists then leave on a helicopter, which Stromberg blows up.

Bond heads for Egypt where an old contact says that he must find a man called Fekkesh in Cairo. When Bond visits Fekkesh's house, an attempt is made on his life. Fortunately he is being kissed by a woman and turns so that she shields him, getting the bullet in her back. He chases the assassin to the roof, where the killer tells him that he can find Fekkesh at the Pyramids before Bond pushes him off the roof.

At the son et lumière at the Pyramids, Amasova is sitting with Fekkesh. Seeing Jaws – Stromberg's steel-toothed assassin

– Fekkesh tries to escape, is cornered and killed. Bond pulls a gun on Jaws, but he escapes. From a diary in Fekkesh's pocket, Bond finds he has an appointment with Max Kalba at the Mujaba Club. Amasova arrives and Bond sees off her two henchmen.

At the Mujaba Club, Bond bumps into Amasova, who knows everything about him. He excuses himself and locates Kalba, the owner of the club. Bond enquires about the tracking device. Amasova arrives at the table to make a rival bid for the details of the device Kalba has on microfilm. Kalba is called away to the phone, where he is killed by Jaws. Bond pursues Jaws and gets into the back of the van he is driving, only to be joined by Amasova.

Jaws drives out to a ruined temple in the desert. There is a confrontation and Amasova takes the microfilm; however, Bond has the keys to the van and takes the microfilm from her while Jaws trashes the van. They escape only to break down in the desert. Eventually, they get a dhow to take them back to Cairo. On the way, Bond checks the microfilm. But Amasova drugs him and takes it back.

In a secret office in another archaeological site, Bond finds Moneypenny, M, General Gogol and Amasova. Britain and the Soviet Union have combined forces to find out what has happened to their submarines. A clue on the microfilm identifies Stromberg's marine laboratory near Sardinia. Bond and Amasova take the train there. In a scene reminiscent of *From Russia with Love* and *Live and Let Die*, Jaws appears. Bond breaks a table lamp, applies the exposed live cable to Jaws's teeth, then pushes him through the window. As much of the compartment has been trashed, Bond is then forced to sleep with Amasova.

On Sardinia, Q delivers a new car. With Bond posing as a marine biologist, he and Amasova are taken out to Atlantis by Stromberg's assistant Naomi. After a short and amicable interview, Bond and Amasova are returned to land. But Jaws has identified them and is ordered to kill them. There is a car chase, where the pursuers are seen off by Q's special defences. Eventually they are pursued by a helicopter flown by Naomi.

Bond drives off the end of a pier and the car turns into a mini-submarine. A rocket fired from the roof destroys the helicopter. Bond then sails out to examine Atlantis. They are attacked by frogmen, but again the car's defences prove robust.

Back at the hotel, Amasova notes that Bond's new cigarette lighter comes from Austria. Bond admits killing her lover and she vows to kill Bond once the mission is over.

Bond and Amasova are then winched down from helicopter to a US submarine. They go to examine Stromberg's new super-tanker *Liparus*, which opens its bow doors and swallows up the submarine. Inside, it joins the other two missing subs. The crew are incarcerated while Bond and Amasova are taken to see Stromberg. He explains that he is going to use the nuclear submarines to destroy New York and Moscow, prompting a nuclear war that will destroy life on land while he begins a new civilization under the sea.

Crewed by Stromberg's men, the British and Soviet submarines set off on their mission, while Stromberg takes Amasova and returns to Atlantis. Bond fights off his guards and frees the captured crews of the submarines. They take over the *Liparus*, but cannot break into control room. Bond achieves this by dismantling a nuclear warhead and using its explosive detonator to blast a hole in the control room's armour-plated wall. He then helps reprogram the target co-ordinates of the nuclear missiles so that the submarines destroy each other. The survivors escape on the American submarine.

The captain then receives orders to destroy Atlantis. Bond persuades him to delay as Amasova is still on board. He sets off on a jet ski supplied by Q. Stromberg to feed Bond to the shark by retracting the floor of the lift. Bond then kills Stromberg. Searching for Amasova, Bond bumps into Jaws and defeats him using a magnetic hoist that attaches to his teeth. Bond dumps him in the pool with the shark, which proves no match for Jaws.

Bond then finds Amasova and frees her. But the deadline has already passed and the US submarine starts firing torpedoes. As

Atlantis sinks, Bond and Amasova escape in a high-tech life-raft. Bond is just opening the champagne thoughtfully supplied by Stromberg when Amasova grabs his gun: the mission is now over and she is going to kill him. But she relents and the two are making love when the life-raft is hauled aboard a British ship where M *et al.* are waiting. Meanwhile Jaws swims away.

Moonraker (1979)

The film of *Moonraker* retains Hugo Drax as the villain, but there is no cheating at bridge at Blades Club and no private ICBM base in Kent. However, Jaws makes a welcome return, though the character appears nowhere in Fleming's books.

The pre-title sequence begins with a 'Moonraker' space shuttle on loan to the UK being hijacked. Meanwhile, Bond is returning to England on a private jet when he is attacked by the air hostess and pilot; the pilot jumps out of the plane with a parachute. Bond is then thrown out without one, by Jaws. A skydiving Bond catches up with the pilot and robs him of his parachute. But Jaws catches him up. Bond breaks free by pulling his ripcord. Jaws's ripcord fails, but his fall is broken by a circus tent.

When Bond reports to M, he is told that the wreckage of the 747 transporting the Moonraker has been found, but there is no sign of the Moonraker itself. Q gives him a new wristwatch that fires darts – armour-piercing or tipped with cyanide. The Moonraker is made by the Drax Corporation and Bond flies to its headquarters in California to investigate. He is taken to meet Dr Holly Goodhead, who gives him a tour of the facilities. This includes a ride on the G-force training centrifuge. Drax's oriental manservant Chang tampers with the control panel so that the machine rotates at near-fatal speeds. Bond saves himself by shooting through the mechanism with Q's wristwatch.

With the help of Drax's obliging helicopter pilot, Corinne Dufour, Bond breaks into Drax's safe where he finds plans for containers made by a specialist glass-blower in Venice. The next day, Bond goes to bid farewell to Drax, who is shooting game. Drax hands Bond a shotgun. Birds fly over. Bond misses; instead he hits a sniper who has been aiming at him from a tree. After Bond has left, Corinne turns up. Drax fires her. She is chased through the wood by Drax's two Dobermans, presumably to her death.

At the glassworks in Venice, Bond spots Holly Goodhead. When she refuses a date, he heads off in a gondola. A knife-throwing assassin appears from a coffin on a floating funeral cortège and kills Bond's gondolier. Bond hurls a knife back, killing the thrower. He then flicks a switch that turns the gondola into a motorboat. After a chase around the canals of Venice, Bond escapes across St Mark's Square when his motor-powered gondola makes a further transformation into a hovercraft.

That night, Bond returns to the glassworks and discovers a secret lab where vials of a clear liquid are being packed into the containers designed by Drax. Bond steals a vial. He deliberately leaves another where it will be knocked over by two men working in lab. As the contents escape, the lab is instantly sealed and the two men die in agony. Bond then has a fight with Chang, who is in kendo gear, destroying the glassworks' museum. Chang is thrown to his death through the glass front of a clock into the square below. Bond then visits Holly Goodhead, who turns out to be with the CIA, and makes love to her. She disappears in the morning, leaving Bond with a CIA-issue poison-tipped pen.

When Bond, M and the British Minster of Defence return to the lab wearing gas masks, they find it has been transformed into a beautiful baroque room where Drax is waiting to greet them. Despite the embarrassment, Bond still has the vial, which proves there was a laboratory there.

Bond arrives in Rio de Janeiro where he searches a warehouse owned by Drax. His pretty assistant Manuela is grabbed by Jaws, who has now been hired by Drax, but she is saved when carnival revellers drag him off. Next day, on an observation platform overlooking an airfield where planes belonging to

Drax's airfreight company are taking off, Bond bumps into Holly Goodhead again.

On the cable car back down to the city, they are attacked by Jaws, eventually escaping by looping a chain over the cable and sliding down. Jaws comes after them in the cable car and crashes through the winch-house. He is extricated by a short blonde woman with glasses, called Dolly. They fall instantly in love. Meanwhile Bond and Goodhead are picked up by paramedics. Bond manages to break free and after a tussle falls out of the ambulance, but Goodhead is unable to escape.

Bond meets up with M in a monastery seconded by the Secret Service outside Rio. Q has discovered that the vial contains a deadly nerve gas that only affects humans, not animals or plants. It occurs naturally in a rare orchid found deep in the Brazilian jungle. Bond heads upriver in search of it in a motorboat modified by Q. He is pursued by Jaws and his henchmen. As they head for a waterfall, Bond escapes on a hang-glider. When he crash-lands, he sees a beautiful woman and follows her into a temple that is full of other beautiful women. Suddenly he is tipped into a pool where he is attacked by a large python. He kills it with Goodhead's poison-tipped pen.

Jaws grabs him and takes him to Drax, who is in control of the launch of a number of Moonrakers. He explains he had to steal the Moonraker that was on loan to the UK because something had gone wrong with one of his. Bond and Goodhead are locked in the bay under the shuttle engines where they will be incinerated, but they escape through a ventilation shaft using another of Q's wristwatch gadgets. They knock out the pilot and copilot of a Moonraker crew and take their place. During their flight, they take a look at their cargo, which consists of a number of good-looking young couples.

Docking at a space station that is cloaked by an anti-radar shield, Bond and Goodhead discover that Drax intends to use the nerve gas to kill the world's population and repopulate it with the offspring of the perfect couples the Moonrakers have brought with them. To foil the plot, Bond and Goodhead turn off the radar jammer, so the space station can be seen from Earth. The Americans launch a space shuttle with troops on board. A space-walking fight breaks out. Drax orders Jaws to throw Bond and Goodhead into the airlock where they will be ejected into space. But Bond remarks that Drax only intends to let perfect specimens survive. This plainly does not apply to Jaws and his lady-love. He turns on Drax.

As the American troops board the space station, Drax flees. Bond pursues, wounds him with Q's dart-firing wristwatch and pushes him out into space. The space station is now disintegrating and the US troops return to the shuttle. Bond and Goodhead are trapped, but make for Drax's Moonraker. Jaws pours two glasses of champagne for himself and Dolly and says, 'Well, here's to us' – his only words in the Bond series.

Bond and Goodhead cannot un-dock so they call for help from Jaws, who remains in the space station with his lady-love. They then plummet earthwards. News comes later that they have survived.

Drax has already released three containers of nerve gas. Bond and Goodhead go after them, shooting them down one by one. Now that they have saved the world, the camera on board the Moonraker is patched though to the White House and Buckingham Palace, revealing Bond and Goodhead making love in weightless conditions.

For Your Eyes Only (1981)

While the movie *For Your Eyes Only* loses most of the plot of the short story, it does include elements and borrows part of the storyline of 'Risico' which is also in the *For Your Eyes Only* collection.

The pre-title sequence begins with Bond visiting his wife's grave. A helicopter has come to take him back to the office. In fact, it has been sent by Blofeld, who we have not seen since the end of *Diamonds are Forever*. Blofeld has a remote control system that electrocutes the pilot. He then uses his remote control panel to send the helicopter spinning madly around the sky. However, Bond manages to climb out of the rear of the helicopter, throw the pilot's body out and take his seat. But as he struggles to take control, Blofeld flies the helicopter into a disused factory. At the last moment, Bond manages to pull the wires out of the control unit on board, then flies the helicopter out of the factory. Blofeld has been sitting in a high-tech wheelchair on top of a roof watching the action. Bond picks Blofeld's wheelchair up on the ski of the helicopter and deposits him down a chimney.

The story begins on board a fishing vessel named the *St Georges* out of Valletta. In fact, it is a high-tech British spy ship. It hits a mine and sinks before the crew can destroy the top secret ATAC (Automatic Targeting and Attack Communicator) equipment on board. The boat has sunk in shallow water off the Albanian coast. Soviet spymaster General Gogol believes a contact in Greece can recover the ATAC for them.

The action switches to a seaplane delivering a young lady who is visiting her parents on board their yacht. Her father is seen with a parrot which repeats whatever has been said. Once the daughter has been dropped off, the seaplane returns and strafes the yacht, killing her parents. These are the Havelocks, though their daughter is named Melina, not Judy.

Bond is told that Havelock senior had been sent to recover the ATAC. Now it is Bond's job. His first lead is Cuban hit man, Hector Gonzales, who killed the Havelocks. He lives near Madrid. Bond parks his car outside Gonzales's Spanish villa, where a pool party is under way. Bond sees a man give Gonzales a suitcase full of money. Bond is then captured. As he is being led away, Gonzales is hit by a bolt from a crossbow. Bond escapes, only to be saved by the archer, who turns out to be Melina Havelock.

Bond's Lotus Esprit blows up when one of Gonzales's henchmen tries to break into it. Instead, they take Melina's Citroën 2CV on a furious car chase. Nevertheless, they get away. Using Q's latest 'identigraph' machine, they discover that the man who delivered the money to Gonzales was Belgian assassin Emile

Leopold Locque, who is thought to be in Cortina d'Ampezzo in northern Italy.

In Cortina, Bond's contact Ferrara introduces him to a Greek named Aris Kristatos, who says that Locque is working for a drug smuggler named Milos Colombo, known in the Greek underworld as the Dove. The two had worked together in the Resistance during World War II. Kristatos has a young protégé named Bibi who is training to be a future ice-dance champion. Bond agrees to escort her to the biathlon.

Shopping in Cortina, Bond spots Melina. He fends off an attack on her by two black-clad men on motorcycles, then persuades her to return to her father's yacht and wait for him there. At the biathlon – after Bond fends off her advances – Bibi points out her friend Eric Kriegler, who is a competitor in the event. After Bond has left Bibi, Kriegler tries to kill him. He is chased by two men on motorcycles and is shot at by Locque. After he has escaped, Bond meets Bibi in the skating rink, where she tells him that Kriegler is an East German defector. She leaves and he has to fend off three assailants in ice-hockey outfits. Back in the car, he finds Ferrara dead. There is a white dove pin in his hand.

Bond then goes to Greece to check out Colombo. At dinner at a casino, Kristatos points out Colombo, who is with a contessa named Lisle von Schlaf. Bond spends the night with her. In the morning, they are walking on the beach when they are attacked by Locque and an accomplice in dune buggies. Locque runs down and kills Lisle von Schlaf. Bond is captured. But frogmen emerging from the sea kill Locque's accomplice. Locque makes off and the frogmen take Bond. They wear the white dove emblem on their wetsuits.

Incarcerated in a yacht, Bond meets Colombo, who tries to convince him that it is Kristatos who is the drug smuggler that works for the Soviets. To prove what he is saying, Colombo takes Bond to Kristatos's warehouse in Albania. During a raid, they discover a huge store of raw opium, plus deep-sea diving suits and floating mines like the one that sank the *St*

Georges. Locque blows up the warehouse and tries to escape. But Bond shots him through the windscreen of his car and rolls him off a cliff.

Using her father's two-man submarine, Melina and Bond recover the ATAC, only to be attacked underwater by Kristatos's men. Kristatos is waiting for them when the two-man sub is winched back on board the yacht. He takes the ATAC and tries to dispose of Bond and Melina by dragging them behind his yacht over a reef, as in the book of *Live and Let Die*. But thanks to Bond's ingenuity, they escape, convincing Kristatos that they have been eaten by sharks.

Back on the Havelocks' yacht, they hear the parrot repeat 'ATAC to St Cyril's'. This turns out to be a mountain-top monastery where Colombo and Kristatos hid from the Nazis during the war. Bond climbs the sheer cliff to operate the winch that allows the others up. Bond recovers the ATAC machine. As he tries to prevent Melina from avenging herself on Kristatos, he pulls a hidden weapon and Colombo kills him.

Gogol has arrived by helicopter. At gunpoint, he orders Bond to hand over the ATAC. Instead he hurls it over the cliff and it smashes on the ground below.

'That's détente, comrade,' says Bond. 'You don't have it; I don't have it.'

Gogol laughs and leaves.

Prime Minister Margaret Thatcher is patched though to the Havelocks' yacht to congratulate Bond. While he and Melina go skinny-dipping, Mrs Thatcher is left speaking to the parrot.

Octopussy (1983)

The main plot of *Octopussy* borrows nothing from the short story. However, a version of Fleming's tale is used as an ingenious backstory. The pre-title sequence begins in an unnamed Latin American country. Bond disguises himself as an army officer in order to place a bomb in a secret installation on an airbase. However, he is quickly captured by the officer he is impersonating. Bond's female assistant then distracts the guards, allowing him to escape on board a mini jet plane. Pursued by a SAM, Bond flies though the hangar containing the secret installation, blowing it up, while Bond escapes safely. He then runs out of fuel, lands, retracts the plane's wings and drives into an ordinary petrol station.

The main story begins in East Germany, where a clown is being pursued by knife-throwing twins. With a knife in his back, the clown survives long enough to reach the British Embassy, where he crashes dead through the French windows clutching a Fabergé egg. The egg is, in fact, a fake and the dead clown was 009. However, the real egg is up for auction in London, possibly as a method of funding Soviet subversion in the West. According to the catalogue, it is 'The Property of a Lady' – a Fleming short story which this part of the plot draws inspiration from.

At the auction Bond bids up the price, while substituting the fake egg for the real one. But exiled Afghan prince Kamal Khan is desperate to get his hands on the egg, paying twice what it is worth. Bond follows him to Delhi. At the casino attached to his hotel, Bond notes that Khan is winning money at backgammon by using loaded dice. He joins the game, using the egg as collateral and beats Khan at his own game. Bond is then pursued through the streets of Delhi by Khan's henchman, the sinister Gobinda. Evading him, Bond ends up in Q's laboratory where Q demonstrates a bugging device he has put in the egg which can be tracked by Bond's Seiko digital watch – the Rolex having fallen by the wayside.

Bond is seduced by the beautiful Magda, who has a tattoo of a blue-ringed octopus on her back. She steals the egg. Gobinda knocks out Bond and takes him to Khan's palace. But Bond escapes from his room using a pen filled with acid, which Q had provided, on the bars on the windows. He overhears Khan talking to dissident Soviet General Orlov. They agree to meet in Karl-Marx-Stadt in East Germany and Orlov orders Khan to kill Bond.

Bond manages to escape from the palace, disguised as a corpse in a shroud. He is then pursued though the jungle in a big game hunt. He escapes. The tattoo on Magda's back leads him to investigate Octopussy's island, which is inhabited only by beautiful women. Bond infiltrates the island under a fake crocodile.

When he meets Octopussy, she asks whether he remembers Major Dexter Smythe. Bond says yes. After a brilliant military career Smythe had been seconded to the Secret Service. His mission was to recover Chinese gold seized in North Korea. Both he and his native guide disappeared and the gold was never found. Twenty years later Bond was sent after him. The guide's body turned up with a bullet in its skull. It came from Smythe's service revolver. Bond traced Smythe to Sri Lanka, confronted him with the facts and gave him twenty-four hours to clear up affairs before taking him back to London. Instead he committed suicide rather than face the disgrace of a court martial. Smythe, it turns out, was Octopussy's father. But rather than seeking revenge, she thanks Bond for giving her father an honourable alternative. During his time in hiding, Smythe had become an expert on octopuses, which is why he gave his daughter the nickname Octopussy.

Bond stays the night and learns that Octopussy owns a circus which is to perform at Karl-Marx-Stadt. However, Khan has sent assassins after him. During their attack, Bond disappears. Octopussy thinks he has been eaten by a crocodile. In fact, he has escaped again under the fake one.

Visiting Octopussy's circus in East Germany, Bond sees Octopussy, Khan and Orlov. Octopussy is a jewel smuggler. She is smuggling Romanov jewels out of Russia in the base of a cannon used by a human cannonball. However, in the Soviet archives it is discovered that Orlov has been replacing the real imperial jewels with fakes. Meanwhile, Khan, Octopussy's associate, has betrayed her. In exchange for the jewels, he has allowed Orlov to replace them in the cannon with a small atomic bomb. The circus's next performance is at a US airbase in West Germany. Orlov reasons that an atomic explosion there will force the West to disarm, allowing the Soviets to invade Western Europe.

Bond spots one of the knife-throwing twins making the switch and kills him. Bond then sets off after the train in Orlov's car. The tyres are blown out, but the wheel rims conveniently fit the train tracks. He clambers on board the speeding train. General Gogol then discovers the stolen jewels in the trunk of Orlov's abandoned car and sets off after Orlov, who is also chasing the train. At the border, he is shot down.

On the roof of the train, Bond fights the surviving knife-throwing twin and Gobinda. Bond and the twin fall off and Bond kills him. Then he steals a car and, pursued by the West German police, crashes into the airbase. Bond eludes security by disguising himself a clown. In the nick of time, he finds the bomb and disarms it.

Bond and Octopussy return separately to India. Using Octopussy's circus girls as commandos, they launch an assault on Khan's palace. Khan and Gobinda flee, capturing Octopussy as they go. Bond follows them. They attempt to escape in a light aircraft. Bond jumps on to the tailplane before it takes off. Clambering over the roof of the plane, he disables one of its engines. Bond and Gobinda fight on the roof of the plane and Gobinda falls to his death. As the plane loses height, Bond and Octopussy jump to safety, while Khan and the plane crash into the side of a mountain.

In London, M and Gogol discuss the return of the jewellery, while Bond recuperates with Octopussy aboard her private boat in India.

Never Say Never Again (1983)

Four months after *Octopussy* came out, Sean Connery returned to the screen in the aptly named *Never Say Never Again*. Apparently, when he retired from the role of Bond after *Diamonds are Forever* in 1971, Connery told the press that he would never play Bond again. His second wife Micheline Roquebrune then said he should 'never say never again' – and is credited for her contribution at the end of the film.

The film begins with a middle-aged but still athletic Bond

infiltrating an enemy compound, subduing and apparently killing several guards along the way. Breaking into the main
building, he fights his way into a bedroom where he finds a
woman tied to a bed. He frees her, but she grabs a hidden knife
and kills him.

At Secret Service headquarters, a new M reviews Bond's
performance on video. The raid had been a training exercise.
Bond is clearly slipping and is sent to the Shrublands health
clinic, while the double-O section is to be disbanded. In the
vault of a bank in France, a meeting of SPECTRE is taking
place. An audacious operation called 'The Tears of Allah' is
being planned. An American air force officer, Captain Jack
Petachi, is addicted to heroin and, to feed his habit, has been
given a corneal implant making his right-eye print an exact
replica of that of the president of the United States. He is being
moved to a convalescent clinic near London, where he will be
under the care of Fatima Blush.

Fatima is wheeling Petachi into Shrublands when Bond
enters. He quickly seduces his physiotherapist. While making
love to her, he hears cries and observes Blush beating Petachi.
Then he sees Petachi testing the eye-print. But Bond is spotted
by Fatima.

The following day in the club's weights room, Bond is set
upon by a large thug. After an extended fight, Bond throws a
beaker of caustic liquid in the man's face. He reels back, impales
himself on broken glassware and falls dead. The label on the
beaker reads: 'James Bond – urine sample.'

At a US Air Force base in Britain, they are testing the deployment of cruise missiles. Petachi sneaks into the sealed control
room and, using the fake eye-print, gives presidential authoriza-
tion for the substitution of nuclear warheads for two dummy
ones. These are successfully deployed. As Petachi flees the base,
Blush forces him to crash his car, then blows it up, killing him.

On his fishing boat, a SPECTRE operative interferes with
the missiles' guidance systems, bringing them down in the sea
nearby where they can be recovered. A cat-stroking Blofeld then

broadcasts a threat to set them off if the nations of the world do not pay a massive ransom within seven days.

The double Os are reactivated. Bond discovers that Petachi's sister Domino is the mistress of sinister billionaire Maximilian Largo and heads to the Bahamas to investigate. On his yacht there – the *Flying Saucer*, a translation of the Italian *Disco Volante* – Largo gives Domino a precious jade pendant with a strange pattern on it called 'The Tears of Allah'. In Nassau, Bond meets Fatima Blush, who invites him on a diving expedition. She seduces him. Then, while they are diving, she places an electronic lure on his back to attract sharks. He finds and removes it. Reaching the surface, he is rescued by a woman he had met at the harbour side earlier.

Back in Nassau, Blush sees Bond and the woman at his hotel. She places a bomb under his bed. However, he is in the other woman's room, making love to her. Meanwhile the British High Commission has discovered that Largo's yacht is on its way to the South of France. Bond flies after him and is met at the airport by his local Secret Service contact Nicole and the CIA's Felix Leiter.

Bond poses as a masseur to give Domino a rubdown at a health spa and discovers that Largo is holding a charity event at the casino that night. Bond crashes the party. He plays a game of world domination devised by Largo, which gives the loser painful, even potentially fatal, electric shocks. Bond bests his host but refuses his winnings in exchange for a single dance with Domino. During it, he tells her that her brother is dead and Largo is the chief suspect.

Returning to his villa, Bond finds Nicole dead. He pursues the fleeing Fatima on a turbo-charged motorbike supplied by Q. Fatima eventually traps him in a dockside warehouse and tries to force him to write down that she is the greatest lover he has ever had. He uses a pen supplied by Q, which fires a small rocket that blows up Blush.

Bond goes scuba diving under the *Flying Saucer*, finds a secret compartment and is sucked in. Largo then heads for

North Africa. Bond is chained up in Largo's medieval castle there, while Largo – convinced that Domino has betrayed him with Bond – tries to sell her off to some unsavoury Arabs. Bond escapes and rescues her. After a spectacular leap over the walls into the sea on a horse, they are picked up by a submarine.

One of the warheads has been found in Washington and defused. They have five hours to find the other one. Bond spots that Largo has anchored near a coastal feature that matches the pattern on Domino's pendant. Largo intends to explode the bomb in an underwater cave there to destroy the whole of the Middle Eastern oil reserves. Bond and Leiter thwart him. But in the ensuing battle Largo escapes with the warhead. Bond is then dropped by helicopter down a well – according to legend formed by the tears of Allah – and catches Largo. Domino turns up in the nick of time and shoots Largo with a spear gun, while Bond defuses the bomb. The two of them retreat to the Bahamas for a holiday. M wants him back but Bond says: 'Never again.' This time Sean Connery, at least, means it.

A View to a Kill (1985)

Roger Moore was also going to say 'never again' after *Octopussy*, as critics already considered him too old for the part. The film owes nothing to Ian Fleming's short story 'From a View to a Kill', except the title. The movie begins with Bond locating the body of 003 in Arctic Siberia and recovering a microchip. Soviet troops ambush him, but he escapes in a submersible camouflaged to look like a small iceberg.

Back in M's office, it is revealed that the Soviet chip that 003 had purloined was an exact copy of a British chip made by a company recently taken over by the Anglo-French Zorin Industries. At Ascot racecourse, Bond sees owner Max Zorin. Zorin's horse Pegasus wins a race against all odds. Trainer Sir Godfrey Tibbett believes that it must have been doped, though it had been cleared before the race.

Through Tibbett, Bond meets French detective Achille Aubergine. During a dinner in the restaurant on the Eiffel

Tower, Aubergine says he intends to investigate the alleged doping at a bloodstock sale at Zorin's. But he is then assassinated by Zorin's mysterious female accomplice May Day. Bond gives chase. May Day parachutes from the Eiffel Tower. Bond appropriates a taxi and gives chase, but she escapes on a speedboat driven by Zorin.

Bond attends the sale masquerading as James St John Smythe with Tibbett as his chauffeur. At a reception at Zorin's château, Bond finds himself cold-shouldered by a young American woman who has taken a large cheque from Zorin. Bond and Tibbett break into Zorin's secret laboratory and discover that Zorin has been using the chip to deliver dope remotely to the horse during the race. They also find a warehouse full of chips. The break-in is discovered. Bond finds his way into May Day's bedroom and sleeps with her to allay suspicion of his other nocturnal activities.

Zorin tricks Bond into a steeplechase. When Bond is about to win, Zorin triggers a remote injection to his horse, which dashes off the track. Bond spots Tibbett's Rolls, gallops alongside and climbs in the window to find Tibbett dead and May Day at the wheel. Bond is knocked out and the Rolls is rolled into a lake. Before the air in the car is exhausted, Bond comes round. He stays underwater by breathing air from the tyre until Zorin and May Day have gone.

Zorin is visited by General Gogol. Though it transpires that Zorin, an East German defector, has been funded by the KGB, he says he wants nothing further to do with them. He has fish of his own to fry.

The action shifts to San Francisco, where Zorin outlines his plans to a number of businessmen in an airship above the bay. He says he wants $100 million from each of them to destroy Silicon Valley, giving them a monopoly on microchips. One refuses and is dropped into the water below.

Bond meets his CIA contact, who reveals that Zorin is a psychopath, the product of a Nazi experiment conducted by Dr Glaub, who is also the scientist behind his horse-doping scam.

Posing as a journalist from the *Financial Times* of London, Bond investigates the disappearance of crabs near Zorin's tightly guarded oil pumping station in San Francisco Bay. Diving near the facility, Bond is also sucked into the pipe, and discovers that Zorin is pumping water into the oil wells, rather than oil out. He also comes across KGB agent Pola Ivanova, who is trying to blow up the facility. Former lovers, they renew their romantic entanglement – though, in fact, Pola is trying to steal a tape of a conversation Bond eavesdropped on electronically. But Bond knows what she is up to and switches the tape. When he reviews the recording of the conversation, he hears Zorin mention Silicon Valley and 'Mainstrike'.

After interviewing a corrupt state official Zorin has bribed, Bond sees the girl who snubbed him at Zorin's reception. Her name is Stacey Sutton and she is a state geologist Zorin has tricked out of her family oil company. Zorin had tried to buy her, but she did not cash the cheque. Bond saves her life when Zorin's men try to kill her at her mansion. Together they go at night to City Hall to search for more information. Zorin catches them. He shoots the corrupt official with Bond's gun so it looks as if Bond killed him, then shuts Bond and Stacey in the elevator and sets fire to the place.

Bond and Stacey escape and make off in a fire truck. Eluding the police in a choreographed car chase, they head for Mainstrike, a disused mine owned by Zorin. They discover it is packed with explosives. Zorin's plan is to set off an explosion that will release the San Andreas and Hayward Faults simultaneously, causing a flood that will engulf Silicon Valley.

Stacey escapes, but May Day and Bond are trapped in the flooded mine. May Day realizes that Zorin does not love her and helps remove the bomb that would trigger a massive cache of explosives. In the process, May Day sacrifices her life. Stacey is picked up by Zorin as he escapes on his airship with Dr Glaub. Bond grabs one of the mooring ropes and is carried over San Francisco. Zorin tries to foul Bond on the Golden Gate Bridge, but Bond lashes the mooring rope to the stanchion.

Stacey escapes on to the supporting cable. Bond and Zorin slug it out and Zorin falls to his death. Glaub tries to throw dynamite at Bond and Stacey, but slips and blows the airship up.

In a final scene, General Gogol arrives at M's offices to award Bond the Order of Lenin, explaining that Russian technological development depended on the breakthroughs made in Silicon Valley. Meanwhile Q locates Bond and Stacey having a shower together in the Sutton Mansion.

The Living Daylights (1987)

The first Timothy Dalton Bond, *The Living Daylights*, does at least take its inspiration from the short story of the same name. Bond is assigned to kill a KGB hit man, who turns out to be a beautiful blonde cello player, and, at the last moment, alters his aim to hit the stock of her rifle. However, in the movie, she is not there to kill a British agent coming over the wall, but rather a KGB general who is defecting. And the action takes place in Bratislava, not Berlin. Although this is the beginning of the main story, the pre-title sequence opens in the cargo hold of a plane over Gibraltar. M is briefing three double-O agents on an exercise to test the colony's defences. The loading ramp lowers and the three agents skydive on to the Rock. One is immediately stopped by the SAS. An assassin shoots another SAS guard, then cuts the rope a second agent, 004, is using to scale the Rock. But before he does that, he slides down a tag. Written on it is '*Smiert spionom*', an alternative transliteration of '*Smert shpionam*' – 'Death to spies'.

Bond sees 004 fall. The man who cut the rope shoots another guard and makes off in a jeep full of explosives. Bond leaps on the canvas roof, cuts his way through and fights with the driver. The jeep goes off a cliff. Bond escapes using his emergency chute, which pulls him out of the jeep before it explodes. He lands on a yacht where a beautiful woman is making a phone call. She offers him a glass of champagne. Roll title sequence . . .

Once Bond has thwarted the blonde sniper, he takes charge of Georgi Koskov, the defecting KGB general, after Saunders, the local Secret Service agent, threatens to report Bond for deliberately disobeying his orders to kill the sniper. Bond takes Koskov to a pumping station on the pipeline that carries gas from the Soviet Union to Western Europe. Koskov is put into a modified scouring plug that is used to clean the inside of the pipeline. Recovered in another pumping station over the border in Austria, Koskov is flown to England in a Harrier jump-jet.

Debriefed in a country house, Koskov says that he has defected because his superior, KGB chief General Leonid Pushkin, drunk with power, has abandoned détente and re-instituted the old policy of 'Death to spies'. However, when Bond, M and the minister leave, Soviet agent Necros breaks into the house and whisks Koskov away in a helicopter.

M orders Bond to assassinate Pushkin at a conference being held in Tangier. But first Bond travels back to Bratislava to find out more about the beautiful cellist who tried to kill Koskov. Her name is Kara Milovy. When she is arrested by the KGB, Bond seizes the opportunity to steal her cello case. In it is the sniper rifle she used. It is loaded with blanks. Bond is in her apartment when she returns the next day. He discovers that she is Koskov's girlfriend, employed as a faux assassin to make his defection look convincing. Bond says that he can reunite her with Koskov in Vienna. She is under surveillance, but they escape using Bond's Aston Martin's defence systems. When these are exhausted, they cross the border using Kara's cello case as a sled.

Meanwhile in Tangier, Pushkin meets with rogue US general Brad Whitaker, who supplies high-tech arms. Pushkin cancels an order and demands his money back. Whitaker later meets with Koskov and Necros. It transpires that they have been aiming to defraud Pushkin then, due to Koskov's supposed defection, get Bond to kill him. To encourage Bond further, Necros is sent to Vienna to kill Saunders, leaving a balloon with '*Smiert spionom*' written on it.

Bond and Kara head to Tangier where Bond seizes Pushkin at gunpoint and demands to know why he has reinstated the

'*Smiert spionom*' policy. Pushkin denies it, so Bond fakes his assassination at the conference, pre-empting Necros's attempt to kill him for real.

While Bond was away, Kara talked to Koskov who told her that Bond was a KGB agent sent to kill him. She drugs Bond's champagne. They are flown to a Soviet airbase in Afghanistan where they escape with the help of Kamran Shah, an Oxford-educated Afghan prince and commander in the mujahedin. Koskov has used Pushkin's arms money to buy diamonds. These are being given to the mujahedin in exchange for raw opium. The profits will be used to buy arms for the mujahedin to fight the Soviets.

When the opium is with loaded on to a plane at the airbase, Bond plants a bomb, but is spotted. During a battle between Shah's men and Soviet troops fighting for Koskov, the plane speeds down the runway with Bond on board. Kara chases after him in a jeep, driving up the loading ramp into the plane. Necros also gets on board. Once they are airborne, Bond and Necros fight – at one point on a cargo net hanging out of the back of the plane. Necros eventually falls to his death.

The plane is badly shot up. After dropping the bomb on a Soviet column pursuing the mujahedin, Bond and Kara manage to escape, rolling the jeep out of the back of the plane as it crashes over a cliff. Bond returns to Tangier, where he kills Whitaker. Koskov is arrested by Pushkin and Kara is given her exit visa by General Gogol, now working for the Soviet foreign office, so she can perform in the West. The film ends, of course, with a romantic scene in her dressing room.

Licence to Kill (1989)

Although *Licence to Kill* is not based on any Ian Fleming title, it does borrow details from some of his work. The story opens with Bond and Felix Leiter on the way to Leiter's wedding. They are stopped by a coastguard helicopter whose pilot reports that the drug baron Franz Sanchez has landed in the Bahamas. Sanchez heads to a villa where he finds his mistress, Lupe

Lamora, in bed with another man. He has the man killed and beats Lupe with a stingray's tail – as in 'The Hildebrand Rarity'. Bond and Leiter ride in the helicopter back to the airfield where they intercept Lupe and Sanchez's henchmen as they arrive in a jeep. But Sanchez has jumped out earlier and escapes in a light aircraft. Bond and Leiter pursue him in the helicopter. Bond is winched down on to the tail of the plane and attaches the winch cable. Then he and Leiter skydive down to the wedding.

After the titles, Sanchez is in custody, but offers $2 million in cash to anyone who will spring him. A Drug Enforcement Agency officer arranges an elaborate escape. After the wedding, Leiter and his bride give Bond an inscribed cigarette lighter with a fierce flame. Later, Sanchez's henchmen capture Leiter and his wife. The wife is killed and Leiter is fed to a shark in a scene akin to that in the novel *Live and Let Die*. Again, Leiter is found barely alive, bearing a note that says: 'He disagreed with something that ate him.'

Bond is determined on revenge for the attack on Leiter. He finds the exotic fish supplier where Leiter was maimed, and breaks in at night to discover that it is a front for drug smuggling. After a fight, Bond is confronted by the DEA agent who arranged for Sanchez to escape. Bond feeds him to the shark.

M has Bond brought to Ernest Hemingway's house in Key West, where he orders Bond to go on assignment to Istanbul. Bond refuses. Ironically, given the title of the movie, he is stripped of his licence to kill. But he won't hand over his gun and escapes. He sails out to the marine research ship belonging to Milton Krest, a name again borrowed from 'The Hildebrand Rarity'. He discovers drugs on board. Again he meets Lupe, who covers for him. He then intercepts a drug transhipment, making off with a light plane carrying $5 million.

Returning to Leiter's house, Bond discovers that Leiter has a rendezvous at a dockside bar in Bimini with ex-CIA pilot Pam Bouvier. There they meet Sanchez henchman Dario. A fight starts. Bond and Bouvier escape. She agrees to fly him to a place called Isthmus. There Bond deposits the $5 million in a bank owned by Sanchez and attracts attention by alternately losing and winning large amounts at Sanchez's casino. Thus making his introduction, Bond offers his services to Sanchez as a professional hit man.

Back at the hotel, Q turns up and furnishes Bond with some essential gadgets including a special sniper rifle, which Bond uses in an attempt to kill Sanchez from an abandoned building overlooking his office. But first he has to set plastic explosives, supplied by Q in a toothpaste tube, to take out the window that is made of bulletproof glass. He detonates the charge, but before he can shoot Sanchez, he is attacked by agents in ninja garb. He comes round tied to a table, to find out that his captors are undercover Hong Kong narcotics agents trying to infiltrate Sanchez's operation. They are joined by a Secret Service agent who says he has orders to return Bond to London. He is about to administer an injection when Sanchez breaks in. His men kill the agents and find Bond unconscious, still tied to the table.

Next morning Bond wakes up in Sanchez's house and plants a seed of doubt in Sanchez's mind concerning Krest, who is about to arrive in Isthmus. With the help of Lupe, Bouvier and Q, Bond withdraws the $5 million from the bank and puts it on Krest's yacht, the *WaveKrest*. Sanchez finds it and kills Krest in a depressurization chamber, rapidly dropping the pressure until Krest's head blows up like a balloon and explodes.

Bond has now proved himself a trusted ally and, after he has surreptitiously slept with Lupe, he is taken by Sanchez to his base with a party of Asian drug buyers. Bouvier follows. Bond learns that Sanchez's scientists can dissolve cocaine in gasoline and transport it in tankers with little risk of discovery. Bouvier has also told Bond that Sanchez has bought Stinger missiles from the Contras, and has threatened to shoot down an American airliner if the DEA interferes in his operations. During Sanchez's presentation, Bond is recognized by Dario. In an attempt to escape, Bond starts a fire in the laboratory which spreads throughout the whole base. Even so, Sanchez has time to grab Bond and put him on the conveyor that drops the bricks of cocaine into a giant shredder, leaving Dario to finish him off. Bouvier arrives and distracts Dario, allowing Bond to feed him into the shredder. As the base explodes, Bond and Bouvier make off after Sanchez and four tankers full of the cocaine-gasoline mixture. Bouvier, at the controls of a Piper Cub, lands Bond on top of one of the trucks. During the chase, three of the tankers are destroyed by Bond or Sanchez's mis-aimed Stingers. Bond and Sanchez end up fighting it out on the top of the last tanker. It crashes. Both survive. Sanchez grabs Bond and is about to kill him with a machete when Bond asks, 'Don't you want to know why?' He pulls the inscribed lighter from his pocket to show Sanchez, who is momentarily distracted. Then Bond flicks it. Sanchez is soaked with gasoline and goes up in flames. Bouvier arrives in the detached train of one of the tankers to take Bond home.

At a party at Sanchez's old home, Bond speaks on the phone to Leiter, who is making a good recovery. Leiter also tells Bond that M might have a job for him, indicating that he will be taken back into the Service. Lupe takes Bond aside, but he rejects her blandishments and goes after Bouvier instead.

GoldenEye (1995)

Pierce Bronson took over as Bond for *GoldenEye*, while Judi Dench became M – mirroring the fact that by then MI5 had a woman, Stella Rimington, as its head. The film takes its title from the name of Ian Fleming's house.

The pre-title sequence begins with 007 breaking into a Soviet chemical weapons facility. Inside, he is met by 006, Alec Trevelyan. They plant explosives, but Trevelyan is captured by Colonel Arkady Ourumov, who ostensibly shoots him. The facility blows up while Bond steals a plane and escapes.

Nine years later Bond meets Xenia Onatopp, a suspected member of the Janus crime syndicate, who has taken as her lover an admiral in the Canadian Navy. She murders the admiral and uses his identity to get on board a Royal Navy frigate where the prototype Tiger Eurocopter – a helicopter whose electronics can survive the electromagnetic pulse generated by a nuclear explosion – is being demonstrated. She steals it, despite Bond's efforts to stop her.

Later Ourumov, now a general, and Onatopp land the helicopter outside a bunker in Siberia, where they massacre the staff and steal the control disk for the new Goldeneye satellite weapon. They then program one of the two GoldenEye satellites to destroy the complex with an electromagnetic pulse, and escape with geeky programmer Boris Grishenko. There is one lone survivor, Natalya Simonova. She arrives in St Petersburg where she contacts Boris, thinking him a trusted colleague. He promptly betrays her to Janus.

In London, M assigns Bond to investigate, but he is not to go after Ourumov out of revenge for Trevelyan's death. Arriving in St Petersburg he meets CIA agent Jack Wade, who takes him to see Valentin Zukovsky, a Russian Mafia head and business rival of Janus. Zukovsky agrees to arrange a meeting between Bond and Janus.

Janus turns out to be Alec Trevelyan, whose death in the chemical weapons facility had been faked to cover his defection. But he is now badly scarred because Bond advanced the timers on the explosives. Bond is about to shoot Trevelyan when he is shot with a tranquillizer dart. He wakes tied up with Natalya in the Tiger helicopter programmed to self-destruct. The two escape using the ejection system.

Arrested by the Russian police, they are interrogated by the Russian Minister of Defence. Ourumov bursts into the room and shoots the minister with Bond's gun. He calls for the guards. Bond punches him and escapes with Natalya into the archives, where a firefight ensues. Natalya is recaptured and taken off in a car with Ourumov. Bond steals a tank and pursues Ourumov through St Petersburg to Janus's armoured train, where he kills Ourumov. Trevelyan and Onatopp escape, locking Bond and Natalya in the train. As Bond cuts through the floor with a laser watch, Natalya uses Janus's computer to locate the dish Grishenko is now using to control the satellite weapons. It is in Cuba. The two escape seconds before the train explodes.

On their way to Cuba, Bond and Natalya meet Jack Wade and swap Bond's car for a light aircraft to search for the dish. Unable to find it, they are shot down. After they have escaped from the wreckage, a helicopter flies over and Onatopp abseils down. She gets Bond in a stranglehold, but he manages to use her weapon to shoot down the helicopter. Still attached by the abseil cord, Onatopp is crushed against a tree and dies.

Bond and Natalya then watch as a lake is drained of water, uncovering the dish. They infiltrate the control station, where Bond is captured. Trevelyan reveals his plan to steal all the money from the Bank of England electronically before wiping all record of the transaction with the remaining GoldenEye satellite weapon, simultaneously destroying the British economy. Meanwhile, Natalya programs the satellite to begin re-entry so it will burn up in the atmosphere. With Natalya now captive, Grishenko tries to save the satellite, while nervously fiddling with a explosive pen provided by Q. Escaping into the dish, Bond sabotages the antenna. High above the dish, he has a fist-fight with Trevelyan, who falls. Bond grabs him, but then releases him after pointing out that, unlike most of his kills, this one is personal. Trevelyan survives the fall, but dies when the damaged antenna falls on top of him while Bond escapes clutching the skid of a helicopter commandeered by Natalya. Grishenko survives the explosion only to be frozen by exploding tanks of liquid nitrogen. Landing safely in a field, Bond and Natalya embrace, imagining themselves to be alone. Wade arrives to reveal that they are surrounded by a camouflaged unit of US Marines. The couple is then whisked off to Guantanamo Bay Naval Base by Marine helicopter.

Tomorrow Never Dies (1997)

The pre-title sequence of *Tomorrow Never Dies* is set on the Russia border where stolen Soviet weapons are being sold to terrorists. The action is being watched remotely in London via

a camera infiltrated by an agent. Among the arms traders identified is 'techno terrorist' Henry Gupta, who is buying a US GPS
encoder. Over M's objections, the Royal Navy launch missiles,
hoping to kill most of the world's terrorists. The camera then
shows that a Soviet plane on offer is carrying nuclear torpedoes,
which could be detonated by the missiles. But it is too late to
recall them. The agent on the ground, now revealed to be 007,
moves in on the attack. In the confusion of bullets and explosions, Bond hijacks the plane and takes off with another plane in
pursuit. Once airborne, the airman in the back seat comes to
and tries to strangle Bond, who reaches for the eject button,
firing the backseater up into the pursuing plane, destroying it.

In the South China Sea, Royal Navy frigate HMS *Devonshire*
is overflown by two Chinese fighters, which inform the Navy
that it is in Chinese territorial waters. The British captain replies
that he is in international waters and will retaliate if attacked.
Nearby a stealth vessel lurks. It launches a sea-drill that punc-
tures the hull of the British ship. As she sinks, the *Devonshire*
fires a rocket that brings down one of the Chinese planes. The
stealth ship's commanding officer, Stamper, contacts his boss,
media mogul Elliot Carver, and tells him that part one of the
operation is complete. In part two, Stamper machine-guns the
survivors in the water, using Chinese ammunition. Meanwhile,
Carver is writing the headline for his international newspaper,
Tomorrow, saying: 'British Sailors Murdered.'

In London, the Royal Navy prepares for war. But M notes
that a mysterious signal was sent on the GPS frequency that
could have sent the *Devonshire* off course. Bond discovers that
the newspaper came out before anyone ashore could have
known about the murder of the British sailors. M also suspects
that the signal came from one of Carver's broadcast satellites
and sends Bond to a reception at Carver's headquarters in
Hamburg for the launch of Carver's new news channel, which
has global coverage with the exception of China.

At the reception Bond meets Carver's wife Paris, an old
flame. Carver also introduces Bond to Wai Lin of the Chinese

government news service. During his conversation with Carver, Bond hints that he suspects Carver's involvement in the sinking of the *Devonshire*. While Carver is making a speech introducing his new channel – pointing out its debut scoop, the sinking of the *Devonshire* – Bond is taken away by Carver's heavies, who try to beat him up. Bond thrashes them, then pulls the plug on Carver's speech. Back in Bond's hotel room, Paris Carver arrives and the two of them sleep together.

The following day, Bond breaks into Carver's headquarters where he spots Gupta. In his safe, Bond finds the GPS encoder device. He takes it and is leaving when Wai Lin breaks in and sets off the alarm. Using a Q-style piton and cable, she escapes easily, while Bond has to fight his way out. Back at his hotel, he discovers Paris dead. The assassin, Dr Kaufman, holds him at gunpoint, while Stamper and his men try to break into Bond's car. The code to open car, Bond says, is on his cellphone – one provided by Q. When Kaufman tries it, he gets a massive electric shock. Bond grabs his gun and kills him.

In the hotel car park, Bond's BMW is surrounded by Stamper's men. Using a remote control provided by Q, Bond drives it away, opens the back window and jumps in. Using all the gadgets Q has built in, he evades his pursuers in a chase around the car park. Eventually he jumps out, leaving the car to speed over the edge of the roof and crash into the Avis office below.

At a US airbase in Asia, Bond meets Jack Wade again. A GPS expert confirms that the *Devonshire* was sent off course before she was sunk and works out where the wreckage is. With Wade's help, Bond makes a HALO dive on the position and scuba-dives down to the *Devonshire*, finding Wai Lin there already. They discover that the frigate's cruise missiles are missing and escape before the ship settles into deeper waters, but surface to be captured by Stamper on a Vietnamese fishing vessel.

Taken to Carver's headquarters in Saigon, they find Carver writing their obituaries, revealing that Wai Lin is with the Chinese People's External Security Force. Carver then outlines his plan to use his media empire to take over the world, after he has destroyed the old world order by starting a war between Britain and China. While Carver goes for a meeting with a General Chang, he leaves Bond and Wai Lin to be tortured by Stamper, a devotee of Dr Kaufman.

Still handcuffed together, Bond and Wai Lin shrug off their captors, then escape by leaping through the window, slowing their fall from the skyscraper by tearing a strip down a huge banner of Carver that decorates the side of the building.

They steal a motorbike and are pursued through the streets of Saigon by a helicopter, downing it by throwing a cable into its tail rotor. While having a shower afterwards, Bond gets romantic, but Wai Lin gives him the slip by unlocking her half of the handcuffs and cuffing him to the pipe. He quickly frees himself and tails her to her hideout. She is attacked by several thugs, but Bond intervenes, finishing them off. Wai Lin reveals that she had been investigating Chang, who she suspected of building a stealth plane. No, a stealth boat, Bond says. They deduce that the boat will use the *Devonshire*'s missiles to start an incident between the Royal Navy and the Chinese fleet which is massing in the South China Sea.

After sending a message to both their governments, they narrow down the stealth boat's berth to one bay. Finding her in the last cove, they board her and plant mines. Wai Lin is captured and Bond overhears Carver revealing his ultimate plan. He will launch one of the stolen British missiles at Beijing. General Chang will take over and Carver will gain access to the Chinese media market. This is possibly a swipe at Rupert Murdoch, who was accused of appeasing the Chinese government to get a broadcast ban lifted.

Bond captures Gupta and offers to exchange him for Wai Lin. But Carver kills Gupta after he tells him that the missile is ready to fire and, consequently, he is no longer needed. However, a grenade planted by Bond in a jar with a small triggering device goes off, causing a huge explosion. The stealth boat is now visible to radar and is attacked by the Royal Navy. Wai Lin shoots up the engines, but Carver goes ahead with countdown to the missile launch. In a fight with Carver, Bond pushes him into the sea-drill. But Stamper has chained Wai Lin and dangles her over an outlet to the sea. She manages to pass Bond some detonation fuses to sabotage the missile and Stamper drops her in the water. In a fight to the death, Bond traps Stamper's ankle under the outlet of the missile's engine. But Stamper clings on to Bond so that he will die with him. Bond cuts himself free and drops into the water as the missile launches and the detonators destroy it along with Stamper and the stealth ship. Underwater, he finds Wai Lin, breathes air into her mouth with a kiss and unchains her. The two surface surrounded by wreckage. Meanwhile M puts out a press release saying that Carver is missing presumed dead while on a cruise, possibly suicide – shades of Robert Maxwell here. Bond and Lin are floating on a makeshift raft together while the Royal Navy hunt for them.

The World is Not Enough (1999)

The film borrows its title from the Bond family motto, revealed by the College of Arms in *On Her Majesty's Secret Service*. It begins with Bond in the offices of a Swiss banker in Bilbao collecting money that is being returned to Sir Robert King. But an MI6 agent has been killed and Bond wants to know who did it. At gunpoint, the banker is about to tell him when he is killed by a knife in the back of the neck wielded by his secretary. One of the banker's henchmen gets the drop on Bond, but is killed by a sniper. Bond then escapes through the window.

Back in MI6 headquarters in London, the money is returned to Sir Robert, an oil tycoon and a personal friend of M. However, the money has been impregnated with a chemical, turning it into a massive bomb that is detonated by a bug in Sir Robert's lapel pin. The bomb blows a hole in the wall. Through it Bond sees the banker's secretary on board a boat in the Thames. She tries to shoot him. He gives chase using Q's latest mini-speed-boat. At the Millennium Dome (now The O_2), she tries to escape on a hot-air balloon. Bond is carried aloft on one of the mooring ropes and tries to persuade her to give herself up. But she prefers to kill herself.

At King's funeral, Bond meets his daughter Elektra. M concludes that the most likely suspect in his murder is a terrorist named Renard. He had been shot earlier by a double-O agent. A bullet had lodged in his brain that would eventually kill him. But first it would leave him with increased powers of endurance and a progressive lack of feeling.

Renard had previously been involved in the kidnapping of Elektra. Sir Robert had turned to M for help. M had told him not to pay the ransom, in the hope that this would lead to the capture of Renard. However, Elektra seduced her guards and killed them, or so she said. Bond realizes that the money returned by the Swiss banker is the same amount as the ransom. It served as a message from Renard that he was going to kill Elektra.

Bond is sent to protect Elektra, who has taken over her father's project, building a pipeline from the oilfield of Azerbaijan to the Mediterranean. He joins her on skis on an inspection of the route of the pipeline. They are attacked by a group of men on 'parahawks' – small fan-driven snowmobiles attached to para-sails. Bond sees them off and protects Elektra from the subsequent avalanche.

While Elektra recuperates in her house in Baku, Bond seeks out his old adversary Zukovsky, who runs a nearby casino. Zukovsky tells him that Renard is an ex-KGB man working for the Russian oil barons who want King's pipeline stopped, as it is a rival to their own. Elektra turns up at the casino and loses $1 million to Zukovsky on the turn of a card.

Secretly Elektra's security chief Davidov meets Renard and a nuclear weapons scientist named Arkov. Renard kills Arkov for failing to kill Elektra with his parahawks. Davidov is ordered to take his place on a secret mission the following day.

Bond takes Elektra home and makes love to her. Then he sneaks out to investigate Davidov. He finds Arkov's body in the back of Davidov's car and takes its place. After Davidov drives to a rendezvous with a plane, Bond appears and disposes of him.

Posing as Arkov, Bond flies to a remote region of Kazakhstan where nuclear missiles are being dismantled in an underground facility. Here Bond meets attractive American Dr Christmas Jones, who is removing the radioactive material. In the silo, Bond finds Renard and his men stealing a nuclear warhead. Bond briefly captures Renard and interrogates him at gunpoint. During their exchange, Renard says, 'There's no point in living if you can't feel alive' – a phrase Elektra has used before. Christmas Jones arrives with security, claiming Bond is an impostor. Bond is forced to drop his gun. Renard's men open fire and escape with the warhead, leaving Bond and Jones trapped in the silo with a time bomb. However, they escape before it goes off.

Bond returns to Baku and confronts Elektra, accusing her of working with Renard. But she has called M. When M then arrives, Bond tries to explain himself, but an alarm sounds. Renard has planted the stolen warhead on an inspection car that is travelling out of control down the pipeline. Bond and Jones use another inspection car to intercept it. When Jones dismantles the device, she finds that only half of the plutonium is there. Bond tells her to let the detonation charge go off. A section of the pipe is blown out. They escape, but have created the illusion that they have been killed.

With Bond seemingly out of the way, Elektra tells M that she killed her father for using her as bait for Renard and had hoped that the bomb had killed M too. M is then imprisoned in the Maiden's Tower on an island in the Bosporus.

Bond and Jones are puzzled as to why Renard only used half of the plutonium. Looking for answers, Bond visits Zukovsky at his caviar factory. They are attacked by helicopters with dangling saw blade machines. Bond downs them, and in the confusion Zukovsky falls into a vat of his own caviar. Before pulling him out, Bond asks him about Elektra's payoff in the casino. Zukovsky tells him that the $1 million was to arrange for his nephew, a Russian submarine captain, to transport some machinery via Istanbul for Elektra.

Bond realizes that Elektra and Renard are interested not in cargo, but in the nuclear submarine itself. Jones points out that if weapons-grade plutonium was loaded into the reactor, there would be a catastrophic explosion destroying Istanbul and blocking the Bosporus. This would render the other pipelines to the Black Sea useless, leaving no competition to Elektra's pipeline direct to the Mediterranean. But before Bond can do anything, he and Jones are captured by Renard. Bond is delivered to Elektra at the Maiden's Tower, while Jones is taken to the submarine moored beneath it.

Despite her love for Renard, Elektra says that she could have given Bond 'the world'. He replies: 'The world is not enough.' Elektra has Bond shackled to an antique device and proceeds to torture him. But Zukovsky and his men invade the tower. Elektra shoots Zukovsky. A dying shot from Zukovsky releases one of Bond's wrists, allowing him to free himself. Pausing only to free M, he chases Elektra up to the top of the tower where, as she refuses to call Renard off, he kills her.

Bond leaps from the tower and boards the submarine. As he kills Renard's men, the sub sinks nose down. Renard is locked in the reactor room with the rod of stolen plutonium. Bond has to swim outside the submarine to get into the reactor room by another entrance. He grapples with Renard, who is able to lock Bond behind a cage door while he inserts the rod into the reactor. But Bond sees a way to eject the rod using a pneumatic pipe. The ejected rod impales Renard, killing him. Bond and Jones escape through a torpedo tube.

Back at MI6 HQ, M, Q and his staff scan satellite imagery, looking for Bond. They find him in Istanbul, making love to Dr Jones.

Die Another Day (2002)
Pierce Brosnan had his last run-out as Bond in *Die Another Day*. It begins with James Bond infiltrating a North Korean military

base belonging to Colonel Tan-Sun Moon, posing as an arms dealer buying weapons with African conflict diamonds. After the diamonds are handed over, Moon's right-hand man Zao discovers Bond's true identity. Bond detonates plastic explosives he has put in the case and diamonds are embedded in Zao's face. Fearing retribution from his father, General Moon, Colonel Moon then flees in a large hovercraft. Bond steals another hovercraft and chases Moon, who tumbles into a waterfall. North Korean troops capture Bond, who is imprisoned and tortured on General Moon's orders.

Fourteen months later, Bond is released in exchange for Zao, who had been captured trying to blow up a summit between South Korea and China and killing three Chinese agents. After medical checks, M tells Bond that his double-O status is suspended as he may have leaked information under duress. Bitter over Zao's release, Bond escapes. With the help of the Chinese, he travels to Cuba, where he traces Zao to a clinic on an offshore island where DNA therapy allows patients to change their identity. In Cuba, he picks up a copy of *A Field Guide to Birds of the West Indies*. And when, in a homage to Ursula Andress in *Dr No*, NSA agent Giacinta 'Jinx' Johnson emerges from the sea in a bikini, Bond pretends to be an ornithologist. They have sex, though neither is aware of the other's true profession.

The following day, Bond locates Zao's room inside the clinic. After a fight, Zao escapes on a helicopter but leaves behind a pendant. Jinx is also at the clinic – and working on the Zao case. She escapes by diving over the wall into the sea where a motor cruiser picks her up. Back in Havana, Bond opens the pendant to find a cache of conflict diamonds, but they bear the crest of British billionaire Gustav Graves.

Bond tracks Graves to a fencing club in London. The two duel with swords. Bond wins and Graves invites Bond to a party he is holding in Iceland. Graves's publicist and fencing partner Miranda Frost is left to make the arrangements.

In a disused London Underground station, Bond meets M, who tells him that Frost is working for MI6, but has failed to uncover any evidence against Graves. Taking up Graves's invitation, Bond arrives at his ice palace in Iceland where he meets Jinx, who is posing as a journalist. Graves then gives a demonstration of his new satellite called 'Icarus', an orbital mirror that, he says, will provide year-round sunshine for crop development.

Bond is spotted snooping around Graves's private quarters where Graves is developing a robot suit that gives high-voltage shocks. He is rescued by Frost, who pretends they are lovers. Though she has previously been frosty with him, they end up in bed together. Meanwhile Jinx infiltrates Graves's quarters, finds Zao but is captured by Graves. She is shackled and left to be killed by Graves's chief torturer, Mr Kil. Bond breaks in and together they kill Kil.

Bond then confronts Graves, working out that he is Moon *fils* who has had his identity altered at the Cuban DNA clinic. Frost arrives, but she is a double agent and turns her gun on Bond. Jinx finds herself locked in her room in the ice palace. Bond escapes and heads off in Graves's jet-powered skate car. Graves calls in three North Korean generals and demonstrates Icarus's real capability, focusing reflected light of the sun down into a concentrated death ray. The ray pursues Bond. He escapes by driving off an ice cliff, after deploying the skate car's braking anchor to break his fall. He then uses the rear cowl as a board and the car's braking parachute to parasurf away across the sea.

Returning to collect his Aston Martin, Bond is pursued by Zao in another car replete with high-tech gadgetry. Meanwhile Graves turns Icarus on the ice palace to drown Jinx. Bond and Zao continue their car chase around the rapidly melting ice palace. Bond uses all Q's modifications, including the facility to render the car invisible, to thwart Zao, eventually killing him by dropping a chandelier on him. He then rescues Jinx from drowning.

Graves has returned to North Korea where there has been a coup by hardliners, ousting his father. They are preparing to invade the South, using Icarus to clear the minefield along the

Demilitarized Zone. Bond and Jinx infiltrate North Korea using experimental stealth air-sleds and parachutes. They follow Graves into his aeroplane, which is also carrying Frost and General Moon. When Moon realizes that Graves is his son, he grabs a gun, but Graves kills him instead.

Jinx fights Frost and kills her. Bond fights Graves, but gets the worst of it because of Graves's high-voltage robot suit. With no one at the controls, the plane strays into Icarus's beam and catches fire. Graves puts on a parachute, throwing the others out. But he cannot resist taunting Bond, who pulls his ripcord. The parachute pulls Graves out of a hole in the side of the plane and into an engine.

Bond and Jinx escape by rolling a helicopter out of the crashing plane, starting the engine just before the helicopter hits the ground. War is averted. In the final scene, in a shack on a remote island Bond is trying diamonds found in Graves's helicopter in Jinx's navel as part of their love play.

Casino Royale (2006)

When Daniel Craig took over as Bond it was decided to take the movie series back to its roots and establish a new timeline. *Casino Royale* would be a screen adaptation of Fleming's first book. It would make no reference to any of the movies that came before and would show a younger and more vulnerable Bond.

The film begins with Bond earning his double-O status. He visits Dryden, the MI6 section chief in Prague, who has been selling secrets. Dryden says he is not afraid because Bond is not a double O – for that you need two kills. A flashback shows Bond killing Dryden's contact. Dryden taunts Bond. 'You needn't worry,' he says, 'the second is . . .' Before he can say 'easier', Bond shoots him and says: 'Yes, considerably.'

In Uganda, the sinister Mr White introduces Steven Obanno, a rebel leader, to Le Chiffre, private banker to terrorist groups worldwide. Le Chiffre uses Obanno's money to short-sell stock in the company Skyfleet.

Elsewhere in Africa, Bond, now a double O, pursues a terror-ist bomb-maker into the Nambutu Embassy. He is surrounded by armed guards. The ambassador tells Bond to let the man go. Bond shoots the terrorist and a nearby gas tank, then escapes in the confusion. In the backpack the terrorist was carrying, Bond finds a cellphone and a bomb.

Back at MI6, M is furious as 007's actions were caught on CCTV at the Nambutu Embassy. But Bond has discovered that a call to the terrorist originated in the Bahamas, and heads there. He traces the call to a man named Alex Dimitrios, an associate of Le Chiffre. To find out more, he beats Dimitrios at poker and seduces his wife. Discovering that Dimitrios is flying to Miami, Bond follows him. After he has deposited a bag, Bond kills him, then follows the man who has picked up the bag to Miami airport. There he tries to blow up Skyfleet's latest prototype, the largest passenger plane in the world. But Bond thwarts him. As a result, Le Chiffre loses over $100 million. Now desperate to earn the money back before Obanno kills him, Le Chiffre sets up the high-stakes match of Texas Hold 'Em in a hotel in Montenegro with an entry fee of $10 million.

The best poker player in the Secret Service, Bond is sent to foil him. The money is put up by the British government, and treasury agent Vesper Lynd is sent to keep an eye on it. Lynd is determined to keep Bond at arm's length, but at the resort in Montenegro they have to pose as a married couple. They are further aided by René Mathis, their contact in Montenegro. The poker players have their entry fees in escrow in a Swiss bank. Each has to specify a bank account where the winnings are to be sent, along with a password. Vesper has the account details, but only Bond knows the password.

On the first hand, Bond loses a large amount of cash. Vesper is furious. During a break in play, Obanno and a henchman turn up and threaten to cut off Le Chiffre's girlfriend's arms with a machete. Le Chiffre does not flinch, but Bond hears her screams. Bond takes them on and, in a fight in a stairwell, kills them. Mathis gets rid of the bodies.

The next day, Bond loses all his money to Le Chiffre. Vesper won't fund him further. However, one of the other players will. It is Felix Leiter of the CIA. In return, Bond must give Le Chiffre to the CIA. At the table, his fortunes revive. But Le Chiffre's girlfriend poisons Bond's Martini with digitalis, inducing heart failure. Bond manages to get to his car. Communicating with medical specialists at MI6 headquarters, he applies a defibrillator from the car's medical kit, but passes out. However, Vesper arrives in time and shocks him back to life.

Shaken, Bond returns to the table. In the final hand, Bond and Le Chiffre bet their remaining money for a pot that has climbed to well over $150 million. Le Chiffre has a full house with three aces and a pair of sixes. But Bond reveals he has a straight flush and wins the game.

Over dinner with Vesper, Bond names his favourite cocktail a Vesper and receives news that the CIA are about to close in on Le Chiffre. However, Le Chiffre kidnaps Vesper. Bond races after them in his Aston Martin, but has to swerve violently when he sees Vesper lying bound in the road. The car rolls several times, knocking him out. Bond is stripped and tied to a chair with the seat cut out. Le Chiffre beats Bond with a knotted rope, demanding he tell him the password for the account where the winnings are lodged. Bond refuses. Finally, Le Chiffre draws a knife and is about to castrate Bond when there are gunshots. The door opens and Mr White appears. He kills Le Chiffre with a single shot to the forehead.

Bond wakes up in a hospital bed. During his recuperation, Bond has Mathis arrested, suspecting he betrayed him. Vesper then agrees to go to bed with Bond. The Swiss banker holding the winnings visits and Bond gives Vesper the password to key in – it is her own first name. Bond declares his love for her. During a holiday with Vesper, he resigns from the Service. They sail to Venice. M calls, asking why the winnings have not been deposited with the Treasury. Bond discovers that Vesper is withdrawing the money from a bank in St Mark's Square. He follows her to a meeting where she hands over the money to a sinister man. He spots Bond, who chases them into a dilapidated building. In a firefight, Bond shoots into the flotation tanks that hold the building up. As it collapses, Vesper is caught in a lift. Bond is unable to extricate her. She locks herself in and drowns, while Mr White makes off with the cash.

M explains that Vesper had a boyfriend who had been kidnapped and she had been forced to hand over the money. Now that Vesper has been found to be the traitor, M wants to release Mathis. Bond says that just because Vesper was guilty does not mean that Mathis is innocent.

'Keep sweating him,' he says.

It seems now that Bond trusts no one. M is pleased, but asks Bond if he needs more time to get over Vesper. Hardened by his experience Bond callously says that it doesn't matter: 'The bitch is dead.'

But M says Vesper has sacrificed her life in exchange for his. From Vesper's cellphone, Bond traces Mr White and shoots him in the leg.

Quantum of Solace (2008)

While *Casino Royale* is an adaptation of the Fleming novel, *Quantum of Solace* owes nothing to the short story of the same name. However, it follows on directly from the preceding movie. The film opens with Bond driving down a road in Italy. A car follows. Inside there is a gunman who opens fire. Bond disposes of his pursuers in typical style. Arriving in Siena during the Palio, Bond opens the boot of his car to reveal Mr White.

In an MI6 safe house, M updates Bond on Vesper's boyfriend, Yusef Kabira. A body carrying his ID was washed up on the coast of Ibiza. However, M had a DNA check done and found it was not him. M concludes that he is still alive. They interrogate White about his secretive organization which, apparently, MI6 knows little about.

'We have people everywhere,' says White.

M's bodyguard, Mitchell, pulls a gun, kills the MI6 guard and attempts to assassinate M. A stray bullet hits White. Bond pursues Mitchell over the rooftops and kills him.

Bond heads to Haiti to track down Mitchell's contact, Slate. After a fight, he kills him. As he is leaving the hotel with Slate's briefcase, Bond is picked up by a woman named Camille Montes. He learns that Slate was ordered to kill Camille by her lover, Dominic Greene. Mistaking Bond for Slate, Camille tries to shoot him, but misses. Bond follows her to the waterfront where he has a meeting with Greene.

Greene is doing a deal with a Bolivian general named Medrano: he will help Medrano stage a coup in exchange for a seemingly barren piece of desert. He gives Camille to Medrano to sweeten the deal. As they head off on Medrano's boat, Bond rescues her, despite her protests.

Bond then follows Greene to a private jet, which flies him to Austria. On the plane, Greene meets with Felix Leiter and the CIA section chief for South America Gregg Beam. Greene produces a picture of Bond and asks the CIA to kill Bond. Beam agrees, while Leiter pretends not to recognize him.

Greene runs a seemingly innocent ecological organization called Greene Planet. But Bond discovers he is also head of a secret society called Quantum, which is holding a meeting at the opera via tiny radio microphones and earpieces given to guests in gift bags. Bond steals one of the bags and breaks into the meeting, telling members of Quantum that they should probably find a more secure place to meet. This panics them and they get up to leave, allowing Bond to identify and photograph them.

After a shoot-out in a restaurant, Bond pushes a member of Special Branch, the bodyguard of Guy Haines, an adviser to the British prime minister, off a building. He is then killed by Greene, and Bond is blamed. M cancels Bond's passport and credit cards. Bond travels to Italy to met René Mathis, who soon forgives Bond for having him arrested and tortured. Mathis then accompanies Bond to Bolivia to investigate Greene's business dealings there. In La Paz, they are greeted by Ms Fields from the British Consulate, who tells Bond that he must return to the UK on the next available flight. Bond disobeys and seduces her in their hotel suite.

Bond meets Camille again at an ecological fund-raiser being held by Greene, where she is embarrassing her former lover in front of wealthy donors. When Bond and Camille leave together, they are pulled over by the Bolivian police, who find a bloodied and beaten Mathis in the trunk of their car. As Bond lifts Mathis out, the police open fire and fatally wound Mathis. Bond takes his revenge.

Bond and Camille drive out into the Bolivian desert and hire an old Douglas DC-3 plane to investigate from the air. They are intercepted by a fighter and helicopter gunship. Bond downs them both, but the DC-3 is crippled and he and Camille escape by parachuting into a sinkhole. While finding a way out, they discover that Quantum is not after oil as everyone suspects. Instead it is stealing the country's supply of fresh water by damming subterranean rivers. Camille reveals that General Medrano murdered her family and she was trying to take her revenge.

Returning to La Paz, Bond finds M there and learns that Quantum have murdered Fields, drowning her in oil to throw them off the scent. M orders Bond to hand over his gun and has him arrested. Bond escapes. He defies M's orders to surrender. M tells her men to watch him because she thinks he is on to something. She still has faith in him.

Although the CIA is out to kill him, Bond arranges to meet Felix Leiter at a local bar. As American special forces move in, Leiter tells him that Greene is paying off Medrano and the police chief at Greene Planet's eco-hotel in the Bolivian desert. At the meeting, Greene forces General Medrano into signing an overpriced utilities contract allowing Greene to supply water to Bolivia.

Arriving at the hotel Bond kills the police chief for betraying Mathis. A hydrogen fuel tank is hit, setting off a series of explosions. Camille stops Medrano raping a hotel maid, then kills Medrano. In the burning building, Bond fights Greene. He rescues Camille from the conflagration and captures the fleeing

Greene. After interrogating him, he dumps Greene in the middle of the desert with a can of motor oil, telling him that he bets he will make it no more than twenty miles across the desert before he considers drinking it. Bond drives Camille to a railway station, where she wonders what she will do now her revenge is complete. They kiss and she departs.

Bond goes to Kazan in Russia, where he finds Yusef Kabira. He is with a Canadian agent named Corinne; he has even given her a necklace like the one he had given Vesper. It is clear that Kabira is a member of Quantum who seduces women in sensitive positions, such as Vesper. M is surprised when Bond does not kill Kabira, but leaves him alive for questioning. As Bond walks off into the night, he drops Vesper's necklace in the snow.

The film ends with the famous gun barrel sequence that traditionally opens Bond films. Then the credits roll.

6. M and Friends

In Ian Fleming's books there is no mention of MI6. However, in *Live and Let Die*, Bond mentions that they are 'always rubbing MI5 up the wrong way' and 'stepping on the corns of Special Branch'. Inter-agency rivalry goes even further in the film *Quantum of Solace* when Bond throws a Special Branch officer off a roof.

Throughout the books, Fleming and Bond talk of the Secret Service, or the British Secret Service. England had an organization collecting foreign intelligence going back at least to the second half of the fifteenth century. Thomas Cromwell ran secret agents in Europe for Henry VIII and Sir Francis Walsingham maintained a network of fifty secret agents abroad while principal secretary to Elizabeth I.

However, today's Secret Intelligence Service has its origins in the Secret Service Bureau set up in 1909 by the Committee for Imperial Defence in response to the growing threat of German naval expansion. It was often known as the Secret Service, the SS Bureau or even the SS. The Bureau's Home Section was to counter foreign espionage and eventually became MI5, while the Foreign Section collected secret intelligence abroad and became the Secret Intelligence Service. However, in a modern liberal democracy no parliament is going to tolerate a secret organization that is not answerable to the electorate outside wartime. So the SIS later masqueraded as MI6 under the pretence that it belonged to military intelligence.

Indeed, during World War I, the Foreign Section did fall under the Military Intelligence Directorate and was known as MI1 (c). Its first head, Commander (later Captain Sir) Mansfield Cumming RN, signed himself simply as 'C' in green ink, a practice continued by his successors – and, indeed, by M. During the war, it carried out successful operations behind enemy lines in Belgium and France and made an important contribution to the Allied victory. However, Cumming did not enjoy being under the auspices of the War Office, which curtailed his independence, and after the war he managed to engineer the return of the Service to the Foreign Office. Until his death in 1923 Cumming maintained a lively interest in the tradecraft of spying, experimenting personally with disguises, mechanical gadgets and secret inks in his own laboratory.

Although SIS was cut back following World War I, it survived because of the need to combat the spread of Soviet Communism, then of Nazism. During World War II, it became Section 6 of the Directorate of Military Intelligence, consequently MI6, before being returned to the Foreign Office after the end of hostilities.

SIS agents were given five-digit code numbers. It appears there were no double-O agents, though. After the publication of *The Human Factor* in 1978, the author Graham Greene, himself a wartime agent, was upbraided by former SIS chief Sir Richard White, who complained that MI6 did not go about killing people. Nor did it work under the cover of 'Universal Export', though its former headquarters at 54 Broadway, just opposite St James's Park tube station, bore the brass plaque of the Minimax Fire Extinguisher Company for many years.

The headquarters near Regent's Park is Fleming's invention, though the SAS does have its HQ there. In the movies, the head office of Universal Export is usually somewhere in Westminster, so the shot can get Big Ben in the background. That way, viewers will know they are in London.

The SIS only officially came into being in 1994 with the passing of the Intelligence Services Bill. Since then its chief has been named and its headquarters on the Albert Embankment at

Vauxhall is hardly a secret. The building appears in the opening sequence of *The World is Not Enough*. Since the fall of the Berlin Wall, the SIS – as it still likes to call itself – sees its role as countering 'regional instability, terrorism, the proliferation of weapons of mass destruction and serious international crime'. These are exactly the tasks James Bond had taken on in the recent movies.

M

Bond's boss M borrowed his single-letter descriptor from Cumming's C. But the letter itself was out of bounds. In 1932, Compton Mackenzie was prosecuted under the Official Secrets Act for writing about C in a book about his adventures in British intelligence in the eastern Mediterranean, *Greek Memories*. However, Fleming knew other spymasters who identified themselves by their initial, including three Ms.

One was Major-General Sir Colin McVean Gubbins who became head of SOE in 1943. A career soldier, he had been with the Allied intervention force in Russia in 1919, then fought in the Anglo-Irish War of 1919–21. In 1939, he helped set up MI(R), where he prepared manuals of irregular warfare which would be dropped, in translation, across occupied Europe to aid the Resistance. In August 1939, he flew to Warsaw to brief the Polish General Staff on sabotage and subversion. After liaising with the Czechs and the Poles in Paris, he returned to England to raise 'independent companies' – the forerunner of the commandos – which he later commanded in Norway, where Peter Fleming saw action. Back in England, he was in charge of setting up 'auxiliary units' of civilians who would operate behind German lines if Britain was invaded. He then became SOE's head of operations and training. As its head, he found he could not sign himself G as the initial was in common use in military acronyms. C was also taken. So he took M from his middle name. Ian Fleming would have known him as he liaised with SOE.

MI5's Maxwell Knight also signed his memos 'M'. He had

been in the British *Fascisti* before joined the security service in 1925. He then used his contacts to break spy rings on both the left and the right. Married three times, he used attractive young women as his agents, though he was convinced that 'more information has been obtained by women agents by keeping out of the arms of the man, than was ever obtained by sinking too willingly into them'. However, one of his agents – and would-be lover – Joan Miller characterized him as an anti-Semitic homosexual, though he was vehemently anti-gay. He was a jazz aficionado who had been taught the saxophone by Sidney Bechet, a fan of the occult and friend of Aleister Crowley. Knight was also the author of two hard-boiled crime novels and, as Uncle Max, a radio and TV naturalist, who also wrote books such as *How to Keep an Elephant* and *How to Keep a Gorilla*. Although they never worked together, Fleming would have known of him and Miller believed that Bond's M was an amalgam of Knight and Fleming's boss at Naval Intelligence, Admiral John Godfrey.

The third M was in the spying game before C came along. Irish-born policeman William Melville was one of the founding members of the Metropolitan Police's Special Irish Branch, now known simply as Special Branch. His job was to foil bomb plots by Fenians and anarchists. He thwarted the 1887 Golden Jubilee Plot to assassinate Queen Victoria, learnt how to pick locks from Harry Houdini and recruited Sidney Reilly, the so-called 'ace of spies' who was believed to have been killed by the Soviets in 1925. It is thought that the detective in Joseph Conrad's 1907 novel *The Secret Agent* is based on Melville. Fleming himself was interested in the fate of Reilly. When, towards the end of World War II, reports from Russia suggested that Reilly was not dead, but had been reprieved on the understanding that he would give the Soviets information about British Intelligence, Fleming gave instructions for a report to be obtained from Brigadier George Hill, best man at one of Reilly's numerous bigamous weddings and a British agent who had been liaising with the NKVD, the forerunner of the KGB, since

1941. Hill was living in Bad Neuenahr in Germany at the time and proved elusive when attempts were made to contact him.

In 1903, Melville retired from the police force and went to set up a new intelligence section for the War Office, another fore-runner of MI5. There he adopted the code name 'M'. Under the pseudonym William Morgan, he recruited agents in Germany. When the Secret Service Bureau was established in 1909, he co-ordinated the Home and Foreign Sections. Although he died in 1918, Fleming would have known of him as Melville was still part of the enduring legend of the Secret Service when Fleming joined Naval Intelligence.

Fleming also knew a famous Z. This was Lieutenant-Colonel Sir Claude Dansey who, as a sixteen-year-old, had been seduced by Oscar Wilde. He was recruited as a spy while serv-ing in the Boer War. After losing his money in the Wall Street Crash, he worked for SIS in Italy, keeping tabs on Mussolini's Fascist movement. Finding the service incompetent, he resigned, allowing the rumour to circulate that he had been sacked for stealing. Meanwhile, he used his contacts to set up a rival operation known as Z Organization after his own code name, Z. When two MI6 agents were captured by the Nazis in the Dutch border town of Venlo in September 1939 and the whole organization was compromised, the Z Organization took over and saved the day. Assistant to the then C, Stewart Menzies, Colonel Z co-ordinated MI6's activities throughout the war. Dansey gets a namecheck in *From Russia with Love*, when Darko Kerim mentions that a Major Dansey was his predecessor as head of Station T.

M's real name only comes out gradually in the books. In *Moonraker*, his first name, Miles, is revealed during a conver-sation with Lord Basildon, chairman of Blades. Then at the beginning of *The Man with the Golden Gun*, to prove that he is James Bond, 007 tells liaison officer Captain Walker that the head of department is Admiral Sir Miles Messervy. This again leads to the suspicion that M is based in part on Fleming's wartime boss, Admiral John Godfrey, a suspicion confirmed in *On Her Majesty's Secret Service* where Bond visits M at his home, Quarterdeck and Fleming notes that the knocker on his front door is the clapper from the brass sea-bell of a former HMS *Repulse*, 'the last of whose line, a battle-cruiser, had been M's final sea-going appointment'. The *Repulse* was Admiral Godfrey's last command before he became head of Naval Intelligence. At one point, Godfrey had asked Fleming to be his biographer. Fleming declined. As it was, Godfrey was less than flattered by any comparison. He complained after Fleming's death: 'He turned me into that unsavoury character, M.'

But there is another anomaly here. In Bond's obituary in *You Only Live Twice*, M says that it was only at the end of the war that he 'became associated with certain aspects of the Ministry's work'. The *Repulse* had gone down in December 1941, so what had he been doing for three and a half years?

William Stephenson, head of SIS in New York, could also have been a model for M. There is a lobby for Maurice Buckmaster, head of the French Section of SOE, as well.

Kingsley Amis noted a stern but paternal streak in the relationship between M and Bond. In the short story 'For Your Eyes Only', for example, Bond is prepared to kill for M over what is, essentially, a private matter. M has a voice or demeanour, Fleming notes, that is alternately angry, brutal, cold, curt, dry, frosty, gruff, hard, impatient, irritable, moody, severe, sharp, short, sour, stern and testy. It is also a voice that Bond 'loved and obeyed', according to *Live and Let Die*. Could M have been a fantasy version of Fleming's own long-dead father? Amis even cites the Oedipus myth when, at the beginning of *The Man with the Golden Gun*, Bond returns after a long absence in a distant land and tries to kill M. In the event, Bond is rehabilitated rather than disciplined. But Fleming's biographer John Pearson has a more intriguing theory: 'There is reason for thinking that a more telling lead to the real identity of M lies in the fact that as a boy Fleming often called his mother M . . . While Fleming was young, his mother was certainly one of the few people he was frightened of, and her sternness toward him, her unexplained demands, and her remorseless insistence on success find a curious and constant echo in the way M handles that hard-ridden, hard-killing agent, 007.'

In *On Her Majesty's Secret Service*, we discover that the old sea-dog M would prefer to live by the sea, near Plymouth or Bristol perhaps. But as he had to be within easy call of London, he had chosen the next best thing – a small Regency manor house on the edge of Windsor Forest. It was on Crown lands and Bond had 'always suspected that "Grace and Favour" had found its way into M's lease'. As head of the Secret Service, M earned £5,000 a year, with the use of an ancient Rolls-Royce and a driver. A pension from the Navy would give him, perhaps, another £1,500. In the 1950s and 1960s, this would have been a decent salary. However, it did not explain how he could afford to be a member of Blades, where a candidate had to show that they had £100,000 in cash or gilt-edged securities. Nevertheless, the club kept bottles of his favourite cheap Algerian red wine 'Infuriator' for him, though the committee would not allow it on the wine list.

At home, it is served by Hammond, M's chief petty officer on the *Repulse*, who had followed M into retirement. Hammond's wife does the cooking at Quarterdeck, though M usually seems to have dined at his club. At home, M 'had one of the stock of bachelor's hobbies' – he painted watercolours, according to the book *On Her Majesty's Secret Service*, though butterfly collecting is substituted in the film. Both at home and in the office, M smoked a pipe. And in *The Man with the Golden Gun*, we learn that M is not the first head of the Secret Service. After Bond's attempt to assassinate him, M turns to his Chief of Staff and says: 'My predecessor died in that chair.'

In *Colonel Sun*, the first post-Fleming novel, M is kidnapped from Quarterdeck and Bond goes to great lengths to rescue him. Then in John Gardner's novel *Win, Lose or Die*, in 1989, M has a daughter and grandchildren – there was always the intimation that he was a widower. Hammond and his wife were killed in *Colonel Sun*. Now he has acquired Mr and Mrs Davison as household staff. According to Raymond Benson's *The Facts of Death* in 1998, M has 'two daughters from the marriage that few people knew about' – including, apparently, Ian Fleming. One is Haley McElwain, who married an American, but is now divorced. She has two children, nine-year-old Charles and six-year-old Lynne, though it is clear she cannot be the same daughter mentioned in *Win, Lose or Die*. By then M has retired from the Service. Bond remains a friend, though continues to address him as 'sir'.

In the early Bond films, M is played by Bernard Lee and is obviously meant to be the same M that Fleming wrote about. In *You Only Live Twice*, he appears in the uniform of a rear admiral. In *On Her Majesty's Secret Service*, when Bond visits Quarterdeck, he is ushered through to see 'the Admiral', now butterfly collector. And in *The Spy Who Loved Me*, General Gogol calls him Miles.

Again, M is not the first head of the Secret Service. In *Dr No*, he boasts that he has reduced the number of casualties among operatives since taking the job.

Bernard Lee famously faced the day fortified by several large Scotches or a bottle of gin. Though he was barely able to stand, when the cameras rolled he was word perfect and acted superbly. When the director said 'cut', he practically passed out. It was said that, when his house burned down, he was so drunk he did not even notice. Lee died during the production of *For Your Eyes Only*. As a result, M was said to be on leave and his lines were shared out among his Chief of Staff, Q and the Minister of Defence, Sir Frederick Gray.

In *Octopussy*, the role was taken over by Robert Brown, who had played Admiral Hargreaves in *The Spy Who Loved Me*. It is not clear in the movies whether Brown is playing Sir Miles Messervy, or that Hargreaves has taken over as M. However, in the continuing book series under Gardner and Benson, Messervy continues as head of the Secret Service until replaced by a female M. The eagle-eyed have spotted that Brown is wearing the insignia of a rear admiral – Messervy's rank – in *The Living Daylights*, while as Hargreaves he wore the insignia of a vice admiral in *The Spy Who Loved Me*. This means that, on becoming M, he would have been demoted.

In 1995, with *GoldenEye*, Judi Dench took over as M. She is definitely a new character as Zukovsky remarks, 'I hear the new M's a lady' and, in *The World is Not Enough*, an oil painting of Bernard Lee as Sir Miles Messervy appears behind her in MI6's Scottish Headquarters. The female M clearly drew inspiration from Stella Rimington, who was head of MI5 from 1992 to 1996. Although she has not been named in the films, Raymond Benson calls her Barbara Mawdsley. In *GoldenEye* she says she studied law at Oxford where she met Sir Robert King. She also admits to being a mother. However, in Raymond Benson's *The Facts of Death*, M is not married and has a boyfriend who is killed. She was also an acquaintance of Sir Miles Messervy. That is implied in *Casino Royale*, where she says, 'Christ, I miss the Cold War': it is plain she has been in MI6 for some time. Early drafts of the scripts for *GoldenEye* suggest that she had a relationship with Bond himself at some time in the past. She has a man in bed with her in *Casino Royale* when woken by a call and in *Quantum of Solace* she is married and has a brief on-screen dialogue with her husband.

Her attitude to Bond is completely different from the old M's. In *GoldenEye*, she calls Bond a 'sexist, misogynist dinosaur, a relic of the Cold War'. Bill Tanner, her Chief of Staff and Bond's closest friend in the Service, refers to her during the film as 'the evil queen of numbers'. Her response is that if she had wanted sarcasm, she would have spoken to her children. But she addresses the perception in a conversation with Bond: 'You think I'm an accountant, a bean counter, more interested in my numbers than your instincts,' she says.

He replies: 'The thought had occurred to me.'

After he returns from fourteen months of torture at the beginning of *Die Another Day*, she shows no sympathy, stripping him of his double-O status and telling him that he is useless to her. However, behind his back in *The World is Not Enough*, she admits, 'He's the best we have . . . although I'd never tell him.'

But she is positively hostile when she finds that he has broken into her home in *Casino Royale* and has found out her real name.

'I thought "M" was just a randomly assigned letter,' he says. 'I didn't know it stood for . . .'

She cuts him short.

'Utter one more syllable and I'll have you killed,' she says.

John Huston plays M in the 1966 *Casino Royale*. When he is killed, David Niven's James Bond takes over. And in *Never Say Never Again*, Edward Fox becomes the new M. He is a martinet who constantly tests agents and has little regard for Bond.

Miss Moneypenny

M's secretary is the redoubtable Miss Moneypenny. In *Casino Royale* we learn that she 'would have been desirable but for eyes which were cool and direct and quizzical'. In *Thunderball*, she has a 'desirable mouth' and 'often dreamed hopelessly about Bond'. In the film, *You Only Live Twice*, she tells Bond that the password in his forthcoming assignment is 'I love you'. When she asks him to repeat it, he refuses by saying he thinks he will remember it. Then in *Die Another Day*, she has a fantasy encounter with Bond, courtesy of Q's virtual reality glasses. He kisses her, sweeps everything off her desk and lays her on it. Even this is interrupted by Q. In reality she was not Bond's type. She owns a poodle and in *Moonraker* she can be found lunching on sandwiches and a glass of milk at her typewriter. A civilian in the books, in the movies she appears in the uniform of a lieutenant in the Wrens.

The principal model for Miss Moneypenny appears to have been Kathleen Pettigrew, the dragon-like guardian of wartime MI6 director Stewart Menzies. To get to see C, as Fleming must have done, he would have had to deal with his terrifying secretary. In early drafts of *Casino Royale*, M's secretary is a 'Miss Pettavel' or 'Petty'. Clearly this was too close to home, so

Fleming borrowed the name Moneypenny from his brother Peter's unfinished novel *The Stett*.

Another possibility is Victoire 'Paddy' Bennett, a secretary in Room 39 who worked with Fleming on Operation Mincemeat. She once described her former colleague as 'definitely a James Bond in his mind'. A pillar of respectability, she became secretary to Sir Julian Ridsdale, long-serving member of parliament for Harwich, married him and was made a Dame of the British Empire for her work as chairwoman of the Conservative MPs' Wives Club.

Then there is Vera Atkins. Recruited as a secretary to F Section of SOE, she went on to become an intelligence officer in her own right and sent more than five hundred agents to occupied France, spending years after the war investigating the fate of the 118 F Section operatives who disappeared in enemy territory. Fleming would have known her through his liaison work, and her obituary in the *New York Times* in 2000 said she was 'widely believed to have inspired the character of Miss Moneypenny'.

It has also been mooted that Moneypenny was based on Margaret Priestley, a secretary transferred to Fleming's 30AU from the Department of Naval Research in the winter of 1943–44. She went on to become a history don at Leeds University.

Another possible model is Joan Bright, who had worked for MI(R) and SIS, before becoming assistant to General Ismay, Winston Churchill's chief of staff in the War Cabinet offices. She first got to know Peter but as he was married Ian began taking her out. They met up at conferences in Washington and Quebec, then flew together to the conference in Cairo, returning together on HMS *London*. After the war, they sailed together on the *Queen Mary* from Bermuda to London. Also on board was Winston Churchill, who had just made his 'Iron Curtain' speech in Fulton, Missouri. It was Joan who introduced them, on the occasion when Churchill made it clear he would rather have met Peter instead. During the 1950s, in his 'Atticus' column in the *Sunday Times*, he plugged the small literary research agency she had set up and used it to check the details of the rocketry in *Moonraker*.

Typist Jean Frampton was dubbed by the press 'Ian Fleming's Miss Moneypenny' when their correspondence was sold at auction for £14,340 in 2008. In his letters, Fleming asked Frampton to copy-edit the manuscript as she retyped it. However, it seems they never met. Fleming's secretary at the *Sunday Times* was Una Trueblood. Mary Trueblood appears as the murdered Caribbean number two in *Dr No*.

Moneypenny has a minor role in the novels, but became a staple of the movies. However, in the 2006 *Casino Royale* she was replaced by a male assistant called Villiers and was missing again from *Quantum of Solace*. In fourteen of the Bond movies, plus the 1967 TV special *Welcome to Japan, Mr Bond*, she was played by Canadian actress Lois Maxwell with a mild Canadian accent. She has also been played by Pamela Salem in *Never Say Never Again*, Caroline Bliss in *The Living Daylights* and *Licence to Kill*, and Samantha Bond in *GoldenEye*, *Tomorrow Never Dies*, *The World is Not Enough* and *Die Another Day*. Barbara Bouchet takes the role of Moneypenny's daughter in the 1966 *Casino Royale*. And in *Octopussy* Moneypenny has an assistant named Penelope Smallbone, who is instantly smitten with Bond, despite Moneypenny's 'thorough briefing'.

In 2005, Moneypenny came into her own with *The Moneypenny Diaries* written by Samantha Weinberg under the nom de plume Kate Westbrook. There have been three books in the series so far – *Guardian Angel*, *Secret Servant* and *Final Fling* – along with a number of short stories. In *The Moneypenny Diaries* she gets a first name – Jane. In Fleming's books she is often referred to as Penny, though that is presumably a contraction of her surname.

Loelia Ponsonby and May

Bond has his own secretary, or at least one he shares with 008 and 0011. In *Moonraker, From Russia with Love* and *Thunderball* she is Loelia Ponsonby. Bond teases her by calling her 'Lil'. The character herself is a tease – Loelia, Duchess of Westminster, was a friend of Fleming's wife and came to stay at Goldeneye.

Bond terrifies Miss Ponsonby when he kisses her at Christmas, on her birthday and before he goes off on a dangerous assignment. She is both 'delectable' and 'virginal'. She was also 'tall and dark with a reserved unbroken beauty to which the war and five years in the Service had lent a touch of sternness. Unless she married soon, Bond thought for the hundredth time, or had a lover, her cool air of authority might easily become spinsterish and she would join the army of women who had married a career.' Bond and two other members of the double-O section had made 'assaults on her virtue'. Eventually in *On Her Majesty's Secret Service*, she left to marry a dull, but worthy and rich member of the Baltic Exchange. By then, she had been replaced by Mary Goodnight, who soon graduates to be a Bond girl.

On the domestic front, Bond is looked after by May, his treasured housekeeper, a grey-haired Scottish woman.

Bill Tanner

M's Chief of Staff Bill Tanner is Bond's closest friend in the Service. A former colonel in the Royal Engineers, he calms Bond's fears in *You Only Live Twice*. They lunch together. However, after Bond tries to kill M in *The Man with the Golden Gun*, Tanner urges M to charge Bond with treason or attempted murder, or simply court-martial him. After that, though, in John Gardner's novels, Bond and Tanner remain friends, even playing a round of golf together in Raymond Benson's *High Time to Kill*. Tanner, a family man, is envious of Bond's freedom.

In the film of *The Man with the Golden Gun*, he appears briefly and is not mentioned by name. Played by Michael Goodliffe, he appears in M's office, discussing the gold bullet with 007 on it sent ostensibly by Scaramanga. In *For Your Eyes Only*, Tanner gets a bigger role, taking over some of the lines originally meant for M. Played by James Villiers, he berates Bond for allowing Melina Havelock to kill Gonzales.

Michael Kitchen plays Tanner in *GoldenEye*, where he calls

M 'the evil queen of numbers', and in *The World is Not Enough*, where he appears discussing the villain Renard. Rory Kinnear took over the role in *Quantum of Solace*. However, in *Tomorrow Never Dies*, the Tanner role is played by Colin Salmon as Charles Robinson. Salmon appears again as Robinson in *The World is Not Enough* and *Die Another Day*.

Felix Leiter

While Tanner may be Bond's friend, his only serious sidekick is Felix Leiter. The name comes from Fleming's American friends, the Leiters, coupled with Felix, the middle name of Fleming's lifelong buddy Ivar Bryce. Leiter makes his first appearance in *Casino Royale*. A blond Texan and former US Marine, he is with the CIA and stationed in Paris. Crucially, he helps Bond out by giving him money to continue playing baccarat against Le Chiffre when he had been cleaned out. Then in *Live and Let Die*, Leiter gets fed to the sharks by Mr Big's henchmen and loses an arm and a leg. In *Diamonds are Forever*, he reappears with a hook for a hand and limping on a prosthetic leg; he is now working for Pinkerton's Detective Agency. Still ostensibly working for Pinkerton's, Leiter turns up in fatigues leading an army contingent at Bond's request to save the US gold reserves in Fort Knox in *Goldfinger*. In *Thunderball*, Leiter has been recalled to the CIA in the emergency following the theft of two nuclear bombs and joins in the underwater fight, despite his disabilities. He stays on with the Company in *The Man with the Golden Gun*. Working undercover as a hotel clerk, he gets the opportunity to save Bond's life during the disastrous train ride.

Leiter continues to work with Bond in the books by John Gardner and Raymond Benson. In *For Special Services*, he even teams up with Leiter's daughter Cedar, who is also working for the CIA. And though his physical disabilities grow progressively worse as he gets older, Leiter manages to acquire a Hispanic girlfriend named Manuela.

In the Bond movies, Leiter remains with the CIA except in *Licence to Kill* where he is seconded into the DEA. Leiter was written in to the first Bond film *Dr No* because the producers had been intending to start the series with *Thunderball*, when Leiter appears prominently, but plans were changed due to legal entanglements. In *Goldfinger*, Leiter starts the story off by delivering a message from M to Bond, telling him to keep an eye on Goldfinger. He then keeps an eye on Bond for M, eventually riding to the rescue after being told of Goldfinger's plans by Pussy Galore. Strangely, having been roughly the same age as Bond in *Dr No*, by *Goldfinger*, Leiter has aged dramatically, now being middle-aged and grey-haired.

In *Thunderball*, Leiter has been rejuvenated and is Bond's indispensable sidekick throughout. In *Diamonds are Forever*, Leiter appears as a customs officer – surely a CIA cover – who clears Franks's corpse when Bond is using it to smuggle the diamonds into the US. He is on hand to help Bond throughout. This is highly suspect as the CIA is forbidden by law from conducting intelligence or counterintelligence operations within the United States, though it has frequently done so.

Leiter again works within the United States in *Live and Let Die*, as well as more legitimately outside the country. In the movie, he avoids being dismembered by sharks. In *Never Say Never Again*, he has mysteriously become a black man. Then in *The Living Daylights*, he is white again and, once more, young, hip and a bit of a ladies' man.

Leiter's encounter with the sharks is delayed until *Licence to Kill*, where he is played by David Hedison, who previously took the role in *Live and Let Die*. Now working with the DEA, he marries, but his wife is soon killed and he is fed to the fishes. Despite extensive injuries he makes a remarkable recovery. So much so that, in *Casino Royale* – as an African-American again – he is unimpeded by any physical disability from helping Bond on his mission. As the 2006 *Casino Royale* restarts the chronology, Leiter has to introduce himself to Bond halfway through the poker tournament. The same actor, Jeffrey Wright, takes the role in *Quantum of Solace*, where Leiter puts his personal friendship to Bond above his duty to his superior, the CIA Section

Chief for South America Gregg Beam. This is a good move as, at the end of the film, Beam is dismissed and Leiter promoted.

In the 1954, TV outing of *Casino Royale*, there is a Clarence Leiter, working for the British Station S, opposite the American agent Jimmy Bond. He is essentially a composite of Felix Leiter and René Mathis from the book, while the name 'Mathis' is transferred to the heroine Valerie Mathis rather than Vesper Lynd. Although Clarence Leiter is supposed to be a British agent, he was played by Australian actor Michael Pate.

Jack Wade and J.W. Pepper

In *GoldenEye*, Bond's CIA contact is Jack Wade, who has little time for cloak-and-dagger passwords and 'stiff-assed Brits'. However, they quickly get to like each other. He reappears in *Tomorrow Never Dies* to arrange Bond's HALO dive on to the wreck of the *Devonshire*.

Another would-be Bond ally in the movies is Sheriff J.W. Pepper. He seeks to arrest Bond after the devastating boat chase in *Live and Let Die* only to be outranked by the Federal and State authorities. In *The Man with the Golden Gun*, he appears as a tourist in Thailand where the car he is perusing in a showroom is commandeered by Bond for another devastating car chase.

René Mathis

Bond's other undercover ally is René Mathis of the Deuxième Bureau. In Fleming's *Casino Royale*, we learn that Bond has worked with Mathis before on the casino job in Monte Carlo. In *From Russia with Love*, he makes a last-minute appearance to arrest Rosa Klebb and, we learn at the beginning of *Dr No*, to save Bond's life by giving him artificial respiration until a doctor turns up. Mathis's name comes up in *Thunderball* in connection with the investigation into SPECTRE. He appears again in Raymond Benson's *Never Dream of Dying* and Sebastian Faulks's *Devil May Care*. There is a youthful Mathis in the Young Bond short story 'A Hard Man to Kill'. Mathis also makes the scene in the 1966 spoof *Casino Royale*. In the 2006 *Casino Royale*, Bond suspects his loyalty and has him arrested and tortured. In *Quantum of Solace*, Mathis, played a second time by Giancarlo Giannini, is persuaded to forgive Bond, who then gets him murdered.

John Strangways

SIS station chief in the Caribbean John Strangways, a former lieutenant commander in the Special Branch of the RNVR, appeared in Fleming's *Live and Let Die* and *Dr No*. He also gets a namecheck in *Diamonds are Forever* and *The Man with the Golden Gun*. He is about thirty-five years old and, in the books, wears a black patch over his left eye. This is dispensed with in the film of *Dr No*. And, as he is killed early on in the movie, he makes no further appearances in the series.

Quarrel

In *Live and Let Die*, Strangways provides Bond with a local guide and physical trainer named Quarrel, a Cayman Islander. He is probably based on Fleming's friend, the champion swimmer Barrington Roper. Quarrel, played by John Kitzmiller, is killed in *Dr No*, so in the film of *Live and Let Die* his role is taken over by his son Quarrel Junior, played by Roy Stewart.

Kerim

Darko Kerim – renamed Kerim Bey in the film – appears in *From Russia with Love* as the long-time head of Station T in Istanbul. With a Turkish father and English mother, M says, he is 'one of the best men we've got anywhere'. He was two inches taller than Bond and broader. Though dissipated and debauched, his face radiated life. As they were both interested in eating, drinking and women, Bond and Kerim became firm friends. Unfortunately, Kerim was killed after one outing on the Orient Express.

Dikko Henderson and Tiger Tanaka

In the novel *You Only Live Twice*, Bond is given a guided tour of the bars and geisha houses of Tokyo by Australian intelligence officer Dikko Henderson, who is based on Fleming's friend Dick Hughes, the Asian correspondent for *The Times*. In the film, there is also a Dikko Henderson, played not noticeably as an Australian by Charles Gray, who went on to play Blofeld in *Diamonds are Forever*. The movie Dikko is a kimono-wearing ex-soldier with an artificial leg, who has settled in Japan. He gets killed, stabbed through the paper wall, when discussing the missing American spacecraft. In the book, Henderson introduces Bond to the head of the Japanese Secret Service, Tiger Tanaka, based on Fleming's friend Torao 'Tiger' Saito. In the movie, Bond is led to Tanaka by his contact Aki. Tanaka studied at Oxford and was naval attaché at the Japanese Embassy in London. During the war, he became a kamikaze pilot, but was saved by the atomic bombs dropped on Hiroshima and Nagasaki. Interested in drinking and women, Tanaka and Bond soon bond.

Ronnie Vallance

Bond's ally at Scotland Yard is Ronnie Vallance, assistant commissioner in charge of Special Branch and the boss of Bond girl Gala Brand in *Moonraker*. Vallance reappears in *Diamonds are Forever*. It is Vallance who discovers that the conflict diamonds from Sierra Leone are being smuggled through London, but as the diamonds are travelling on to the US he needs the help of the Secret Service and Bond. As the drugs in the short story 'Risico' are coming from Italy, Vallance co-opts a reluctant M and Bond again.

In *On Her Majesty's Secret Service*, he becomes, more formally, Sir Ronald Vallance of the CID. M phones him at home on Christmas Day to discover him reading a report on teenage prostitution. Then in 'The Property of a Lady', Bond uses Vallance's name to establish his credentials when visiting the Fabergé egg dealer Wartski. Vallance also appears in Kingsley Amis's *Colonel Sun* where he is called in after M has been kidnapped.

Captain Troop and Sir James Molony

In *From Russia with Love*, Bond is irritated by the Secret Service's paymaster Captain Troop, head of admin. They sat together on a committee of inquiry in the aftermath of the defection of Burgess and Maclean and fell out over the recruitment of 'intellectuals' to the Service. The eminent neurologist Sir James Molony appears in *Dr No*, *On Her Majesty's Secret Service*, *You Only Live Twice* and *The Man with the Golden Gun*, usually expressing concern about the state of Bond's health, his drinking, smoking etc.

General Gogol

As head of the KGB, General Gogol should be Bond's archenemy. In his first appearance in the film *The Spy Who Loved Me*, it is clear that he has sent agents to kill Bond. But soon M and Gogol form a pact to find out what is happening to their submarines. He makes a brief appearance in *Moonraker* warning that if the Americans fail to destroy Hugo Drax's space station, the Soviet Union will take action.

In *For Your Eyes Only*, he tries to buy the ATAC unit from Kristatos. When Bond throws it over a cliff, Gogol stops his guard shooting Bond. Bond then remarks that the destruction of the ATAC is part of the policy of détente; Gogol laughs and leaves without saying another word. Then in *Octopussy*, Gogol opposes General Orlov's plans to invade Western Europe. Gogol is responsible for Orlov's death, while the plan is thwarted by Bond, putting them on the same side once again.

Gogol tries to stop renegade KGB agent Max Zorin destroying Silicon Valley. And when Bond succeeds, Gogol awards him the Order of Lenin. By *The Living Daylights*, Gogol has been transferred to the Foreign Ministry and arranges the visa that allows Kara Milovy to play in the West. He is played throughout by Walter Gotell, who made his first appearance in Bond movies in *From Russia with Love*, where he was a villain. He played Morzeny, head of training on SPECTRE Island.

Valentin Zukovsky

More recently, Bond has found another reluctant Russian ally, Valentin Dmitrovich Zukovsky, played by Robbie Coltrane. A former KGB officer, Zukovsky has become a Mafia boss. In a previous encounter, Bond had shot him in the leg, leaving him with a permanent limp, and stolen his car and his girl. However, in *GoldenEye* and *The World is Not Enough*, he is willing to help Bond because there is money involved. He has made his last appearance in *The World is Not Enough*, as Elektra King killed him.

7. Gimmicks, Guns and Gadgets

Bond's most enduring ally is Q. In the first novel *Casino Royale*, M tells Bond to 'have a talk to Q about rooms and trains, and any equipment you want'. Then in *Live and Let Die*, M tells Bond to contact 'Q' to arrange to have a skin graft on the back of his hand. But it is 'Q Branch' that supplies his diving gear. In *Diamonds are Forever*, Q Branch deals with US documentation as well as supplying an attaché case that conceals a gun, silencer and thirty rounds of .25 ammunition.

Q Branch again supplies the equipment in *From Russia with Love*. This time the attaché case conceals two flat throwing knives as well as fifty rounds of .25 ammunition. Inside the lid are fifty gold sovereigns. There are cyanide pills in the handle, which Bond flushes down the lavatory, and a silencer for his Beretta is hidden inside a tube of Palmolive shaving cream in an 'otherwise guileless sponge-bag'. However, this time, Q is up against a tricky foe. The KGB has supplied assassin Red Grant with a copy of *War and Peace* that fires bullets from the spine.

In *Goldfinger*, Bond got Q Branch to send a crate of limpet mines to Station H in Hong Kong. In *On Her Majesty's Secret Service*, Q Branch supplies a new Rolex because the shops are shut. Q Branch has also given Mary Goodnight a string of pearls, one of which has a suicide pill in it, but she can't remember which.

Fleming admitted: 'It is the gimmicks in my books, rather

than the more or less straightforward plots, that stay in people's minds.'

In fact, the gimmicks in the books are few and far between. But Fleming always insisted that they were based in reality – as were Q and Q Branch. In the book *The Man Who Was 'Q'*, author David Porter identified the real Q as wartime SOE quartermaster Charles Fraser-Smith. Fleming knew him from his liaison work. Fraser-Smith produced buttons with compasses in them, cigarette lighters that concealed cameras, cigarette holders that doubled as telescopes, flying boots with hidden knives, miniature radios in sandwich boxes and numerous other 'Q gadgets', as he called them – taking their name from World War I Q ships, which were warships disguised as unarmed freighters and trawlers. Fraser-Smith's devices were used to help prisoners of war escape and by SOE agents working behind the lines. Even produced were garlic-flavoured chocolate so agents would have an authentic aroma the moment they set foot in France, and containers for hidden documents with a left-handed thread, as Fraser-Smith believed that the 'unswerving logic of the German mind' would mean that no German would ever think of trying to unscrew something the wrong way. Fraser-Smith was particularly amused by Fleming's use of his hollowed-out golf balls in *Diamonds are Forever*. He used hollow golf balls to conceal compasses or messages and they were sent out to prisoners of war. They fooled the Germans because they could actually be used to play golf. Golf balls filled with diamonds would be too heavy, he pointed out, and would fool no one.

In the movies, there is some confusion about the origins of Q. Occasionally the technical wizard played in seventeen of the Bond films by Desmond Llewelyn is referred to as Major Boothroyd or 'the armourer'. In the novel *Dr No*, the armourer Major Boothroyd replaces Bond's Beretta with a Walther PPK, his name being borrowed from Fleming's arms expert Geoffrey Boothroyd. The Beretta's silencer got stuck in his clothing and Major Boothroyd, introduced by M as 'the greatest small-arms' expert in the world', considers it a 'ladies' gun'. The armourer also recommends, for more stopping power, the .38 Smith & Wesson Centennial Airweight. At the end of *Dr No*, Bond cables that the Smith & Wesson is no match for a flame-thrower – though, it seems, he has used a Remington carbine to good effect. However, Bond had not been using a Beretta exclusively up until then. In Chapter One of *Casino Royale*, he keeps a .38 Colt Police Positive with a sawn barrel under his pillow, though he carries a flat .25 Beretta with a skeleton grip in his chamois leather shoulder-holster. He also carries a .45 Colt Army Special in a concealed holster under the dashboard of his 4.5-litre Bentley with Amherst-Villiers supercharger. Bond is equally adept with the .38 Colt Detective Special he took from Tee-Hee in *Live and Let Die*. *Moonraker* opens with Bond practising with a Colt Detective Special and during his car chase with Drax he finds that .45 Colt Army Special under the dashboard again. In *Diamonds are Forever*, M has given him a new Beretta. He has put tape around the skeleton grip, filed the firing pin to a point and sawn the blunt foresight.

Although Bond has been issued with new firearms, the Aston Martin DB3 he picks up from the car pool in *Goldfinger* still carries a long-barrelled Colt .45 in a concealed compartment under the driver's seat. Bond could have had the Jaguar 3.4, but he preferred the DB3 because of its up-to-date triptyque and its inconspicuous colour – battleship grey. It also had extras: switches to alter the type and colour of the lights, reinforced steel bumpers, a radio pick-up tuned to receive signals from a 'homer' and 'plenty of concealed space that would fox most Customs men'. Bond uses a long-barrelled Colt .45 again in 'A View to a Kill'.

In *Thunderball*, Bond is back in a Bentley again – this time a 1954 Mark II Continental. Some rich idiot had crashed it into a telegraph pole on the Great West Road. Bond bought the wreck for £1,500 and Rolls-Royce straightened the bend in the chassis and fitted a new Mark IV engine with 9.5 compression. For another £1,300, he had the old cramped sports saloon body removed and turned it into a two-seater convertible, painted battleship grey, and with upholstery of black morocco. 'She went like a bird and a bomb and Bond loved her more than all the women at present in his life rolled, if that were feasible, together.'

Not far into the book the car gets badly damaged in an explosion after an assassination attempt on Bond. Nevertheless, in *On Her Majesty's Secret Service*, the old Continental Bentley – with the 'R' type chassis, the big six engine and a 13:40 back-axle ratio that he had now been driving for three years – is back on the road again. The Bentley Convertible remains with him through *You Only Live Twice* and 'The Living Daylights'.

In *The Spy Who Loved Me*, Bond is said to carry a Smith & Wesson Police Positive – a gun that does not exist. However, from Vivienne Michel's description, it is thought to be an S&W Centennial Airweight, a replacement for the one Bond lost in *Dr No*. And as a sniper in *The Living Daylights*, Bond uses a .308-calibre International Experimental Target rifle built by Winchester with a curled aluminium handle at the back of the butt that extended under the armpit and held the stock firmly in to the shoulder. An adjustable pinion below the rifle's centre of gravity allowed the stock to be nailed into its grooved wooden rest. The armourer had also had the usual single-shot bolt action replaced by a five-shot magazine, in case Bond missed first time.

Boothroyd says that the Walther PPK, which becomes Bond's trademark, should be carried in a Berns Martin triple-draw holster. A sprung holster, it would work well carried under the shoulder, but could cause trouble if worn inside the waistband of this trousers as Boothroyd recommends. Bond solves the problem by wearing it in a stitched pigskin holster inside his waistband in *On Her Majesty's Secret Service*.

In the film of *Dr No*, Major Boothroyd is played by Peter Burton. He becomes an increasingly important character as he imparts much of the technical information Fleming litters the books with. Bond drives a Sunbeam Alpine in Jamaica, but it has no special modifications. The only serious gadget in the movie has not been supplied by Q. It is Dr No's dragon – a swamp-buggy fitted with a flame-thrower and metal cladding to give it a menacing appearance.

Llewelyn takes over the role of Q in *From Russia with Love*, supplying Bond with his attaché case full of tricks. As well as the ammunition, the throwing knife and the fifty gold sovereigns taken from the book, the case also contains an AR-7 .22 sniper rifle and a magnetized tin of talcum powder containing a cartridge of tear gas. The case's catches have to be turned horizontally to prevent the tear-gas cartridge exploding. Kerim Bey – has a folding sniper's rifle provided by Q, which he uses to kill Krilencu. Bond has a box camera that conceals a reel-to-reel tape recorder which he uses when he interrogates Tania. But the enemy has the best gadgets. The assassin Red Grant has a watch with a retractable piano wire that he uses to garrotte his victims, while Rosa Klebb has spikes in the toes of her shoes that are treated with poison.

In the film, Bond is seen driving a Bentley Mark IV convertible. Its only high-tech gadgetry is a phone – which itself was remarkable in 1963. Bond also has a pager, new then, and an electronic bug detector to ascertain whether his phone has been tapped. The plot revolves around the Lektor – Spektor in the novel – code machine. Based on the German World War II Enigma cipher machine, it is rigged to explode when British technical experts examine it.

By *Goldfinger*, Llewelyn is solidly established as Q, a hard-working technician who is annoyed by Bond's flippant attitude and the lack of respect he shows for Q's gadgets. He is shown in his workshop where assistants are working on gas-spewing parking meters, a Thermos flask that contains a bomb, and a bulletproof coat designed to withstand machine-gun fire. Here, Q introduces Bond to his new fully modified Aston Martin DB5. It has machine guns mounted under the front indicator lights, a bulletproof shield that emerges to protect the back window and revolving licence plates that are valid in Britain,

France and Switzerland. Concealed in the rear light clusters are high-powered oil jets. Other devices produce a rear smoke-screen and dispense nails to foil pursuing vehicles. There is a revolving tyre-slasher that emerges from the hubs, a weapons control panel in the centre armrest and a radar screen that tracks a homing device – another of Q's devices.

Q warns Bond not to touch a little red button in the top of the gearstick.

'Why not?' asks Bond.

'If you do, you'll release a section of the roof and engage, then fire the ejector seat,' says Q.

'You're joking,' says Bond.

'I never joke about my work' is Q's put-down.

On a lighter note, Bond appears in the opening sequence with a snorkel disguised as a seagull. Again the enemy is not without gadgets. Goldfinger has a state-of-the-art industrial laser which he aims to cut Bond in two with, starting at the most delicate parts. Then there's Oddjob's lethal bowler.

In *Thunderball*, Q is flown to the Bahamas to demonstrate the latest underwater equipment to Bond. This includes a mini breathing unit and an underwater camera, at a time when they were still rare. Though Llewelyn was indeed flown to Nassau, the scene was actually filmed in Pinewood Studios with Q wearing a suitably colourful shirt. Bond is also provided with an underwater propulsion unit that straps to his air tanks, Geiger counters concealed in a watch and a camera, and a tape recorder concealed in a book. When Bond is stuck in a cave, the 'radioactive' capsule he has swallowed guides Leiter and a helicopter to the rescue. Bond then fires a mini-flare through a hole in the roof.

The Aston Martin DB5 makes another appearance. At the beginning of the film, Bond makes his escape from Bouvar's château using a Bell Textron Rocket Belt developed for the US military. At the end, Bond and Domino are rescued by a Skyhook, where a modified plane catches a wire attached to a weather balloon, then hauls the passengers on board.

SPECTRE's gadgets include a rocket-firing BSA Lightning motorbike, a fully armed hydrofoil with an underwater compartment, 'gamma gas' to knock out the crew of the V-bomber and an underwater sled for carrying the atomic bombs. Blofeld also has the chairs of his staff wired, so he can electrocute any who fail.

Q flies to Japan to deliver the tiny gyrocopter Little Nellie to Bond in *You Only Live Twice*. This was not just a cinematic prop, but a genuine prototype built and flown by Wing Commander Kenneth Wallis. Just ten feet long, she had a top speed of 180 miles an hour and weighing just 250 pounds she could lift twice that. In the film, she is armed with two front-mounted machine guns, two rocket launchers firing heat-seeking air-to-air missiles, two rear flame-throwers with a range of eighty yards, two smoke ejectors, aerial mines dropped by parachute and a flight helmet carrying a camera.

During the filming of the aerial battle, aerial cameraman John Jordan was leaning out of a helicopter to get a better shot when another helicopter was caught in a gust of wind and was blown closer. The rotor blade severed his leg, which had to be amputated. Nevertheless, he continued working. He developed a special harness hanging eighteen feet below the helicopter for filming aerial shots of the action sequences in *On Her Majesty's Secret Service*. But the following year, he was filming *Catch-22* over the Gulf of Mexico when another plane passed close by. He was sucked out of the open doorway and fell two thousand feet to his death.

Tiger Tanaka also had a helicopter in *You Only Live Twice*. It was fitted with a gigantic electromagnet which picked up the villains' car and dumped it in the sea. Bond watches the action on a TV screen in Aki's specially modified Toyota 2000 GT, but who is doing the filming is never explained.

You Only Live Twice is the only Bond movie in which he does not drive. He is, however, provided with an electronic safe-cracking device and special breathing apparatus when, at the beginning of the film, he is buried at sea in Hong Kong harbour.

And along with an array of ninja weapons, Tanaka shows Bond guns that fire jet-propelled ammunition that explodes on impact and gives him a rocket-firing cigarette which he uses to kill the guard and let the ninjas in.

However, SPECTRE has a rocket named Bird 1 that captures US and Soviet spacecraft. Helga Brandt has a stun grenade concealed in her lipstick when she escapes the Cessna, leaving Bond to his fate. And Blofeld has a retractable bridge in his office that dumps those who have failed him into a pool of piranha.

Q appears briefly at the beginning of *On Her Majesty's Secret Service*, showing Bond radioactive fluff that can be used as a tracking device. At the end, he turns up at Bond's wedding to offer: 'If you need anything . . .'

Bond replies with a smile: 'Thanks Q, but I've got all the equipment – and I know how to use it.'

During the scene where Bond breaks into the office of Blofeld's lawyer in Bern, he has delivered another electronic safe-cracking machine which doubles as a photocopier. Bond also had a Minolta Minox B spy camera – standard issue for spies at that time – which he uses to photograph a map in Blofeld's lair. The DB5 returns, this time with a sniper rifle in the glove compartment. Tracy drives a Ford Cougar, though in the books it's a Lancia Flaminia Zagato Spyder.

Q appears in Las Vegas in *Diamonds are Forever*, but again shows a mastery of the gadgetry by winning jackpots on a line of one-armed bandits. Earlier Q has provided Bond with false fingerprints so that he can pass as smuggler Peter Franks. He also matches the voice simulator Blofeld uses to imitate Willard Whyte. Bond uses a standard mountaineer's piton gun to break into Whyte's penthouse apartment and carries a razor-sharp finger trap in his pocket which foils one of Blofeld's bodyguards when he tries to disarm him.

Blofeld, on his side, has the whole building rigged with CCTV, a moon buggy which Bond borrows to make his escape, Honda three-wheeled dirt bikes for the chase, a diamond-encrusted satellite and a Bathosub in which he tries to escape from his oil-rig headquarters. The assassins Wint and Kidd provide a bomb hidden inside a 'bombe surprise'.

As the film is set largely in America, Bond gets to drive Tiffany's Mustang Mach 1 in a car chase around Las Vegas.

By then, Q had become such an important part of the Bond formula that Llewelyn made a publicity tour of the US, showing off the gadgets. However, he was dropped from *Live and Let Die*.

But that does not mean Bond was short of gadgets. He has a Rolex watch that can, magnetically, deflect a bullet at long range. It is also used to unzip the dress of Italian agent Miss Caruso. And it has a built-in buzz saw that Bond uses to free himself when he is tied up in Kananga's lair. He uses a hang-glider to infiltrate Kananga's island headquarters at night and a radio transmitter concealed in the cigarette lighter of CIA agent Strutter's car to contact Felix Leiter, leading Bond to quip: 'A genuine Felix lighter.'

He communicates with Quarrel Jr in Morse code via a radio transmitter concealed in a hairbrush. It also contains a bug detector which Bond uses to sweep his room.

The enemy has fewer gadgets. Whisper fires a poison dart from his right wing mirror, killing the agent driving Bond into Manhattan. Tee Hee has a prosthetic steel arm whose pincers bend the barrel of Bond's pistol at right angles. On San Monique, Kananga protects his poppy fields with scarecrows that have CCTV cameras in their eyes and guns in their mouths.

As well as trying to drive from the back of a car speeding down the Franklin D. Roosevelt River Drive, Bond gets to drive an old London double-decker bus, making it a single-decker when he goes under a low bridge during a car chase. But the most famous chase involves four Glastron speedboats powered by Evinrude jet propulsion motors.

In *The Man with the Golden Gun*, the slightly flustered Q provides Bond with a prosthetic third nipple so he can imper-sonate Scaramanga. The only other gadgets do not come from

Q Branch. There is the solar agitator which promises to provide limitless energy from the sun, Scaramanga's golden gun, his high-tech junk and his AMC Matador which, with wings attached, becomes a light aircraft. Bond himself drives an AMC Hornet hatchback with Sheriff Pepper in the car chase through Bangkok.

After the film, Llewelyn was asked by the president of the Ian Fleming Foundation to donate one of Q's suits to a private Bond Museum in the US. However, he had none to offer. The crumpled tweeds Llewelyn wore were his own.

Q's workshop has shifted to the inside of an Egyptian pyramid in *The Spy Who Loved Me*, where a lethal tea tray is used to decapitate a dummy. Bond has abandoned his Rolex for a Seiko with a built-in ticker-tape messaging device, which summons him from a romantic tryst in an Alpine cabin. He is armed with a ski pole that doubles as a rifle. He also has a cigarette case and lighter that, together, operate as a microfilm viewer. However, he loses the microfilm because his KGB opposite number has a cigarette that puffs out a sleeping draught.

Later Q turns up in Sardinia with the latest gadget-laden Lotus Esprit, though before he can explain how it works Bond drives off. During a car chase, it sprays concrete on the windscreen of the pursuing car. Then as it runs off the end of a pier, it transforms into a two-seater submarine armed with a sea-to-air missile that knocks out the helicopter hovering above. It has torpedoes, a mine dispenser and a device for producing an underwater smokescreen. And Bond makes his final assault on Atlantis on a wet bike, a seated version of a jet ski not commercially available when the film was made.

The enemy is impressively equipped too – and not the least of the arsenal are Jaws's metal teeth. Bond is pursued by a motorbike with a heat-seeking sidecar packed with explosives, a helicopter armed with machine guns and a two-man mini-submarine armed with torpedoes. Stromberg's supertanker *Liparus* can open its bows to swallow submarines. The hovercar used to carry men and machinery around inside the *Liparus* is also used as an escape vehicle, jettisoning its outer shell as it exits through a pothole to reveal a speedboat inside.

But Stromberg's greatest achievement is Atlantis, a marine facility off the coast of Sardinia that can sink beneath the waves or rise above them. It is full of gadgets, including a bay for helicopters, an elevator with a retractable floor that dumps unwanted guests into a shark tank, a dining table with a gun fitted underneath it and an escape capsule conveniently stocked with champagne and caviar.

Q Branch moves to a monastery in Brazil in *Moonraker*, where Q's assistants demonstrate explosive bolas and a machine gun concealed inside the mannequin of a Mexican taking a siesta. Q himself helps identify the source of the rare orchid Drax plans to use to make a deadly gas that will kill all human life, but leave other life forms unaffected. Bond is equipped with another Seiko, this time containing an explosive charge and a remote detonator, used to escape from under the Moonraker. A dart-gun concealed in the wristband can fire both armour-piercing and cyanide-tipped darts which Bond uses to escape from a centrifuge and kill Drax. He has a mini-camera the size of a cigarette lighter – engraved, curiously, with his supposedly secret code number, the middle 0 concealing the lens.

His cigarette case has an X-ray facility, allowing Bond to see the internal workings of the lock of Drax's safe so he can open it. Bond also has a motorized gondola for a boat chase around Venice which transforms itself into a hovercraft to cross St Mark's Square. In Brazil he has a Glastron hydrofoil armed with rear-firing, heat-seeking torpedoes and floating mines, as well as a detachable hang-glider that Bond escapes on as the boat plunges over a waterfall.

Bond's CIA counterpart, Dr Holly Goodhead, has a handbag that contains a dart-firing diary, a flame-throwing atomizer, a radio transmitter-receiver and aerial, and a pen containing a hypodermic syringe of poison which Bond uses to kill Drax's pet python. The US troops sent to thwart Drax are armed with the laser guns previously seen being tested by Q Branch.

Drax is well kitted out with space shuttles – one fully armed – that can launch without a first-stage rocket, as well as covert launch facilities, a space station and a secret lab to produce poison. He also has Jaws's teeth to depend on, until Jaws eventually turns against him.

While Q's gadgets are impressive, his most memorable line comes at the end of the film. When Bond and Dr Holly Goodhead are pictured in an amorous embrace in space, Q says: 'I think he's attempting re-entry . . .'

In *For Your Eyes Only*, a visit to Q's workshop reveals his technicians working on a spiked umbrella that snaps closed when exposed to water and a spring-loaded plaster cast. Again Bond has a Seiko watch, this time equipped with a two-way voice communicator. The plot revolves around the ATAC – Automated Targeting Attack Communicator – which was stolen from the British spy ship *St Georges*, disguised as a trawler and sunk by a mine.

Q's 3D Visual Identigraph is used to identify the villain Emile Locque. However, Llewelyn had difficulty saying his lines while operating a computer for the first time. So Roger Moore suggested that Bond take over as the computer expert, operating the machine while taking over Q's lines as well. Later Q turns up disguised as a priest in a church in Greece complete with phoney beard. Bond appears in the confessional box and says, 'Forgive me, father, I have sinned . . .'

To which Q answers: 'That's putting it mildly, 007.'

Bond gets through two Lotus Esprits during the course of the film. The first self-destructs when Hector Gonzales's men try to break into it, leaving Bond to embark on a car chase in a 2CV. When Q provides a second Esprit, Bond quips: 'I see you've managed to get the Lotus back together again.'

Bond and Melina use the *Neptune* mini-submarine to hunt for the wreck of the *St Georges*. They are attacked by a one-man sub armed with robotic drills and pincers. Melina, then Bond, is pursued by enemy henchmen on motorbikes equipped with spiked tyres for use in the snow and machine guns mounted on their handlebars. Bond also takes a hair-raising ride on a heli-copter after the pilot is electrocuted and control is taken over by Blofeld using a remote control pad attached to his wheelchair.

Q Branch sets up in Udaipur, India, for *Octopussy*, concealed behind a movie poster that is automatically replaced once Bond has driven through it. Here the relationship between Bond and Q is further developed. When a high-tech Indian rope trick goes limp, Bond remarks: 'Having problems keeping it up, Q?'

Later on board a hot-air balloon, Bond asks: 'Can you handle this contraption, Q?'

'It works by hot air,' replies Q.

'Oh, in that case you can,' says Bond.

Q even gets lucky with a number of Bond girls, after the balloon lands on Octopussy's women-only island. He shrugs off their kisses, saying, 'Later, perhaps.' Indeed, later, Llewelyn got to undertake a publicity tour with two of them. He had to carry a letter from the producers explaining that the replica Walther PPK, stage daggers, replica piton gun, explosive tin of talc and finger trap he was carrying were props from movies.

In the pre-title sequence of *Octopussy*, Bond attempts to blow up an aircraft hangar with a suitcase bomb. He escapes on an Acrostar mini-jet, concealed in a horsebox. Bond has a watch with a radio direction finder in it. Then Q provides a Seiko watch with TV screen, a Mont Blanc pen containing acid and an earpiece that works with the bug he has placed inside the Fabergé egg.

Bond also has a mini-submarine disguised as a crocodile. On land, he conducts a car chase from the back of a tuk-tuk in India and in a stolen car in Germany. Apart from a stolen nuclear bomb, the best the opposition can come up with is a spinning saw that operates like a yo-yo.

In *Never Say Never Again*, Kevin McClory's remake of *Thunderball*, Q was played by Alec McCowen and is addressed by Bond as Algernon. But here Q Branch is depicted as chroni-cally under-funded compared with the mainstream Eon movies.

Greeting the returning Sean Connery, Q says, 'Good to see

you Mr Bond. Things have been awfully dull around here. I hope we're going to see some gratuitous sex and violence!' To which Bond replies: 'I certainly hope so.'

Q provides Bond with a rocket-firing pen he uses to kill Fatima Blush and a watch equipped with a laser that he uses to cut his bonds in Largo's castle.

Bond is seen driving a Bentley once again, as he does in the 1966 spoof *Casino Royale*. Later he takes to a motorbike for a high-speed chase, then to a bicycle pretending to be Leiter's trainer.

The villains have the best equipment again, including a false eye used to fool the warhead loading system with a plug-in retinal scanner. Fatima has a device which she sticks on Bond's air tanks to attract sharks. The *Flying Saucer* is also suitably equipped with a wet-sub for carrying the bombs.

Q appears wearing a top hat and morning suit with Bond, M and Moneypenny at Ascot in the line of duty in *A View to a Kill*. Bond has a ring with a miniature camera in it. He uses his electric shaver to detect bugs. A credit card opens locks electronically. Polarizing sunglasses allow him to look through darkened windows and he has mini-photocopier that scans Zorin's cheque, picking up the indentations left when he wrote the previous cheque to Stacey.

Zorin has a supercomputer which establishes Bond's identity. His secret laboratory produces implants that, when activated by a device in the jockey's whip, administer performance-enhancing drugs directly into the muscles of the horse. Desk lamps in his château monitor the conversations of his guests. His sidekick May Day uses lethal butterflies to dispose of Achille Aubergine in the restaurant on the Eiffel Tower. The plot revolves around a microchip that withstands the electromagnetic pulse from a nuclear explosion. And Zorin travels by an airship which has a retractable stairway that turns into slide to get rid of unwanted passengers.

Bond begins the film by returning to a luxurious submarine disguised as an iceberg. Then, while pursuing May Day, he is reduced to conducting a car crash in a commandeered Renault taxi, which keeps going even after it is sheared in half. After that he gets to ride in Sir Godfrey Tibbett's Rolls-Royce with Sir Godfrey masquerading as his chauffeur. The film ends with Q operating a remote-controlled Snooper – a dog-shaped surveillance machine – that finds Bond in the shower with heroine Stacey Sutton.

Q branch came up with a host of new gadgets for *The Living Daylights*, though at the time Llewelyn himself found that he could not operate the automatic ticket barrier at the Lancaster Hotel in London without the help of the management. He demonstrates a portable boombox with a built-in bazooka, saying: 'It's something we're making for the Americans . . . it's called a ghetto blaster.' There's also a revolving sofa that swallows anyone who sits on it. Q provides Bond with a modified keychain. Activated by the first notes of 'Rule Britannia', it emits gas that will stun anyone within five feet. Q says that it will disorientate any normal person for up to thirty seconds. To which Bond replies, 'You don't find too many normal people in this business, Q . . .' It also contains an explosive charge activated by a wolf whistle and a lock-pick that Q says will open ninety per cent of the world's locks. Then there are miniature binoculars that fit in spectacle frames and the Walther sniper rifle with an infrared scope.

Koskov is smuggled to the West using a special vehicle that fits inside a gas pipeline. Meanwhile Bond has upgraded to an Aston Martin Vantage/Volante. The Vantage is a convertible which Q's assistants are seen 'winterizing' into a hardtop Volante. In reality, they are two different cars. In the car chase, it has bulletproof windows, retractable ski outriggers for driving on snow, retractable tyre spikes for driving on ice, guided missiles behind the fog lamps with the target display projected on the windscreen, police-band radio and lasers in the hubcaps that cut a police car from its axles. Again it has a self-destruct.

In the enemy's arsenal are explosive milk bottles used to free Koskov from the MI6 safe house, a watch with an alarm that

Pushkin uses to summon the guard and a high-tech assault rifle that Whitaker uses along with a bulletproof face mask that deflects Bond's shots.

In *Licence to Kill*, Q turns up in the hotel suite in Isthmus City which Bond and CIA pilot Pam Bouvier are sharing – platonically – with a suitcase containing 'everything for the man on holiday', reminding a disgruntled Bond: 'If it hadn't been for Q Branch you would have been dead long ago.' After demonstrating the contents, Q heads off to bed in one bedroom, while Pam takes the other, leaving Bond to trot off disconsolately after Llewelyn, saying, 'I hope you don't snore, Q.'

Bond is provided with a toothpaste tube full of plastic explosives which can be detonated by a cigarette packet; he also has a cummerbund containing a rappelling rope that allows him to abseil down the front of Sanchez's headquarters, a Polaroid camera that projects a high-powered laser, a signature gun disguised as a Hasselblad camera that can be reassembled as a sniper rifle with an optical palm reader allowing only the designated user to fire it, and an exploding alarm clock – 'Guaranteed never to wake up anyone who uses it,' says Q.

Q also poses alternately as a chauffeur, a crew member on board a harbour patrol vessel and a gardener with a walkie-talkie in the handle of his rake. Meanwhile Bond swims undetected past the video camera on the bottom of the *WaveKrest* disguised as a manta ray. The *WaveKrest* is naturally replete with a fleet of high-tech vessels, including the three-man mini-sub *Shark Hunter II*, while Bond gets to drive a high-powered speedboat and a Kenilworth tanker full of petrol mixed with cocaine.

After his antics as a field agent, Q returns to the workshop in *GoldenEye*. He appears in a wheelchair with his leg in a cast that fires a missile. Also on test in the workshop are an X-ray document scanner disguised as a tea tray, an office ejector seat and a phone box with a concealed airbag that traps the occupant when triggered.

When Bond makes a quip about an explosive pen, Q chides him: 'Oh, do grow up, 007.' The pen contains a C4 grenade that is armed with three clicks of the pen, then disarmed by another three clicks. Q also introduces him to the latest BMW Z3 Roadster, some months before it was available to the general public. According to Q, it was equipped with an ejector seat, parachute braking, a radar system and Stinger missile. None of these are used and the car only makes one brief appearance on a Caribbean island where he swaps it with Jack Wade for a light aircraft.

Q also reminds Bond, yet again, to return all the equipment in pristine condition. Then as Bond examines what he takes to be another new gadget, Q barks: 'Don't touch that . . . that's my lunch.'

The pre-title sequence begins with Bond bungee-jumping from the top of a dam. Before the bungee cord recoils he uses a piton gun to attach himself to the top of a blockhouse. The piton gun conceals a laser which he uses to cut through a steel plate to gain entry. With an electronic code-cracker he then unlocks the door to the chemical storage area, where he rigs the storage tanks with magnetic mines.

Bond also has a rappelling belt. The buckle fires a piton into the ceiling, then seventy-five feet of fine steel cable uncoil. His Omega watch contains a laser that can cut through armour plating to allow him and Natalya to escape from Trevelyan's train that is about to blow up.

His DB5 has a complete communications centre in the dashboard and a seduction kit comprising a chilled bottle of Bollinger (not Bond's usual brand of champagne) and a rose. Bond also rides a Cagiva motorbike taken from a Soviet soldier during the pre-title sequence and a Russian T55 tank in a car chase through St Petersburg. Xenia Onatopp drives a Ferrari 355 and she and Ourumov make off with a state-of-the-art Tiger Eurocopter. Trevelyan has satellite weapons that can knock out any electronic network on earth using electromagnetic shock waves.

In *Tomorrow Never Dies*, Q turns up at Hamburg airport as an Avis representative in a red jacket to deliver Bond's latest car. Bond reminds him that he needs maximum insurance cover because 'accidents do happen'. Q then introduces Bond to a BMW 750iL which features twelve STS missiles mounted under the sunroof, a security system that gives anyone tampering with the car an electric shock and dispenses tear gas, a cable cutter that emerges from the BMW bonnet logo, bullet-proof windows and bodywork, tyres that re-inflate at the touch of a button, a metal spike dispenser under the rear bumper, magnetic flash grenades and a hidden safe that slides out from under the glove compartment. Most ingenious of all, it can be driven remotely from an Ericsson cellular phone which has a built-in TV front- and rear-view monitor. Unfortunately, Bond returns the BMW to Avis, not in pristine condition, but from the top of the building over the road. The DB5 is also in evidence in the film.

The Ericsson mobile phone also features a stun gun and a fingerprint scanner that allows Bond to open Carver's safe. And it emits a laser beam that can cut through steel, plus a detachable antenna that doubles as a lock-pick. Bond also has a cigarette lighter that doubles as a grenade.

Bond's ally Wai Lin has her own array of high-tech gadgets hidden in her Saigon headquarters – computerized maps that pinpoint any location on earth, a statue of a dragon equipped with a flame-thrower, a fan that throws out spikes when opened, a sliding walls that reveals an armoury of sophisticated weapons and an Omega watch that doubles as a detonator. Her earrings double as lock-picks. She has a device attached to her wrists that fires a piton and cable, allowing her to walk vertically down walls, and she gives Bond a sleek Walther P99, which takes sixteen rounds of 9 mm bullets, rather than six rounds of 7.65 mm, not including the round in the chamber. It is thanks to Wai Lin that Bond abandons his old Walther PPK, first made in 1931, in favour of the new Walther P99 of 1997 vintage.

Together they ride through the streets of Saigon on a BMW R1200 motorbike. Along the way there is a booby-trapped rickshaw. The story revolves around a top secret GPS encoder and, as well as his global satellite TV and media empire, Carver has a stealth ship, and a sea-drill that eventually kills him.

The time finally came for Q to retire, and *The World is Not Enough* introduces his successor, played by John Cleese. Bond says to Q: 'If you're Q, does that make him R?'

Cleese then demonstrates an inflatable ski jacket that blows up to form a protective sphere. This saves Bond and Elektra's lives when they get caught in an avalanche. Bond's latest Omega watch provides light inside. It conceals a tiny grappling hook and fifty feet of high-tensile wire. Q's technicians have also come up with a bagpipe that doubles as a flame-thrower.

Bond is again armed with a Walther P99, but this one is rigged with a 'flash-bang' charge, remotely detonated by a button on his spectacles after he has been disarmed. He has another pair of glasses, whose X-ray vision capability allows him to see who is carrying concealed weapons in Zukovsky's casino. It gives Bond the added advantage of seeing women in their underwear.

The boat Q says he has built for his retirement in commandeered by Bond for a high speed chase down the Thames. The jet-powered craft has a draught of only three inches, though it is seen travelling on dry land down a street in Docklands and through a restaurant using rocket propulsion. It is submersible and is armed with torpedoes, so it is difficult to imagine how Q plans to spend his retirement. No matter. It bursts into flames after Bond is catapulted on to the mooring line of a hot-air balloon.

Q Branch also provided a BMW Z8. Again the car has a remote-control facility, a sonic device to overhear conversations in nearby buildings, titanium plating and armour, the very latest in intercepts, surveillance and countermeasures, and six beverage holders. Surface-to-air missiles hidden behind the headlamps bring down a helicopter armed with giant revolving tree-trimming saws. But a second helicopter uses its revolving saws to cut the car in half.

'Q's not going to like this,' says Bond.

Bond and Elektra are also pursued by parahawks – propeller-driven snowmobiles suspended under paragliding canopies. This time Bond and Christmas Jones get shot through a pipe-line and Bond has a new lock-picking credit card device. Again the baddies have the best weapons. This time it is the reactor of a nuclear submarine that will blow up if loaded with weapons-grade plutonium.

Although Bond does not get on with the new Q at first, in *Die Another Day* he refers to him as 'Quartermaster' then finally as 'Q'. They also swap quips.

'You're cleverer than you look,' says Bond.

'Ah yes, the legendary 007 wit,' says the new Q. 'Or at least half of it.'

He demonstrates a sonic ring that allows the wearer to break 'unbreakable glass'. His Omega watch – Bond's twentieth, Q remarks – features a detonator and a laser cutter. Q also provides a mini breathing device like the one used in *Thunderball*. As the film marked the fortieth anniversary of the Bond series and the twentieth movie under the Eon franchise, there are numerous references to gadgets used in previous films.

The new Q proudly reveals Bond's new car – only there doesn't appear to be one. The Aston Martin Vanquish has the latest cloaking device that uses high-tech imaging to render the car virtually invisible. It has two auto-aiming machine guns mounted under the hood, front-firing rockets behind the main air intake grille, cannons under the chassis, a seat with a spring-loaded ejection system and central console to control all the gadgets. The Aston Martin is pitted against Zao's Jaguar XKR, which has rockets in the door panels, machine guns in the front grille, a rear-mounted Gatling gun and mortars mounted in the trunk. Jinx drives a Ford Thunderbird which has no special features. Perhaps the NSA doesn't have the budget.

The film begins with Bond surfing into North Korea on a surfboard that stows C4 explosives, detonators, communications equipment and a Walther P99 and silencer in a hidden compartment. Bond also gets to ride on Graves's jet-power skate car. Again the baddies have all the best gadgets. As well as an ice palace and a device to give respite to the sleepless, Graves has Icarus, a satellite that can beam down an intense ray of energy reflected from the sun. This harks back to *Diamonds are Forever*.

Q's most fantastic device in *Die Another Day* is a virtual-reality combat simulator. Using special glasses, weapons and computers, Bond undergoes a realistic scenario inside the MI6 building. Moneypenny later uses it to simulate a romantic encounter with Bond. Q interrupts, only to say, 'Hard, isn't it?'

In the brooding atmosphere of the Daniel Craig movies, there is no place for a quipping Q. But Bond still needs his gadgets. He has a microchip tracking device implanted in his arm and puts a similar device in Le Chiffre's inhaler. He has a modified Sony Ericsson K800 cellphone with built-in GPS and a digital camera that can take pictures extra-fast. He drives an Aston Martin DBS with a glove compartment filled with assorted tools and weaponry, including a communications centre and high-tech first aid kit with a portable defibrillator. The vehicle itself appears not to have any special features apart from a bulletproof windscreen. Bond also wears a standard issue Omega Seamaster wristwatch.

The enemy are also short of gadgets in the new *Casino Royale*. Carlos has an explosive key chain which he intends to use to blow up the fuel tanker and Skyfleet's prototype airliner. But Bond hooks it over Carlo's belt loop instead.

In *Quantum of Solace*, the Walther PPK, Aston Martin DBS and Omega Seamaster all make their return. This time Bond has a Sony Ericsson C902 mobile phone with a built-in identification imager, capable of compiling a composite facial image of a potential suspect even when the person being photographed is looking to the side. This phone can also receive information immediately regarding the suspect as it is tied into the MI6 data mainframe. At MI6 they have the latest Microsoft Surface touch-screen computer interface. They use a similar device to compile information concerning possible suspects and relay them back to Bond via his cellphone.

Q also supplies Bond with an eyepiece he uses to eavesdrop on Dominic Greene, while Greene uses a hydrogen fuel cell to power his desert lair. It seems that technology is rapidly catching up with both Q and the Bond villains. Nothing they come up with these days seems even remotely outlandish.

8. The Girls

Along with the guns and the gadgets, the other staple of Bond is the girls. In the books Bond sleeps with just fourteen women; in the movies he has clocked up over sixty conquests – not an unusually high total for a man approaching middle age. They are all, of course, beautiful. But not flawless. The girls in the books are not pin-ups. They have physical and emotional defects that make them real. Though sometimes vulnerable, they are strong, independent, assertive women who do not wait to be rescued by the macho hero. In several instances, it is the girl who rescues Bond rather than the other way around. They usually drive faster than he does and are sexually experienced. Bond makes little effort to seduce them. They go to bed with him on their own initiative, because they want to and they find him sexually attractive. Even if they try to keep him at arm's length, they are drawn to him by experiencing shared dangers. Bond girls are always part of the plot, not a mere adornment.

Vesper Lynd
The first Bond girl is Vesper Lynd in *Casino Royale*. It is thought that she is based on Krystyna Skarbek, a Pole who worked for SOE during the war under the name Christine Granville. In the book, Vesper works for Section S, which deals with the Soviet Union, and is sent to Royale-les-Eaux under the guise of a radio salesperson assisting René Mathis. Bond is annoyed, until he

sets eyes on her. Then he is 'excited by her beauty and intrigued by her composure'.

Vesper is the prototype Bond girl. She wears her black hair long and natural. She is suntanned and wears little make-up 'except on her mouth which was wide and sensual'; her eyes are deep blue and wide apart. Her clothes are plain, but elegant. She wears little jewellery and her breasts are 'fine'. Like Bond, she drinks and smokes.

She is named Vesper, she says, because she was born on a very stormy evening, which her parents wanted to remember. 'Some people like it, others don't,' she says. Bond promptly names his special Martini after it.

Having survived their run-in with Le Chiffre, Vesper visits Bond in hospital every day and, much to his surprise, he develops feelings for her. They take a holiday together and become lovers. However, before meeting Bond, she was in love with a Polish officer in the RAF. When he returned to Poland after the war, he was arrested by the Russians, who said they would keep him alive if she worked for them as a double agent. But then she became attracted to Bond and, when she decided to have an affair with him, she told them that she would not work for them any more, knowing her previous boyfriend would have to die. She hoped that she and Bond could escape together to South America and she would have his baby. However, SMERSH is on her tail. Knowing she can never escape them, she commits suicide.

Although at the end of *Casino Royale* Bond says 'The bitch is dead', he continues to hold a torch for her. In *Diamonds are Forever*, he skips the track 'La Vie en Rose' because it holds memories for him. In *Goldfinger*, when Bond is drugged and thinks that he and Tilly Masterton have died and gone to heaven, he wonders whether he would introduce her to Vesper there. Then *On Her Majesty's Secret Service* – the tenth novel – begins with Bond making his annual pilgrimage to visit Vesper's grave in Royale-les-Eaux.

However, she does not seem to be uppermost in Bond's mind

when he is ogling the black girls in Harlem in *Live and Let Die*. All he can think of during the frenzied fan dance of G-G Sumatra is her small, hard, bronze, beautiful, oiled body as it goes into a series of juddering spasms.

Solitaire

Then he meets twenty-five-year-old clairvoyant Solitaire. Solitaire is, after all, 'one of the most beautiful women Bond had ever seen'. Her hair is blue-black and shoulder-length; her eyes blue, disdainful with a touch of humour. Unusually for a Bond girl, it is implied that she is a virgin. Mr Big, who intends to marry her, says she will have nothing to do with men – that's why, in Haiti, they call her Solitaire. Bond doubts this and, sure enough, after letting herself be kissed on the train she quickly shows herself to him naked and appears disappointed that he can't make love to her.

Solitaire's real name is Simone Latrelle. Bond imagines that she comes from a plantation house – she has the face of the daughter of a French colonial slave-owner and the pale skin of white families who have lived too long in the tropics. Her parents died; the house was sold. She worked as a governess, a companion, a secretary – 'all of which meant respectable prostitution'. Then in the sleazy nightclubs of Port-au-Prince, she performed a mysterious act that involved magic, until Mr Big turned up one night.

Although she has diamond earrings and a thin diamond bracelet, she wears no rings. Her nails are short and unpainted. Her mouth is 'sensual' with a hint of cruelty, but at their first meeting Bond's eyes are drawn to her breasts and the valley between them. She then teases him with her nudity, but Bond is impeded by a broken finger and the need to maintain vigilance that night. Later she is stripped naked and the two of them are tied together, but as they face being dragged over a reef this is hardly erotic. In fact, they do not consummate their relationship in the book, though there is every prospect that they will do so on the holiday Bond is planning. And when Bond returns to the

Caribbean in *Dr No*, he thinks of Solitaire and wonders what has become of her; but he leaves it there.

Gala Brand

However, back in England for *Moonraker*, Bond forgets all about Solitaire. Instead, he gets to work with Gala Brand, a Special Branch officer posing as Drax's personal assistant. Her full name is Galatea, after the cruiser her father was serving on when she was born. This is either the HMS *Galatea* commissioned in 1914 and scrapped in 1921, or the HMS *Galatea* commissioned in 1935 and sunk in 1941. So either Gala is between thirty-four and forty-one when the book is published in 1955 – making her the oldest Bond girl – or between fourteen and twenty – making her the youngest. However, she had been in the Wrens before joining Special Branch, so she seems to have been the oldest.

On taking the assignment, Bond gets to see her personnel file. Though he is unimpressed with the photograph of her in her police uniform, he reads on: 'Hair: Auburn. Eyes: Blue. Height: 5 ft 7. Weight: 9 stone. Hips: 38. Waist: 26. Bust: 38. Distinguishing marks: Mole on upper curvature of right breast.' The latter clearly interests him. However, he makes little progress with her. She is a dedicated policewoman. Although she finds Bond attractive, she dismisses him as a playboy. Walking on the beach in Kent, Bond persuades her to strip down to her underwear to go swimming, but she undresses demurely behind a rock. In the water, Bond seizes the opportunity to kiss her. She curses him, but afterwards sunbathes in her bra and panties while Bond ogles the 'pointed hillocks of her breasts' and 'the mystery of her tightly closed thighs'. Then the explosion that covers them with leaves them naked, but in the circumstances this is hardly erotic.

During their escape from Moonraker's silo they are forced together again. At the end of the book, Bond plans to take her away on holiday to a farmhouse in France. She turns him down. Instead she is going to marry another policeman. This is a solitary example in the books of Bond not getting his wicked way.

Tiffany Case

In *Diamonds are Forever*, Tiffany Case proves a tantalizing prospect. When he goes to meet her in her hotel room, he finds her
half-naked in front of the dressing table mirror. Wearing only a
black bra and lace panties, 'the splay of her legs whipped at
Bond's senses'. Her skin is lightly tanned. Again she wears no
make-up except deep red lipstick on her 'sinful mouth'. She
does not paint her nails, which pleases Bond. At first, he does
not know her name. Seeing 'Miss T. Case' on a label on her
luggage, he speculates on what the T stands for. Two of the
possibilities he comes up with are Teresa and Tilly – the names
of two future Bond girls.

Later, Leiter fills in her background. Tiffany's mother had
been a madam in San Francisco. When she refused to pay
protection money, gangsters wrecked the place and gang-
raped sixteen-year-old Tiffany, turning her against men. She
worked as a hat-check girl, taxi-dancer, movie extra and a
waitress until she was twenty, when she decided to drink
herself to death. But she saved a child from drowning and got
her name in the paper. A rich woman took an interest, got
Tiffany to Alcoholics Anonymous and took her around the
world as her companion. Eventually Tiffany went back to San
Francisco to live with her mother, who had given up the business. But Tiffany found this dull, went on the lam again and
ended up working in a club in Reno where she got to know the
gangsters who were smuggling diamonds.

In New York, Bond persuades Tiffany to have dinner with
him. 'I'm not going to sleep with you,' she says and warns him
not to waste his money. But after caviar and champagne, she
softens. Outside the door of her hotel room, Bond notices that
her eyelashes are wet. She tells him to be careful because she
does not want to lose him, then kisses him fiercely. But when he
tries to return the kiss she tells him to get away from her, and
slams the door in his face.

After Bond has been beaten up by the gangsters at Spectreville,
Tiffany rescues him. On a romantic cruise back to England, she

is kidnapped and Bond gets to rescue her. They live together for a few months. By the beginning of *From Russia with Love*, she has left him and returned to the US with a Marine Corps major who had been on the military attaché's staff at the embassy. Bond did not have the energy or the desire to find a temporary replacement. Maybe this was why he was so eager to go to Istanbul to collect Tatiana Romanova, even when her invitation is so obviously as trap.

Tatiana Romanova

Tatiana's story is that she saw Bond's picture in the MGB's central files. M believes that such a thing could happen and convinces Bond. After all, the head of Station T has reported that she is 'very good-looking'.

A twenty-four-year-old corporal in the MGB – *Ministerstvo Gosudarstvennoi Bezopastnosti* or Ministry of State Security – Tatiana has been chosen to seduce Bond. She does not know that she is merely the bait to lure him to his death. One of her boyfriends compared her to the young Greta Garbo. Her brown silky hair falls to her shoulders and has a curl at the end. Her skin is pale with an ivory sheen at the cheekbones. Her eyes are blue and, again, set widely apart, with natural eyebrows and long lashes. Her mouth is also wide with the hint of a smile at the corners and the lips are full and finely etched. Her body is firm. She had trained as a ballet dancer until she grew too tall, but continues to keep fit by figure skating and walking to work. Her arms and her breasts are faultless, but the muscles of her buttocks have hardened and her backside 'jutted like a man's'.

In her interview with Rosa Klebb, Tatiana is forced, tearfully, to admit that she has had three lovers – one at seventeen, a second at twenty-two, then a third she had met skating the previous year. When she is shown a photograph of Bond, she finds him good-looking. She does not know whether she can fall in love with him, but has no choice but to accept the assignment. However, she flees from Klebb's attempted seduction. Klebb concludes that she is prudish and needs more training.

However, she does not seem at all prudish when she turns up in Bond's bed in Istanbul naked except for a black velvet ribbon around her neck and black silk stockings. Perhaps the training worked. But then she did not know about the camera crew behind the one-way mirror in the honeymoon suite. They travel on the Orient Express as husband and wife. After that, no more is heard of her.

Honeychile Rider

Bond can be forgiven for forgetting about Tatiana when Honeychile Rider emerges from the sea naked except for the belt around her waist. When he whistles along to her tune, she does not cover her body with the two classic gestures, leaving her 'beautiful firm breasts' jutting 'towards him without conceal-ment'. Then a hand goes to the knife on her belt, ready to defend herself. Like the other Bond girls, she has blue eyes, set wide apart, and a wide mouth. This time, her hair is ash blonde, but again it hangs to her shoulders. They spend some time in conversation before she becomes self-conscious about her nakedness. Even then she is in no hurry to get dressed, more concerned about her shells than her clothing.

Like Solitaire, Honeychile is the daughter of an old colonial family. She was orphaned at five when the plantation house, Beau Desert, burned down. She lived in the cellar with her black nanny until she died when Honeychile was fifteen. Then a drunken white overseer, who she hated, hit her, breaking her nose, and raped her. She killed him with a poisonous spider – 'He took a week to die.'

She supports herself by collecting and selling shells. Then, when she has saved up enough money, she intends to go to America and have her nose fixed by a plastic surgeon. After that she would become a call girl until she has made enough money to buy back her parents' plantation, and get married and have children.

Bond wants to take care of her. At twenty, Bond considers her just a child, though there is nothing childish about her body or her personality. She is highly intelligent and more than capable of taking care of herself. But when she invites Bond to share her sleeping bag, he declines, even when she says they do not have to make love.

After they are captured by Dr No's men, Bond and Honeychile are locked in a suite together. She undresses to have a bath and flings her arms around him. He kisses her and fondles her left breast – 'Its peak . . . hard with passion'. But he decides that this is no time to make love as they are in danger, so he threatens to spank her if she does not get into the bath.

Bond frequently threatens to spank girls. He wanted to spank Vesper in *Casino Royale*. In *From Russia with Love*, he tells Tania that if there were a bit more room in their compartment on the Orient Express, he would put her across his knee and spank her. In *Goldfinger*, Bond decides that it would be ungallant to spank Tilly Masterton 'on an empty stomach'. In *For Your Eyes Only*, he threatens to give Judy Havelock 'such a spanking you won't be able to sit down for a week'. And in *Thunderball*, he even threatens to give Miss Moneypenny such a spanking that she will have to do her typing on a block of Dunlopillo. But she doubts he would have the strength to spank her that hard after going to the health farm and living off nuts and lemon juice for two weeks.

Honeychile appears naked again when Dr No's men strip her and stake her out to be eaten by land crabs. Finally Bond and Honeychile do make love in her cellar home at Beau Desert. Returning to Jamaica six books later in *The Man with the Golden Gun*, he recalls his time with Honeychile at Beau Desert. The last he heard, she had married a doctor called Wilder in Philadelphia and has two children. She never wrote.

Jill and Tilly Masterton

Bond does not give Honeychile a second thought when he creeps into Jill Masterton's hotel room to find her in a black brassiere and black silk briefs. Her pale blonde hair hangs heavily to her shoulders. Her eyes are blue and her skin suntanned.

Her face is beautiful and she is unselfconscious about her splendid body. But unlike other Bond girls, she paints her nails.

Bond forces Goldfinger to book a compartment on the train to New York for Bond himself and Jill, taking the girl as a prize. She has been starved of sex and makes love to Bond five times on the journey. But then she returns to Goldfinger, who has Oddjob paint her naked body with gold paint, killing her.

Next a pretty girl overtakes him in a Triumph TR3. She has a gash of red lipstick, and black hair tied back under a spotted handkerchief. In Macon, Bond reverses his Aston Martin into her car and gives her a lift to Geneva. She is a beautiful girl, 'the kind who leaves her beauty alone', and throws out her fine breasts against her taut silk blouse in a way that is both provocative and challenging. However, Bond thinks there is something faintly mannish about her.

He meets her again when she tries to kill Goldfinger. He has to restrain her and she explains that she is Tilly Masterton, Jill's sister, out for revenge. Although they stay together for much of the book, there is little chance of her becoming a Bond girl as she instantly falls for Pussy Galore when she meets her. The feeling is mutual and Pussy calls Jill 'yummy'.

Pussy Galore

Pussy is obviously a lesbian, yet Bond has little trouble seducing her once Tilly has been killed by Oddjob.

'They told me you only liked women,' says Bond.

'I never met a man before,' says Pussy, explaining that she had been put off men after being raped by her uncle at the age of twelve.

Unfortunately she is going straight to Sing Sing and asks James to write to her. It is not clear whether he does as there is no further mention of her. But then she had violet – sometimes blue-violet – eyes and long nails painted silver, so she was not really his type.

Mary Ann Russell

'A View to a Kill' finds Bond in Paris looking for a girl, willing even to pay her fifty thousand francs for her company that evening while knowing that he would be disappointed. But then a tall girl with pale skin and blonde hair turns up. This is Mary Ann Russell. She is number 765 from Station F. Bond is wanted. She worries about him taking unnecessary risks, telling him off when he reports by phone each evening. He invites her to dinner, promising pink champagne and gypsy violins. In the end when Bond gets the worst of it in a fight with enemy assassins, she turns up to save him.

Judy Havelock and Liz Krest

In 'For Your Eyes Only', Bond is held up at arrow-point by a bow-wielding Judy Havelock. Again the heroine has pale blonde hair which falls to her shoulders. She has a beautiful face with a wild, animal look to it, a wild sensuous mouth, high cheekbones and silvery grey eyes. After they have killed the baddies, Bond says he is taking her to London to meet M. But first he must take her to a motel. He has already promised her a spanking. Although she says she is twenty-five, she seems a lot younger – more concerned about the deaths of her dog and her pony than those of her parents.

There are no Bond girls in 'Quantum of Solace' or 'Risico', but in 'The Hildebrand Rarity' Bond makes off with Mrs Krest, presumably to comfort the widow who has almost certainly just killed her husband.

Patricia Fearing

In *Thunderball*, Bond is saved from the traction machine by nurse Patricia Fearing. To aid healing, she brings him brandy and gives him a massage wearing mink gloves. He asks her to marry him because 'you're the only girl I've ever met who knows how to treat a man properly'. Later he enjoys her 'strong, smooth body' on the squab seats from her bubble car high up on the Downs.

Domino Vitali

In Nassau, Bond meets Domino Vitali. After going to school in Cheltenham and attending RADA, Domino returned to Italy after her parents were killed in a train crash. Unable to make a living as an actress, she became the mistress of millionaire yacht-owner Emilio Largo.

She has a Brigitte Bardot haircut, a small upturned nose and a snarling, half-pouting mouth. Her breasts are high with a deep cleavage. Bond can tell she is a wilful, sensual girl – 'a beautiful Arab mare who would only allow herself to be ridden by a horseman with steel thighs and velvet hands, and then only with curb and saw bit – and then only when he had broken her to bridle and saddle'. But he can see she belongs to another man, another rider who has to be unseated first.

While skin diving, she gets sea-egg spines in her foot. Bond sucks them out. Then they make love and go skinny-dipping before Bond tells her about the death of her brother. Thanks to Bond, Domino gets caught with a Geiger counter by Largo, who tortures her with a lighted cigar. She survives to rescue Bond when Largo is trying to kill him. When they are in hospital together, Bond makes it to her room, but collapses before he can take things any further.

Vivienne Michel

In *The Spy Who Loved Me*, Fleming gives the Bond girl's point of view. The protagonist Vivienne Michel is five foot six with blue eyes and brown wavy hair which she one day wants to give a 'lion's streak' to make her look older. Originally from Quebec, she was orphaned at eight when her parents died in a plane crash. Brought up by a widowed aunt, she was sent to a finishing school in England at the age of sixteen. She was losing her virginity to her boyfriend in a box in a cinema in Windsor when they got caught and humiliated. Then they completed the act in a field. Two weeks later, she received a letter saying that he was marrying someone else as his parents did not approve of 'foreigners', presumably because she is a French-Canadian.

Vivienne then got a job with a German news agency and started sleeping with her boss. She became pregnant, but he would not marry her because he had inherited strong views about 'mixed blood'. However, he arranged for her to have an abortion in Switzerland and gave her the money.

At the time of the action, she is twenty-three. She thought she had a good figure until the English girls at her finishing school told her that her behind stuck out too much, and that she should wear a tighter bra. In fact, she does without one during the tale – surely a rebellion against her strict convent education.

An outdoor girl, she has high cheekbones which make her look 'foreign'. Her nose is too small and her mouth too big, so she looks sexy when she doesn't want to. She considers herself sanguine, a romantic tinged with melancholy, but also wayward and independent to a degree that worried the sisters at the convent and her teachers at finishing school.

When Bond turns up, he has a 'quality of deadliness' that makes her think that he may be another gangster. But he is good-looking and when she uses her hands to hide her nakedness, he smiles and she thinks things might be all right.

When they think they have killed off the gangsters, Vivienne insists that she is not going to leave Bond that night, adding chastely, 'I'll sleep on the floor.' Bond says that, if she is going to sleep on the floor, he will sleep on the floor too – though 'it seems rather a waste of a fine double bed'.

Without a second thought, Vivienne strips off to have a shower. She soon finds a naked Bond in the shower with her, washing her body. Then they dry each other. Usually, Fleming brushes over the details of sex. But in *The Spy Who Loved Me*, Vivienne screams during orgasm. It is nothing like what she has experienced with her two previous boyfriends. She knows that Bond has taken her as his reward – though she had fought alongside him. Soon he will be gone. But that does not matter. 'All women love semi-rape,' she decides.

While Vivienne muses on her feelings of love, Bond sleeps. Then Sluggsy reappears. After Bond has finished him off, he and Vivienne make love again. In the morning, he leaves an address, care of the Ministry of Defence, where he can be contacted – by letter or cable, not by telephone. By the time she rides away on her motor scooter she has forgotten his number, but everything else about him is written on her heart. Although the gangsters dismissed her as a bimbo, she has proved she is anything but.

Tracy and the girls of Piz Gloria

On Her Majesty's Secret Service is positively heaving with Bond girls. Again, Bond cannot resist a girl that overtakes him in a sports car. This time is it is La Comtesse Teresa di Vicenzo. He even finds the boom of her white Lancia's twin exhaust sexy. The girl driving is pretty, with a shocking pink scarf tied around her hair. He has always found women who drive 'competitively' exciting. They race, but she gives him the slip before the turn-off to Royale-les-Eaux.

When he sees her again at the Hotel Splendide, he is told that she is 'a lady . . . who lives life to the full'. She turns up in the casino with golden hair down to her shoulders, gold arms, beautiful golden face with bright blue eyes and shocking pink lips. She is wearing a plain white dress. When she cannot pay, Bond seizes the opportunity to help her out. Afterwards when he approaches her in the bar, she introduces herself as Tracy – 'Teresa was a saint. I am not a saint' – and tells him her room number. He is to come later for the most expensive piece of love of his life: 'I hope it will be worth it.' Bond has no complaints.

When he arrives at her room, she tells him to take his clothes off. There is to be no conversation. He can do what he likes. He should be rough with her, treat her like the lowest whore. Afterwards she says it was heaven, and that he should come back in the morning and do it again. Then he hears her crying. They do it again in the morning, but when he makes plans to take her for lunch, she tells him he is a lousy lover and throws him out.

Later, Tracy tries to kill herself. It turns out that she is half

Corsican, half English, and that her mother died ten years before. As head of the Union Corse, her father Marc-Ange Draco was unable to give her a settled home. She threw herself into the world of the international jet set, then married an Italian count who took her money and ran off, leaving her with a baby daughter. The child died of spinal meningitis. In grief she has become suicidal.

Draco offers Bond £1 million to marry her. Bond declines, but agrees to see her again. In the mean time, he visits Blofeld's mountain-top lair, Piz Gloria, where he meets ten gorgeous English girls. They are 'air-hostess types' with 'beautiful, sunburned faces and a succession of splendid, sweatered young bosoms'. Bond falls for Ruby, a bosomy blonde with large blue eyes. That night, he breaks out of his room and into hers, where he takes his clothes off. She is waiting naked for him. Her hair smells of new-mown grass, her mouth of Pepsodent, and her body of baby powder. The sound of the evening breeze give a certain 'friendship' to their act of physical passion.

Ruby comes to his room for a kiss before Bond flees Piz Gloria. Pursued by Blofeld's men, Bond is rescued by Tracy in a short black skating-skirt and a shocking-pink fur-lined parka. At a tearful goodbye at Zürich airport, Bond realizes that he may never find another girl like Tracy. She is beautiful in bed and out, brave, adventurous, resourceful and exciting. Her life is not cluttered up with friends, relatives and belongings. She seems happy to let him get on with his life and she seems to love him. She says she will wait for him in Munich. He dreams about her on the plane to London.

He mentions her in his report and when eating Christmas pudding with M he thinks of Tracy. Bond phones her to tell her that he is making arrangements for them to get married at the British Consulate in Munich. He then calls Draco. His wedding present is to be the raid on Piz Gloria. After the raid, Bond makes his way to Munich, where they marry. Bond refuses Draco's £1 million. As they head off on their honeymoon, Tracy is killed by Blofeld, leaving Bond heartbroken.

Geishas

His heartbreak aside, in Tokyo at the beginning of *You Only Live Twice*, Bond propositions an ageing madam named 'Grey Pearl' who, he believes, will 'certainly possess talents in the art of love making which will overcome any temporary lassitude on my part'. However, he has already been promised a 'geisha pillow' in the person of the youthful 'Trembling Leaf' who we learn has 'pretty hands' and soft skin. She kisses invitingly and he has been told that she is a geisha of the lower caste. As she has not been educated or cultured like her high-caste sisters, she might agree to provide more 'robust services' in private for a high price.

In a bathhouse, Bond is introduced to eighteen-year-old Mariko Ichiban – the name means 'Number One Truth'. She wears little shorts and a tiny brassiere which she dispenses with in due course. Tanaka explains to Bond that she will undress him, wash him, massage him, feed him, shave him, cut his hair and do whatever he likes. As she removes his trousers, he lifts her chin and kisses her on her soft, bud-like mouth. Afterwards he is a new man.

Kissy Suzuki

Tanaka then arranges for Bond to meet twenty-three-year-old Kissy Suzuki, who was once dubbed 'the Japanese Garbo'. But she hated Hollywood because it was assumed that her body was for everyone. The only person who treated her honourably was David Niven, so she named her fishing cormorant after him.

Her fellow fishing girls are beautiful with 'proud, rather coarse-nippled breasts' and gleaming, muscled buttocks. Kissy is a little taller than the rest and first appears naked, though wrapped in a blanket. Her teeth are even and protrude through her lips no more than a European woman's. Her breasts and buttocks are firm and her stomach flat, making her figure as appealing as any Bond has seen in the cabarets of Tokyo.

When they go fishing, she does all the work. In the evening, she pulls off his bathing pants, lays him on a futon and walks along his back from his buttocks to his neck. Then she washes and dries him, tending his sunburnt skin with milk. After that she tells him to go to sleep.

Bond tells her about his mission, explaining that he will go back to England afterwards. She says, no, he will stay for a long time because she has prayed for it in the local shrine. But when she takes off her kimono to swim the strait to the castle, she tells him to 'stop looking at my Black Cat'.

After Bond has killed Blofeld, Kissy rescues him and she looks after him. However, the blow to the head has left him impotent. But she buys some herbs and a pillow book, and restores his virility. Consequently, she becomes pregnant – the only Bond girl to do so. But Bond has left before she can tell him.

Tiffy and Goodnight

Although Bond's amnesia is cured by the time he heads back to Jamaica in *The Man with the Golden Gun*, all memory of Kissy seems to have been wiped. When he visits the whorehouse at No. 3½ Love Lane, he meets Tiffy, an octoroon with *café-au-lait* skin, bold, brown eyes, tiny ankles and wrists, and a fringe of silken black hair, suggesting a hint of Chinese blood in her. She offers him the services of two of the girls; one of them is big, but Bond says that he prefers girls like her. We know Bond likes black girls like the ones he saw in Harlem in *Live and Let Die*. But Tiffy says she only does it for love. Bond is chatting her up, possibly convincing her she should extend a public service, when Scaramanga comes in. However, waiting in the wings is secretary-turned-Bond-girl, Mary Goodnight.

An ex-Wren, she has blue-black hair, blue eyes and a 37-22-35 figure. When she first arrived at the double-O section, there was a £5 sweep on who would bed her first. Bond had been equal favourite with 006, an ex-Royal Marine commando, but he was in love with Tracy at the time, which put him out of the field and he considered himself a rank outsider. However, after Tracy's death, Mary mothered him, getting him to comb his hair and straighten his tie before he went to see M, and in 'The Property of a Lady' he resists the impulse to 'ruffle up the inviting nape of Mary Goodnight's golden neck'.

In *The Man with the Golden Gun*, she has been posted to Jamaica where she assists Bond. He cannot resist kissing her and fantasizes about being with her, naked, under a mosquito net. She looks after him when he is in hospital and invites him to convalesce *à deux* in her villa. But we are not told whether Bond claims his sweepstake winnings.

The nearest Bond gets to a Bond girl in *Octopussy* is when, in 'The Living Daylights', he decides not to kill the blonde sniper with the cello case. He does better the movie, of course. In fact, he does well in all the Bond movies.

Ursula Andress, Eunice Grayson and Zena Marshall

In the first Bond film, Ursula Andress, as Honey Ryder, emerges memorably from the sea in her white bikini. After being captured, she and Bond are stripped naked to be decontaminated. Ursula, at least, wears a flesh-coloured bodysuit. In the film, she is the daughter of a marine biologist, who disappeared while exploring Crab Key, a fate she almost shares.

But Honey is not the first woman Bond beds in *Dr No*. This is Sylvia Trench, played by Eunice Gayson, who flirts with Bond while playing chemin de fer at the posh London casino, Le Cercle. When Bond enquires about her name, she answers: 'Trench, Sylvia Trench.' She then asks about his and he answers, famously, 'Bond, James Bond.'

When he returns home to his apartment, he finds her playing golf, wearing one of his shirts. As a result, Bond delays his departure to Jamaica. First, he has to go 'immediately'; then it is 'almost immediately'.

Next comes Miss Taro, played by Zena Marshall, secretary to Mr Pleydell-Smith, the British Colonial Secretary. In the book, she merely works as an agent for Dr No, conveniently losing the files on Crab Key. In the movie, Bond invites her out. Instead she invites him to her house in the Blue Mountains. On the way, he is pursued and eludes the 'Three Blind Mice' assassins. Miss Taro is then ordered to keep Bond occupied, which she does until Bond has her arrested.

He does not bed Dr No's other agent, the photographer – Miss Chung in the novel – letting her go after exposing her film.

Daniela Bianchi

Sylvia Trench appears again in the opening scenes of *From Russia with Love*. Bond is picnicking with her in a punt when Moneypenny pages him. But instead of rushing to headquarters, Bond pulls up the hood of his Bentley.

In Turkey, after he has saved the life of Vavra, the gypsy leader, Bond asks him to stop the fight between the two gypsy girls, Vida and Zora, played by Martine Beswick and Aliza Gur. In that case, Vavra says, Bond must choose which girl he thinks deserves to win. The film implies that the decision-making process takes all night.

But the centre of romantic attention is Soviet agent Tatiana Romanova, who in the film is unwittingly working for SPECTRE. As in the book, she appears naked in his bed in Istanbul with only a black velvet ribbon around her neck. At the end of the movie, Bond is having a romantic encounter with Tatiana in a gondola and drops the film of them making love in the canal. Tatiana was played by former Miss Rome, Daniela Bianchi, who gave up acting soon after.

Shirley Eaton and Honor Blackman

Kerim Bey has a girl of his own in *From Russia with Love*, who saves his life by luring him away when the limpet mine goes off. Played by Nadja Regin, she is the traitorous cabaret girl Bonita who nearly lures Bond to his death in his next film *Goldfinger*.

The main story of the movie begins with Bond surprising Jill Masterton, played by Shirley Eaton, in her bedroom in her undies. She later turns up in Bond's bed, only to be discovered later, dead and covered in gold paint. This makes her the first Bond girl to get bumped off. Her sister Tilly, played by Tania

Mallet, takes over the role of heroine. However, Bond does not bed her and she is killed by Oddjob. In the movie, Pussy Galore's lesbian tendencies are only implied. However, she is head of a team of female stunt pilots and, when Bond tries to charm her, says: 'I'm immune.' At thirty-seven, Honor Blackman, playing Pussy, is the oldest of the Bond girls. She succumbs in the end.

Molly Peters, Luciana Paluzzi and Claudine Auger

In *Thunderball*, physiotherapist Patricia Fearing, played by Molly Peters, initially rejects Bond's advances. But after the incident with the traction table, she fears that he will report her and succumbs in the shower. She later turns up, not unwillingly, in his room. And when he leaves Shrublands, he says that he will see her again 'another time, another place'. This is a reference to the 1958 movie *Another Time, Another Place*, Connery's first Hollywood role where he starred alongside Lana Turner.

Martine Beswick turns up again in *Thunderball* as local MI6 agent Paula Caplan. She is killed by SPECTRE agent Fiona Volpe, played by Luciana Paluzzi, who has already seduced 007. However, after a pursuit through the Junkanoo, she is killed by a bullet intended for Bond.

The final Bond girl is Domino Derval, Emilo Largo's mistress, played by former Miss France, Claudine Auger. The bored beauty becomes Bond's willing lover, risks her life for him and saves his life by killing Largo.

Daliah Levi, Jacqueline Bisset, et al.

The 1967 spoof *Casino Royale* is also replete with Bond girls. Though Niven's Bond has retired, he plainly still has lead in his pencil. Although he is grieving over the love of his life, Mata Hari, he finds himself entertained and undressed by eleven nubile Bond girls – SMERSH agents pretending to be M's daughters. One of them – Buttercup aka 'Daddy's little thermometer' played by Angela Scoular – ends up with him in his bath.

Although SMERSH agent Mimi posing as M's widow, played by Deborah Kerr, insists that he must 'comfort her', claiming it is her 'widow's due', Bond refuses her and she dismisses him as a 'ninnogaywillycouf'. Taking over as M, Bond discovers that his successive replacements have been variously 'stabbed to death in a ladies' sauna bath', 'burnt in a blazing bordello', 'garrotted in a geisha house', etc. So Bond decides that he must find an 'anti-female-spy device' – a man who is desirable to all women but indifferent to their blandishments. Consequently, 'Coop' ('Sounds like something for keeping birds.' 'That's me.'), played by Terence Cooper, a 'Kama Sutra Black Belt', is sent for training in a gym full of beautiful girls in exotic outfits. Coop resists them all except 'The Detainer', played by Daliah Levi, who boasts, 'I don't do anything, but, unless you're one of them, you do'.

Bond then recruits millionairess Vesper Lynd, played by Ursula Andress, to recruit baccarat-player Evelyn Tremble (Peter Sellers) by seducing him. Bond also recruits his own daughter Mata Bond, played by Joanna Pettet, who is now working as the living Eastern goddess 'Celestial Virgin of the Sacred Altar' – 'Figuratively speaking, of course'. When Tremble arrives at Casino Royale he is greeted in his room by Miss Goodthighs, played by Jacqueline Bisset, who tries to drug him with doped champagne, but is thwarted by Vesper Lynd.

While Mimi is now a nun collecting donations from MI6 – 'This department has always been very helpful to needy girls' – the villain Dr Noah has kidnapped the Detainer and had her stripped and strapped down to a couch – 'I learnt that in the Boy Scouts.' The Detainer escapes, while Vesper Lynd has apparently fallen in love with Bond and tries to lure him to Casino Royale. However, Bond overpowers her, then organizes a mass assault on the casino.

Although this is all very silly compared with the other Bond movies, it has more than its share of Bond girls. There are over two hundred beautiful women in the picture and the movie poster proudly promises that this 'is *too much* for one James Bond'.

Tsai Chin, Akiko Wakabayashi and Mie Hama

You Only Live Twice begins with Bond in bed with a Chinese girl, played by Tsai Chin, in Hong Kong. She leaves the bed, pushes a button and the bed folds up into the wall. Then two men burst into the room firing machine guns. It is part of an elaborate plot to make it appear that Bond is dead.

In Tokyo, Bond is very much alive when he is pampered by Japanese girls who bathe him and groom him for his assignment. He is also aided by Japanese Secret Service agent Aki, played by Akiko Wakabayashi, who does not hesitate to mix business with pleasure. However, when they are sleeping together at the ninja school, she is killed by poison intended for 007. To maintain his cover, Bond then has to marry Kissy Suzuki, played by Mie Hama. He is disappointed to discover that they are married in name only. But Kissy helps him on his mission, even climbing the volcano in a bikini provided by the publicity department.

Diana Rigg, Angela Scoular and Catherine von Schell

The film *On Her Majesty's Secret Service* also starts with Bond rescuing the Comtesse Teresa 'Tracy' di Vicenzo, played by Diana Rigg, then bedding her. They fall in love. But Bond seems to forget about that when he turns up at Blofeld's Alpine eyrie surrounded by his 'Angels of Death', who include former Miss Norway Julie Ege, Anouska Hempel and Joanna Lumley. He is seduced by two of them – Ruby Bartlett, played by Angela Scoular, who writes her room number on his thigh, and Nancy, played by Catherine von Schell. Nevertheless, as in the book, Bond and Tracy get married and are heading off on their honeymoon when she gets shot.

Jill St John

In *Diamonds are Forever*, Bond meets Plenty O'Toole, played by Lana Wood. Impressed by his winnings at the craps table, she goes back to his room with him. However, before they can get down to business, she is thrown topless out of the window to land safely in the hotel's swimming pool. Later she is drowned in Tiffany Case's swimming pool after being mistaken for Tiffany, who had earlier usurped Plenty's place in Bond's bed.

Tiffany herself is played by Jill St John. She was named after the jewellery store when her unmarried mother gave birth to her. Initially a streetwise diamond smuggler, she turns into a bimbo after prolonged exposure to Bond. Although they are last seen travelling to England together, this is the last we see of Tiffany.

The film also introduces two other extraordinary Bond girls – the bikini-clad Bambi, played by Lola Larson, and Thumper, played by Trina Parks in a leotard. These two acrobatic girls are guarding Willard Whyte and give Bond a beating until he finally bests them in the swimming pool.

Madeline Smith, Jane Seymour and Gloria Hendry

Live and Let Die begins when M interrupts Bond at home with missing Italian agent Miss Caruso, played by Madeline Smith, who hides in the closet. In New York, he meets Mr Big's clairvoyant mistress Solitaire, played by Jane Seymour. Her powers, it is implied, come from the fact that she is a virgin. However, the tarot cards seem to predict that she and Bond will become lovers. On San Monique, Bond meets the beautiful, though dizzy, CIA agent Rosie Carver, played by Gloria Hendry, who quickly succumbs. This is Bond's first interracial – and interagency – sex. After she is dead, Bond again pursues Solitaire, seducing her with a deck stacked with the tarot card showing 'The Lovers'. Having lost her virginity, she has lost her powers and has signed her own death warrant. But Bond kills Mr Big and his henchman and they disappear together into the night in an Amtrak couchette.

Britt Ekland and Maud Adams

In *The Man with the Golden Gun*, Bond catches up with Mary Goodnight, played by Britt Ekland, who Bond has previously overlooked. She is now an MI6 agent stationed in Hong Kong and comes to his bedroom in her nightie, But Scaramanga's mistress Andrea Anders, played by Maud Adams, turns up. Mary is shoved unceremoniously into a closet while Bond and Andrea make love. Bond promises to rescue her from Scaramanga if she will help him recover the Solar Agitator. Discovering that she has betrayed him, Scaramanga has her killed. It seems she wants to leave him because he only makes love to her before he kills someone, to improve his aim. Scaramanga also abducts Mary Goodnight, who spends much of her time on his private island wearing a bikini. But she ends up with Bond on a slow boat to Hong Kong.

Sue Vanner, Barbara Bach and others

The Spy Who Loved Me begins with Bond making love to a beautiful woman, played by Sue Vanner, in an Alpine chalet. Although played by a different actress – Fiona Fullerton – she is supposed to be Pola Ivanova, who turns up with General Gogol in *A View to a Kill*. When visiting Sheikh Hosein, played by Edward de Souza, who was at Cambridge with Bond, 007 finds himself waylaid by four beautiful Arab girls, played by Felicity York, Dawn Rodrigues, Anika Pavel and Jill Goodall.

The heroine is Anya Amasova, played by Barbara Bach. As agent Triple X and a major in the KGB, she matches Bond at every turn and even threatens to kill him when she learns that he killed her lover. She finds herself up against Stromberg's bikini-clad henchperson Naomi, played by Caroline Munro. After Bond kills Naomi and rescues Anya from the wreck of Atlantis, she decides not to kill Bond after all. Again Bond moves on.

Corinne Cléry, Lois Chiles and Emily Bolton

In *Moonraker* Bond is taken by helicopter to Drax's California headquarters by Corinne Dufour, played by Corinne Cléry. He then meets Dr Holly Goodhead, played by Lois Chiles, who singularly fails to fall for his charm. Corinne does, though, and he makes love to her in order to gain access to Drax's safe. Drax sees this as an act of betrayal and has her killed. Bond meets

Holly again in Venice. She turns out to be a CIA agent and treats him as a one-night stand. In the morning, he awakes to find her gone. Travelling on to Rio, Bond passes the time with local agent Manuela, played by Emily Bolton. Then he bumps into Holly again. She is kidnapped. Bond heads into the jungle where he discovers a temple full of beautiful women. It is a front for Drax's covert launch site. Bond is captured and imprisoned under the exhaust of a Moonraker with Holly. They escape. Together, with the help of the US Marine Corps, they thwart Drax and are last seen making love in weightless conditions somewhere in orbit.

Cassandra Harris and Carole Bouquet
Bond is still grieving over his late wife Tracy when *For Your Eyes Only* opens. When Bond goes after the assassin Hector Gonzales, he is saved by Melina Havelock, played by Carole Bouquet. She is strong-willed and courageous, and there is no hint of romance between them before the end of the film. Along the way, teenage ice-skater Bibi Dahl, played by Lynn-Holly Johnson, turns up in his bed, but he emphatically declines. He also encounters the Countess Lisle von Schlaf, played by Cassandra Harris, wife of Pierce Brosnan. The Austrian countess turns out to be a down-to-earth girl from Liverpool. She is the mistress of Milos Colombo and Bond spends the night with her in the hope of learning more. In the morning she is killed as they walk along the beach together. Colombo does not mourn his dead mistress, nor is he angry with Bond for sleeping with her. Bond and Melina hook up again and locate the ATAC together. They end up back on Melina's yacht where she strips off, saying that her body is 'for your eyes only'.

Kristina Wayborn and Maud Adams
Octopussy begins with Bond being assisted by a raven-haired girl in a white dress, named Bianca, played by Tina Hudson. When he is arrested, she facilitates his rescue by distracting the guards with her legs. Soon Miss Moneypenny's assistant

Penelope Smallbone, played by Michaela Clavell, is mooning over him.

In India, Bond is seduced by Octopussy's right-hand woman Magda, played by Kristina Wayborn, who says in bed, when her champagne glass is empty, 'I need refilling.' Bond then gets out to Octopussy's island which is positively heaving with Bond girls, some of whom are seen swimming naked. Octopussy, played by Maud Adams, getting a second bite of the cherry, is not annoyed with Bond and sleeps with him, possibly out of gratitude as he had allowed her beloved father to commit suicide rather than face disgrace.

As the head of the Octopus cult she has revived, Octopussy is a powerful woman. After Bond disarms the atomic bomb in Germany, her female acolytes storm Kamal Khan's palace in India. And when the dust has settled, Bond recuperates with Octopussy on her private boat.

Prunella Gee, Barbara Carrera, Valerie Leon and Kim Basinger

Never Say Never Again begins with Bond rescuing kidnap victim Wendy Leech, who stabs him. At Shrublands, Patricia Fearing, played this time by Prunella Gee, treats Bond with the mink mitten borrowed from the book. With his suitcase full of gourmet goodies, he soon seduces her.

In the Bahamas, he meets Fatima Blush, played by Barbara Carrera, who takes him deep-sea diving, making love to him several times on the way. Then she tries to kill him, but he is rescued by a woman he had met in Nassau earlier, played by Valerie Leon. Back at his hotel, they make love in her room, which saves him from the bomb Fatima has left under his bed.

On the trail of Emile Largo in the South of France, Bond charms his way past the receptionist at a health spa, played by Jill Meager, and gets to massage Largo's mistress Domino Petacchi, played by Kim Basinger. At the casino that night, Bond renounces all his winnings for one dance with Domino. Returning to his rented villa, he finds his attractive Secret

Service sidekick Nicole, played by Saskia Cohen Tanugi, dead. Bond chases her killer, Fatima, and kills her with a rocket-firing pen, provided by Q, after she forces him to write that she is the best lover she has ever had.

Bond goes on to rescue Domino when she is chained up to be sold off to Arabs in North Africa. After escaping, they share a cabin and a shower on board an American submarine. She turns up to rescue Bond and kill Largo once more. They are last seen living together in a villa on the Bahamas.

Kimberley Jones, Tanya Roberts, Grace Jones and Fiona Fullerton

At the beginning of *A View to a Kill*, Bond escapes from Arctic Siberia in a luxurious submersible, piloted by a beautiful Bond girl, played by Kimberley Jones. She addresses him as 'Captain Bond'. He replies: 'Call me James, it's five days to Alaska.'

Then, at a party at Max Zorin's château, Bond meets Stacey Sutton, played by Tanya Roberts, who rejects him. However, he does end up in bed with May Day, played by Grace Jones, who tries to kill him several times during the course of the film. In California, Bond meets up again with Pola Ivanova, this time played by Fiona Fullerton. She beds Bond, but is only after one thing – the tape.

It then becomes clear that Stacey is also an enemy of Zorin. At the climax of the film, Bond saves her life a number of times and they end up in the shower, observed by Q and his robotic dog 'Snooper'.

Kell Tyler and Maryam d'Abo

In the pre-title sequence of *The Living Daylights*, Bond ends up on board the yacht of a bored beauty, played by Kell Tyler, aka Belle Avery. But from then on he is uncharacteristically faithful to the beautiful cellist Kara Milovy, played by Maryam d'Abo, the woman he was initially ordered to kill. He does no more than the usual amount of flirting with the glamorous new Miss Moneypenny, played by Caroline Bliss, replacing Lois Maxwell who had played the role since *Dr No*. Thanks to Bond, Kara eventually gets her papers to play in the West.

Carey Lowell and Talisa Soto

It is Leiter's love life that takes centre stage at the beginning of *Licence to Kill,* not Bond's. He gets married. Bond barely even gets a look-in with Leiter's secretary. However, he is soon teamed up with feisty CIA pilot Pam Bouvier, played by Carey Lowell, who is more of an antagonist than a help. In Isthmus City they share a suite, not a bed. Nevertheless, she gets fiercely jealous when Bond beds Lupe Lamora, played by Talisa Soto, the mistress of the villain Franz Sanchez. This is not the first time she has been unfaithful, but when Sanchez caught her last lover, he had his heart cut out, then punished her with his whip.

Bouvier uses her beauty to distract the opposition, repeatedly rescuing Bond. Somehow Bond overlooks Loti, a Hong Kong narcotics agent played by Diana Lee-Hsu, a former *Playboy* playmate. At the end Bond picks Bouvier over Lupe, who turns her attentions to the president of Isthmus.

Famke Janssen and Izabella Scorupco

In *GoldenEye*, the new female M calls Bond a 'sexist, misogynist dinosaur'. Although she does not retract this, Bond is, once again, up against intelligent, resourceful, independent women. However, he starts out with Caroline, played by Serena Gordon, a nervous assessor who is giving Bond an MI6 field evaluation when he becomes involved in a car chase with Xenia Onatopp, played by Famke Janssen. Xenia is later seen having kinky sex with a Canadian admiral, who she strangles with her thighs before stealing his identity papers. She dresses exotically and enjoys cigars, which she smokes in a suggestive manner.

Bond's heroine is GoldenEye programmer Natalya Simonova, played by Swedish singer and actress Izabella Scorupco. Though a dowdy apparatchik at the beginning, she blossoms as the picture progresses. There is little opportunity for them to become romantically involved until the very end when Natalya commandeers a helicopter to rescue Bond and they end up in a field – only to be interrupted by Jack Wade and a platoon of Marines.

Teri Hatcher and Michelle Yeoh

Bond doubly antagonizes Elliot Carver, the villain of *Tomorrow Never Dies*, by stealing his GPS encoder and his wife Paris, played by Teri Hatcher, who had been a former lover. Carver has her killed. Bond then teams up with Chinese Secret Service agent Wai Lin, played by Michelle Yeoh. She seems to be immune to Bond's seductive charms. When they take a shower together, they are fully clothed. But Bond is plainly taken with her. When he captures Gupta, he tries to exchange him for Wai Lin. Finally, when the fighting is over and Carver's stealth ship has sunk, the two of them have a romantic scene on a raft while the Royal Navy hunts for them.

Serena Scott Thomas, Sophie Marceau and Denise Richards

At the beginning of *The World is Not Enough*, Bond finds himself unfit for duty again. However, his status is soon changed after a mutual examination with MI6's medical officer Dr Molly Warmflash, played by Serena Scott Thomas. Bond is sent to look after Elektra King, played by Sophie Marceau. She rejects him at first. He finally beds her, but she is in love with the terrorist Renard. Bond teams up with the ballsy nuclear-weapons decommissioner Dr Christmas Jones, played by Denise Richards. They end up making love in Istanbul and her unusual surname leads to Bond's line: 'I thought Christmas only came once a year.'

Halle Berry and Rosamund Pike

Die Another Day gives us another of those Bond girl moments – akin to Honey Rider emerging from the waves in her bikini. This time Halle Berry as Giacinta 'Jinx' Johnson emerges from the sea in an orange bikini – earning her the ranking of *FHM* magazine's number one sexiest Bond girl. That night they make love, demonstrating that Bond has lost none of his old flair. There was a worry on that score earlier in the picture when Bond rejected the massage girl Peaceful Fountains of Desire, played by Rachel Grant, because she was a Chinese agent. Earlier in his career, Bond would have made love to her first and asked questions later.

It transpires that Jinx is with the NSA – America's National Security Agency. She is more than a match for Bond until she has to be rescued from the melting ice palace. In a poll Jinx has been rated the fourth toughest woman on screen of all time.

Later he meets Gustav Graves's publicist, fencing partner and MI6 agent, Miranda Frost, played by Rosamund Pike, who is frosty with Bond at first. She says: 'I know all about you, 007: sex for dinner and death for breakfast.' She melts after they have to pretend to be lovers. They make love, then Frost is exposed as a traitor. She has been working for Graves all along. She is the one who betrayed him to the North Koreans and she only slept with Bond so she could tamper with his gun. There is a jealous confrontation between Jinx and Miranda. After Bond has rescued Jinx from the ice palace, she has a fight to the death with Miranda with swords on Graves's private plane. Miranda, who is a gold-medal-winning Olympic fencer, taunts Jinx with the words: 'I can read your every move.'

'Read this, bitch,' says Jinx, before stabbing her with a dagger concealed behind a copy of *The Art of War*. Then together Jinx and Bond escape from the disintegrating plane.

Finally Moneypenny, played by Samantha Bond since *GoldenEye*, gets lucky when Bond flings her on the desk and begins to make love to her. It is, sadly, all an illusion.

The film ends with Jinx and Bond together in a remote cabin.

'See, it's a perfect fit,' we hear Bond say.

'Leave it in,' says Jinx.

'It's got to come out sooner or later,' says Bond.

'No, leave it in, please,' says Jinx. 'Just a few minutes more.'

Then we see that Bond is trying the blood diamonds for size in Jinx's navel.

When Bond says that they have to hand the diamonds in, Jinx says: 'Still the good guys, huh?'

'I'm still not sure how good you are,' says Bond.

'I'm so good,' purrs Jinx.

'Especially when you're bad,' says Bond.

Eva Green

The new darker Bond played by Daniel Craig in *Casino Royale* has little time for womanizing. However, he is attracted to Treasury agent Vesper Lynd, played by Eva Green, who wears a necklace showing an 'Algerian love knot'. Though she rejects him at first, she warms when they have to pretend to be a married couple. She saves his life when a wire from his defibrillator becomes detached. By the end of the picture they have fallen in love and are about to live happily ever after when Bond discovers that she has betrayed him. Although she contrives her own death in the sinking Venetian house and has been blackmailed into her betrayal, Bond concludes sulkily: 'The bitch is dead.'

Olga Kurylenko and Gemma Arterton

Nevertheless, in *Quantum of Solace* he is still cut up about Vesper. On the flight from Italy to Bolivia, Bond gets drunk – a first – and, in a conversation with Mathis, broods on Vesper and his sense of betrayal. Clearly he is nursing a broken heart. However, he has already met the altogether sassier Camille Montes, played by Olga Kurylenko, who was formerly the mistress of the villain Dominic Greene. At first, in a case of mistaken identity, she tries to kill Bond, then, against her will, is rescued by him from the grasp of General Medrano. It is later revealed that she is only trying to get close to him because she wants to kill him. When she was a child, Medrano had murdered her father and, in her presence, raped her mother and sister, then strangled them.

Arriving in La Paz, Bond is met by Strawberry Fields, played by Gemma Arterton, an MI6 agent sent from the British Embassy to send him home. She arranges for him to stay overnight in a run-down hotel, posing as a teacher on a sabbatical. Bond says, 'I'd rather sleep in a morgue', then whips her off to a swish hotel where he seduces her. In a scene reminiscent of Jill Masterton's death in *Goldfinger*, Strawberry Fields is found dead in his bed, her naked body covered in oil.

Bond hooks up again with Camille Montes. They kill Medrano and Greene. Then Bond puts her on the train home unmolested – making Camille that rare thing, a Bond girl he does not seduce. Bond finally expiates his grief over Vesper by catching up with her former boyfriend – who was not kidnapped at all but colluded in her blackmail – and handing him over to the authorities for questioning. We know he is finally over Vesper when he drops her necklace in the snow. Plainly, he is now free to pursue fresh Bond girls.

9. The Villains

The other memorable element of the James Bond formula is the diabolical villains and their extraordinary plans for world domination or their fiendish schemes to make money. While Bond and Leiter stand up for staunch Anglo-American ideals, the villains are almost always beastly foreigners – even though several have become naturalized Brits or Americans.

Le Chiffre

In *Casino Royale*, Le Chiffre not only needs to make money, but also is a member of SMERSH, which is committed to the Communist takeover of the world. His origins are unknown. According to his Secret Service file, he was first encountered as an inmate of Dachau displaced persons camp in the American Zone of Germany in June 1945. He was apparently suffering from amnesia and paralysis of the vocal cords, both thought to be feigned. After therapy, he could talk again but continued to claim total loss of memory. He was issued papers as a stateless person, adopting the name 'Le Chiffre' – 'The Numeral' in French – as he was 'only a number on a passport'. He also used the aliases 'The Number', 'Herr Nummer', 'Herr Ziffer', etc., all translations or variations of Le Chiffre.

In 1953, when the book was first published, he is thought to be about forty-five. Five foot eight inches tall, he weighs around eighteen stone or 252 pounds. He has a pale complexion and is clean-shaven. His hair is red-brown with a brush cut, while his eyes are very dark brown with the white showing prominently around the iris. He has a small, rather feminine mouth with expensive false teeth. He is thought to be of Mediterranean origin with some Polish or Prussian blood, though he has small ears with large lobes, which were believed to indicate some Jewish ancestry. Given that many Bond villains seem to be of East European extraction, one can't help thinking that Fleming is betraying some of the anti-Semitism that affected people of his class at that time.

Le Chiffre's hands are small, well-tended, hirsute. His feet are also small. He dresses well, usually in dark double-breasted suits. He chain-smokes strong French Caporal cigarettes, but uses a de-nicotinizing holder and, at intervals, uses a Benzedrine inhaler.

He is fluent in German and French, though with the hint of a Marseilles accent, rarely smiles and never laughs. An expert driver of fast cars, he is adept with small arms and in other forms of combat, carrying razor blades in his hatband, the heel of his left shoe and his cigarette case. He is an accomplished gambler with a good knowledge of accountancy and mathematics.

His file also mentions that he is 'a formidable and dangerous agent of the USSR, controlled by Leningrad Section III through Paris'. He has a large sexual appetite and enjoys flagellation. Otherwise an admirable agent, his predilections are exploited by his mistresses, one of whom, a Eurasian, works for Station F. She reported that he was on the brink of a financial crisis, discreetly selling jewellery and a villa in Antibes.

Le Chiffre is always accompanied by two armed guards. One of them, a thin man named Basil who is thought to be German, takes pleasure in beating up Bond. The other, a moustachioed man with a southern French accent, threatens to shoot Bond in the spine with a gun disguised as a walking stick in the casino when Le Chiffre is losing.

Peter Lorre brought a sinister East European feel to the role in the 1954, TV adaptation, Orson Welles less so in the 1966 film version, where Le Chiffre was also trying to raise money by selling compromising pictures of world leaders. In 2006's updated version, Le Chiffre is thought to be an Albanian who acts as banker to the world's terrorists. He retains the Benzedrine inhaler, but also seems to be suffering from the condition haemolacria, which causes him to weep blood. He has a girl-friend Valenka, but also has to compete with two rival villains, Steven Obanno and Mr White, who kills him.

Mr Big

In the book *Live and Let Die*, Bond comes up against Buonaparte Ignace Gallia, also known as Mr Big because of his height and bulk. He has no known vices except women, which he consumes in quantities. He doesn't drink or smoke. However, he has a chronic heart disease which gives his skin a greyish tinge. He had been initiated into voodoo as a boy, then worked as a truck driver in Haiti before emigrating to the US. He worked as a hijacker in Legs Diamond's gang. At the end of Prohibition, he bought a half-share in a Harlem nightclub and ran a string of black prostitutes. His partner was found at the bottom of the Harlem river in 1938. Called up in 1943, he was sent as an OSS agent to Marseilles, where he worked closely with a Soviet agent. Decorated by both the French and the Americans at the end of the war, he disappeared for five years, when he was thought to be in Moscow. Returning to Harlem in 1950, he bought three nightclubs and a chain of brothels, paying his lieutenants gener-ously. He also started a voodoo temple and used the rumour that he was a zombie – even Baron Samedi himself – to control the African-American underworld. To Bond it is clear that he is a member of SMERSH. He has a number of henchmen includ-ing The Whisper, McThing, Sam Miami, The Flannel, Blabbermouth Foley, The Robber, Butch, The Lifer and Tee-Hee Johnson, who breaks Bond's finger before Bond takes his revenge by kicking him down the stairs.

In the film, Mr Big also owns the Fillet of Soul chain of restaurants. He doubles as Dr Kananga, prime minister of the Caribbean island of San Monique, who is growing opium there as he plans to swamp the US with heroin. Baron Samedi appears as a separate character and, in the movie, Tee-Hee Johnson has lost his arm. He survives to the end of the film when Bond throws him out of the window of a speeding train.

Sir Hugo Drax

There are similarities between Sir Hugo Drax, the villain in *Moonraker*, and Le Chiffre. He was found among the survivors of an Anglo-American liaison post that had been blown up by the German Werewolves during the Ardennes Offensive of 1944. He had lost half his face and, like Le Chiffre, seemed to be suffering total amnesia. After scouring the War Office records of missing men, he adopted the identity of one Hugo Drax, an orphan who had worked in the Liverpool docks before the war and had no next of kin.

The newly renamed Drax then left the country for about three years after the war. When he resurfaced, he was dealing in Columbite, an ore vital in the production of jet engines. Trading in futures, he made himself extremely wealthy, then gave his entire holding of Columbite to Britain to make the Moonraker. This earned him a knighthood.

Physically Drax is repulsive. He is six foot tall with exceptionally broad shoulders and a large square head with a powerful nose and jaw. His face shows the ugly signs of reconstruction. His reddish hair is centre-parted to cover scars on his temples. Puckered skin covers half his face. His right eye is considerably larger than his left because the skin used to rebuild his eyelid has contracted and the eye will not close properly, leaving it painfully bloodshot. Plastic surgery also failed to match his right ear to his left, but they are partially obscured by sideburns that have grown down to his lobes. He also has hair on his cheekbones, and a large moustache covers his protruding teeth that only show when he makes one of his short, braying laughs. Bond dismisses him as a loud-mouthed boor and a snob.

Drax sweats incessantly, chain-smokes cork-tipped Virginia cigarettes and bites his nails. Like Le Chiffre he has hairy hands.

His clothes are expensive. He favours double-breasted suits with turned-back cuffs and velvet smoking jackets. He wears silk shirts with modest cuff-links, possibly Cartier, and a plain gold watch.

Eventually Drax confesses to Bond that he is not English at all, but German – 'a Kraut,' he says. His real name was Graf Hugo von der Drache. Thanks to his English mother, until he was twelve, he was educated in England, where he was bullied mercilessly for his foreign name and his 'ogre's teeth'.

'Then I could stand this filthy country no longer and I completed my education in Berlin and Leipzig,' he says.

At twenty he went to work in the family's armaments factory, where he learnt about steel, aircraft and Columbite. When the war started, he joined the Nazi Party. By the time he was twenty-eight he was a lieutenant in a Panzer regiment. He enjoyed their easy victories over the British Army in France. Then he joined the Foreign Intelligence Service of the SS, where he took the opportunity to exact more revenge on Englishmen. During the Ardennes Offensive – also known as the Battle of the Bulge – he led a German commando unit in American uniforms through the lines. When the battle was lost, he stayed behind with the 'Werewolves'. They came across an Anglo-American liaison post and sent two men with a jeep full of explosives to blow it up. Meanwhile Drax killed a despatch rider and rode off on his bike wearing a British uniform. He was shot up by a German plane and taken to a field hospital at the liaison post. Drax was there when the post was blown up.

During his recuperation he made his plans for further revenge on the English for what they had done to him and his country. The British authorities made it easy for him to adopt a new identity. When he got out of hospital, he murdered a Jewish moneylender and stole £15,000 from his safe, then fled to Tangier where he started trading in Columbite.

Once he had earned £20 million, he returned to establish himself in London. Then he went back to Germany to recruit 'loyal' German technicians and his henchman Krebs, a specialist in torture who had also been with the Werewolves. Moving on to Moscow, he outlined his plans to blow up London. The Soviets gave him an atomic warhead, and Dr Walther, a top scientist from Peenemünde who masterminded the Moonraker project. The test payload of instruments supplied by the British was taken back to Stettin.

Bond considers Drax a remarkable case history – a combination of galloping paranoia, megalomaniac hatred and desire for revenge – and concludes that this must have something to do with his teeth. But thanks to the intervention of Special Branch and Bond, Drax is thwarted and, eventually, hoisted with his own petard.

In the movie, Drax, played by French actor Michael Lonsdale, is not the 'vulgarian' Bond sees him as in the book. He has forgone his mansion on the cliffs in Kent for a French château which he has had transported to California. He has also bought the Eiffel Tower, but could not get an export licence. He is now a cultivated man and is sometimes seen at the grand piano playing Chopin. However, he is ruthless with those he perceives as enemies, setting his Dobermans on helicopter pilot Corinne Dufour, who he suspects has betrayed him to Bond. Like his counterpart in the book, he is a megalomaniac whose company, space-shuttle manufacturer Drax Industries, is a front for his messianic plan to kill everyone on earth and repopulate the world with perfect specimens he has hand-picked and kept safe in his space station. Bond, Goodhead and the US Marines put paid to that.

In the film, Drax also has two henchmen – Chang, the oriental assassin, and Jaws, the seven-foot-two strongman with steel teeth. It seems he also has steel testicles, which clank when Bond knees him in the groin. This does not prevent him falling in love with Dolly, or turning against Drax in the end. Like many Bond villains, Drax commands countless hordes of uniformed men willing to sacrifice their lives for their master or the cause.

Karl Stromberg

Jaws also appears in the movie *The Spy Who Loved Me*, where the villain is Karl Stromberg, played by Austrian actor Curd Jürgens. Like Drax, the webbed-fingered Stromberg is a well-businessman, the owner of a shipping line, who lives in a palace, though Stromberg's can sink beneath the waves. He also has a messianic plan to wipe out all life on land and create a new civilization underwater. As well as Jaws and an army of followers in bright orange jumpsuits, he employs the wonderful Naomi who also tries to kill Bond and Amasova, pursuing his Lotus Esprit in her well-armed helicopter.

In the book, *The Spy Who Loved Me*, the villains are not nearly so grand. They are mere petty crooks, common-or-garden gangsters, though Sluggsy Morant makes a remarkable reappearance after he was thought to have drowned in a lake.

The Spang Brothers

In *Diamonds are Forever*, the villains are the Spang brothers, who head the Spangled Mob. Jack Spang operates the London branch of the House of Diamonds in Hatton Garden, as Rufus B. Saye, and the diamond-smuggling operation as the mysterious ABC. He is killed at the end of the book when Bond shoots down his helicopter. The other brother is Seraffimo, head of the Las Vegas branch of the family, who runs the casino in the Tiara Hotel. He has a fixation about the old West. He also employs the two creepy killers Wint and Kidd. Bond shoots Seraffimo Spang and kills him. Wint and Kidd pursue Bond and Tiffany on board the *Queen Elizabeth*, where they kidnap Tiffany. Bond rescues her and kills them.

Jack Strap, who takes over Spangled Mob after the deaths of Jack and Seraffimo Spang, joins Goldfinger in his raid on Fort Knox in the book and film, while the last reference to the Spangled Mob comes in the book, *The Man with the Golden Gun* – Scaramanga had worked for them as a hit man.

Ernst Stavro Blofeld and Irma Bunt

Wint and Kidd reappear in the movie of *Diamonds are Forever*, though the Spang brothers are absent. This time they are working for Ernst Stavro Blofeld, whose surname is borrowed from Norfolk farmer Tom Blofeld, a contemporary of Fleming's at Eton and father of the cricket commentator Henry Blofeld.

Blofeld is Bond's arch-adversary. He appears in three of the books – *Thunderball, On Her Majesty's Secret Service* and *You Only Live Twice* – and seven of the Bond films – *From Russia with Love, Thunderball, You Only Live Twice, On Her Majesty's Secret Service, Diamonds are Forever, Never Say Never Again* and *For Your Eyes Only*, though he only makes an appearance there in the pre-title sequence.

Intriguingly, Blofeld shares a birthday with Ian Fleming. He was born on 28 May 1908 in Gdynia, Poland, of a Polish father and a Greek mother. After graduating in economics and political history from Warsaw University, he studied engineering and radionics at the Warsaw Technical Institute. At twenty-five he obtained a modest post in the central administration of the Ministry of Posts and Telegraphs, using information gleaned from the telegrams passing through his hand to make money buying and selling stocks on the Warsaw Stock Exchange.

Anticipating the outbreak of World War II, Blofeld made copies of top secret telegrams and, pretending to be running a network of spies, sold them to Nazi Germany, then the Americans and Swedes. Before the German invasion of Poland in 1939, he destroyed all records of his existence and moved to Turkey, where he worked for Turkish radio and set up an intelligence organization. During the war, he sold information to both sides. After the defeat of Rommel in North Africa, he decided to back the Allies and, at the end of he war, was awarded numerous medals by the Allied powers. Blofeld then moved temporarily to South America before founding SPECTRE, an organization of twenty other villains with its headquarters in Paris's Boulevard Haussmann.

Like other Bond villains Blofeld is a physically large man,

weighing twenty stone, or 280 pounds – he had been an amateur weight-lifter in his youth but had run to fat. His hands and feet were long and pointed. He has black eyes which, like Le Chiffre's – and Mussolini's, *Thunderball* tells us – have the whites showing all the way around the iris. His face is large, white and bland, and his black silken eyelashes could have belonged to a woman. The jut of his jaw suggested authority. His nose is squat, his mouth thin and cruel and he has violet-scented breath from the cachous he sucks.

Besides his extraordinary physical appearance, Blofeld has a relaxed manner, a quality of inner certainty and a powerful animal magnetism which leads Fleming to compare him to Alexander the Great, Genghis Khan, Napoleon – even Adolf Hitler. In his one brief appearance in *Thunderball*, he wears a well-cut double-breasted suit with roomy trousers to contain his vast belly. His wiry black hair is crew cut and there are no bags under his eyes or any other side of debauchery, illness or ageing.

By *On Her Majesty's Secret Service*, he appears in casual wear – at first, in a black woollen slip. He has lost a lot of weight and is now around twelve stone, or 168 pounds, though his flesh has not become saggy. There have been other changes. His mouth is now full and friendly with an unwavering smile. There are wrinkles on his brow. His hair is now long and white; his nose aquiline, rather than short and squat. His eyes are disguised by green contact lenses and his heavy earlobes are gone, perhaps to help support his claim to the de Bleuville title – as the Bleuvilles were said to have no lobes.

In *You Only Live Twice*, he swaps his suits for a silk kimono, or a suit of medieval Japanese armour when out in the suicide garden. His white hair has receded. He now has gold teeth, and a grey-black moustache that droops at the ends, mandarin-style.

Blofeld, it is said, neither drank nor smoked, ate little and had never been known to sleep with anyone of either sex. In *On Her Majesty's Secret Service* and *You Only Live Twice*, he seems to have had some sort of relationship with Irma Bunt, apparently based on a shared enjoyment of inflicting pain. However, in John Gardner's novel *For Special Services*, Blofeld's daughter Nena makes an appearance and Bond sleeps with her, although she has only one breast. She is ostensibly the daughter of Blofeld's French mistress. She can hardly have been Irma Bunt's.

When Bond first meets Bunt in Switzerland, he notes that she looks like a sunburnt wardress. She has a square, brutal face with yellow eyes and an oblong mouth without humour or welcome and with blisters at the side which she licks. Her hair is brown and flecked with grey, tied in a tight bun at the back. Her body is short and strong, and she is dressed 'unbecomingly' in tight trousers and a windcheater.

She is little more attractive in Japan, though as Frau Emmy Shatterhand, née de Bedon, she purports to be the wife of Blofeld aka Dr Guntram Shatterhand. Her mousy hair is still tied back in a bun, her eyes yellow. Her face is puffy and square, and her thin mouth still reminds Bond of a wardress. Besides, when Bunt first appears in *On Her Majesty's Secret Service*, Blofeld's right nostril has already been eaten away by what Bond assumes is tertiary syphilis, though it has been repaired by the time Bond sees him again in Japan. Whatever their relationship, it is clear that Bunt encourages Blofeld in his madness.

In the films of *From Russia with Love* and *Thunderball*, Blofeld only appears stroking his trademark white cat. Seen from the rear, he has a full head of black hair. It is only in *You Only Live Twice* that Bond meets him face to face. There Blofeld is played by Donald Pleasence with a bald head and a long scar down the right-hand side of his face, and Blofeld adopts the collarless Nehru jacket that also becomes his marque.

Blofeld is played by Telly Savalas in *On Her Majesty's Secret Service*, where Irma Bunt makes her only appearance and fires the fatal shot that kills Tracy. The actress playing her, Ilse Steppat, died just after the film came out.

In *Diamonds are Forever*, Blofeld is played by Charles Gray. While Pleasence and Savalas are bald, Gray has silver-grey hair.

Blofeld is bald again and confined to a wheelchair in *For Your Eyes Only*. Then in *Never Say Never Again*, he is played by Max von Sydow with a full head of grey hair and a bow tie.

Rosa Klebb

In *From Russia with Love*, Rosa Klebb is a super-bad Irma Bunt. In the book she is a colonel in SMERSH which, Fleming says in the author's note, is portrayed accurately as it was in 1956 when he wrote the novel. Klebb is head of Otdyel II – 'the Department of Torture and Death'. She is a sadist who keeps a bloodstained smock and a low camp stool in her office. It was said that Rosa Klebb would let no torturing take place without her: 'She would take the camp-stool and draw it up close below the face of the man or woman that hung down over the edge of the interrogation table. Then she would squat down on the stool and look into the face and quietly say "No. 1" or "No. 10" or "No. 25" and the inquisitors would know what she meant and they would begin. And she would watch the eyes in the face a few inches away from hers and breathe in the screams as if they were perfume.'

Studying the victim's eyes, she would quietly change the torture, picking another number – 36 or 64 – and the torturers would do something else. Then she would coo softly: 'There, there my dove. Talk to me, my pretty one, and it will stop. It hurts. Ah me, it hurts so, my child. And one is so tired of the pain. One would like it to stop, and to be able to lie down in peace, and for it never to begin again.'

Klebb is also portrayed as a predatory lesbian. After the interview with Tatiana in her apartment, she appears in a semi-transparent nightgown with a brassiere consisting of two large pink satin roses underneath and old-fashioned knickers of pink satin. She has also taken off her glasses and applied a heavy coat of mascara and rouge and lipstick – 'She looked like the oldest and ugliest whore in the world.' No wonder Tatiana fled.

However, strangely, given her power, when she examines Tatiana to judge her suitability for seducing Bond she only gets her to take off her jacket. When she examines Red Grant for his suitability to kill Bond she gets him to strip – only to hit him in the solar plexus with a knuckleduster.

In the movie, she is portrayed by Lotte Lenya as more of a comic-book villain and has left SMERSH to joined SPECTRE, where Blofeld, played here by Anthony Dawson (who played the duplicitous Professor Dent in *Dr No*) with voice dubbed by Eric Pohlmann, refers to her as 'number three'. She still shows a marked propensity for uniforms and sensible shoes – albeit with daggers in the toes.

Red Grant

Donovan 'Red' Grant is even more of a villain in Fleming and Bond's world. He is a traitor. The chief executioner of SMERSH, he was the son of a German weight-lifter and an Irish waitress who was paid half-a-crown – 12½p – for a quick assignation on the damp grass behind a circus tent outside Belfast. Born in 1927, the twelve-pound boy was name Donovan after his father's ring-name 'The Mighty Donovan'. His mother died six months after he was born and he was brought up by an aunt in the village of Aughnacloy, near the border with the Republic. He grew up healthy and strong, but was quiet, communicating with other children only with his fists and taking anything he wanted. Feared and disliked, he made a name for himself boxing and wrestling at local fairs where his guile and the bloodthirsty fury of his attack gave him victory over older and bigger foes. This brought him to the attention of Sinn Fein and local smugglers, who used him as a strong-arm man.

When he was sixteen he began to experience strange feelings that came once a month, around the time of the full moon. First he strangled a cat. The following month he throttled a sheepdog. The month after that he slit the throat of a cow at midnight in a neighbour's shed. It made him feel good. Fearing that he would get caught, he would ride his bicycle further out into the countryside to kill chickens and geese. Then one night he slit the throat of a sleeping tramp. After that he began cruising the countryside at dusk looking for girls who were out meeting their boyfriends. He would kill them, though he would not interfere with them sexually. Killing, alone, slaked his desire.

When he was nearly eighteen, he grew careless and strangled a woman in broad daylight and hid her body in a haystack. Police reinforcements and journalists combed the area, looking for the 'Moon Killer'. Grant was stopped several times on his bicycle, but his cover story was that he was in training. By then, he was a contender for the light-heavyweight championship of Northern Ireland, which he eventually won after half killing a sparring partner.

Although the war was over, he was called up for National Service and sent to England for training. There he took to drink to suppress his murderous instincts. When the full moon came round, he would disappear into the wood near Aldershot with a bottle of whiskey and drink himself unconscious. Trained as a driver in the Royal Corps of Signals, he was posted to Berlin during the Soviet blockade. He fought in the Army boxing championships, but the finals took place on a full moon and he was disqualified for persistent fouling. The whole stadium was in uproar, but the worst booing came from his own regiment. Scheduled to be sent home, he was sent to Coventry by his colleagues. As no one would work with him, he was made a despatch rider. One day, after making a pick-up at Military Intelligence Headquarters, he seized his opportunity to speed across the border. Skidding to a halt outside a pillbox in East Berlin, he demanded to see the Soviet Secret Service. The secret papers he brought with him convinced them that he was serious. When he was finally interviewed by a colonel in the MGB, he said he wanted to work for the Soviet Secret Service as an assassin. They put him to the test, sending him back into the Western sector of Berlin to kill a man. He was then sent to Moscow, where he underwent more tests and learnt Russian. A psychological assessment concluded that he was a manic-depressive whose cycle coincided with the full moon. He was also found to be an asexual narcissist with a high tolerance of pain. Otherwise he was in superb health, but poorly educated, though he possessed a low cunning. Plainly he was a danger to society and it was thought that the best thing to do was kill him.

However, with the continual purges in the Soviet Union, there was a shortage of executioners. There was a need for his talents. Consequently his name was changed to Granitski and he was assigned to SMERSH Otdyel II. But first he was sent to the Intelligence School of Foreigners in Leningrad for political education. His written work was poor, but he mastered the basics of spycraft. His end of term report read: 'Political value nil, operational value excellent' – just what Otdyel II wanted to hear.

After a year, he was sent to the School of Terror and Diversion outside Kuchino for advanced training. Twice during the year, without warning, he was taken at full moon to a Moscow jail where, with a black hood over his head, he was allowed to carry out executions with various weapons – ropes, axes, sub-machine guns. At the same time he was given electrocardiograms. His blood pressure was measured and other medical tests were performed on him. From time to time, prison execution sessions were laid on as a reward for having carried out an assassination in cold blood – that is, when there was no full moon.

He was made a Soviet citizen, given the rank of major with pension rights dating back to his defection, paid five thousand roubles a month, with a holiday villa in the Crimea, and put to work in the Eastern sector of Berlin. He was given two bodyguards to stop him 'going private'. And once a month he was taken to a jail to carry out as many executions as deemed necessary.

Grant had no friends. Everyone who came into contact with him hated and feared him. He did not care. The one thing he thought about were his victims and his own rich internal life. The only distraction was the occasional massage administered by a topless girl and, of all things for a man who had turned his back on Britain, the occasional novel by P.G. Wodehouse. For his peculiar talent, he was richly rewarded. He had a money clip made of a Mexican $50 piece, holding a substantial wad of notes, a gold Dunhill cigarette lighter, a gold cigarette case with a turquoise button made by Fabergé and a gold wristwatch made by Girard-Perregaux with a face that also showed the date and, of course, the phases of the moon. In time he rose to become SMERSH's chief executioner – that is, the top executioner in the whole of the Soviet Union. The only way he could climb any higher would be to kill another country's top assassin – James Bond, say.

In *From Russia with Love*, he has a body that sends his masseuse's pulse racing. It is the finest body she has ever seen, but – though she knows nothing about him – she is terrified and revolted by its rugged perfection. His head is small, his neck sinewy. His tight golden red curls have a classical beauty and hang down to the nape of his neck. There is fine golden hair on his back and his pale skin is red from sunburn.

In the movie he is played by Robert Shaw with bleached blond hair. Like Rosa Klebb, he is now working for SPECTRE rather than SMERSH and is first encountered on SPECTRE island where he is being trained by the sinister Morzeny, played by Walter Gotell, who went on to play the genial KGB spymaster General Gogol. The plan to discredit and assassinate Bond is cooked up by chess master and SPECTRE number five Kronsteen. When the plot fails, he is killed by Morzeny with a knife tipped in poison.

There is another villain in *From Russia with Love*, the Bulgarian enemy of Kerim Bey – Krilencu, who is working for SMERSH. In the film, Kerim Bey kills him as he emerges through Anita Ekberg's mouth. In the books it is Marilyn Monroe's. This is because Cubby Broccoli was plugging his own movie *Call Me Bwana* starring Ekberg and Bob Hope.

Grant gives himself away by ordering red wine with the fish – something no gentleman would do. However, Bond overlooks this social gaffe until it is too late. Also, in the film credits he is listed as Donald Grant, rather than Donovan.

Dr Julius No

Dr No is another sinister foreigner. Like other Bond villains he takes time to explain himself. Born in Peking, he is the illegitimate son of a German Methodist missionary and a high-born Chinese girl. To his parents, he was an encumbrance. Robbed of parental love, he was brought up by an aunt. In Shanghai he went to work for the Tongs and got his first taste of murder, theft, arson and conspiracy. This, he considers, was his rebellion against the father who betrayed him. He freely admits to loving the death and destruction of people and things, and became adept at criminal techniques.

There was trouble. But No was too valuable to kill, so the Tongs smuggled him into the US. In New York, he became treasurer of the Hip Sing Tong, controlling over a million dollars. In the 1920s, the Tong wars broke out, pitting the Hip Sings against the On Lee Ongs. Hundreds were killed on both sides. No joined in the murder, torture and arson with delight. But the police moved in, in force and the ringleaders were jailed. However, shortly before the Hip Sings were raid, No received a tip-off, emptied the Tongs' safe and went to ground in Harlem with a million dollars in gold. Foolishly he did not flee the country. The leader of his Tong in Sing Sing gave orders for his men to find No. They spent a night torturing him, but he would not tell them where the money was. In the end, they cut off his hands, so that people would know that his corpse was the corpse of a thief. Then they shot him and left him for dead. However, he was one of those rare individuals who have their heart on the right-hand side of their body so the bullet did not kill him.

When he left hospital, he invested all his money in stamps so it could be carried easily and, anticipating World War II, would be proof against the inflation that would come with the hostilities. Then he changed his name to Julius No – there is no mention of what his name was beforehand. He took the first name Julius after his father, and the surname No to symbolize his rejection of him and all authority. He changed his appearance, wearing built-up shoes and undergoing traction to make himself taller. He had his hair taken out by the roots, his nose thinned, his mouth widened and his lips sliced. He swapped his mechanical hands for wax ones inside gloves, he said, though on Crab Key he had pinchers. And he threw away his glasses and began wearing contact lenses. Then he moved to Milwaukee – where there were no Chinese people – and enrolled in medical school, he says, because he 'wished to know what this clay is capable of'.

Having completed his studies, he left America and travelled around the world, calling himself doctor because people shared confidences with doctors and it allowed him to ask questions without arousing suspicion. Finally he settled on Crab Key, where he has lived for fourteen years, earning money selling guano. He spent what he earned building his secret lair, giving it the façade of a sanatorium in case the authorities visited.

He uses his base on Crab Key to electronically sabotage US missiles from the testing centre on 'Turks Island' three hundred miles away on behalf of the Russians, who have trained his men and given him a million dollars' worth of equipment. To make his business even more profitable he is putting out feelers to the Communist Chinese. And he plans to go further, bringing the missiles down near Crab Key and selling the prototypes for millions. If discovered, he would simply divert the rockets so that they landed in Havana or Miami – even without a warhead they would cause considerable damage – and escape in the resulting confusion. Now that Bond and Honey know the secret they cannot be permitted to live. But Dr No assures them that their passing will not be in vain. He intends to torture them to death, record their endurance and, at some point in the future, publish his findings. Plainly Dr No is a sadist. He tells them that he has already had a black woman eaten alive by land crabs. It took her three hours to die. Now he wants to repeat the experiment with a white woman for the sake of comparison. Dr No relates the details with obvious relish – telling Honeychile how she will be staked out naked and how her warm body will feel the first cuts of the crabs' pincers.

In the book, Dr No wears a kimono, not the Nehru jacket worn by Joseph Wiseman in the film. His biography is slightly different in the movie. He escaped from the Tongs in China with his hands intact and $10 million, and fled to the US. There he took an interest in nuclear physics that cost him his hands. On Crab Key he has mechanical hands rather than hooks and his lair is disguised, rather prosaically, as a disused bauxite mine. No longer a freelance criminal, he is a member of SPECTRE. And he dies because his mechanical hands cannot grip well enough to pull him out of boiling radioactive cooling water; instead, more fittingly, he is buried under a mountain of guano.

Auric Goldfinger

Like Drax in the book of *Moonraker*, Auric Goldfinger is an immensely rich Bond villain who can't help cheating at cards – though, again, he does not need the money. He also cheats at golf. Colonel Smithers at the Bank of England says that Goldfinger was born in Riga. Junius Du Pont speculates that he was Jewish, judging by his name. Escaping before the Baltic states were taken over by the Soviet Union under the German-Soviet Non-Aggression Pact of 1939, Goldfinger arrived in England in 1937. He came from a family of goldsmiths and jewellers – his grandfather had refined gold for Fabergé. Smithers suspected that he arrived with a belt full of gold coins that he probably stole from his father. After he was naturalized, he began buying up pawnbrokers throughout Britain, putting his name – Goldfinger – over the door. He sold cheap jewellery and bought old gold, and did very well. By the end of the war, Goldfinger was rich enough to buy a large house at the mouth of the Thames, an old Brixham trawler and an armour-plated Rolls-Royce Silver Ghost built for a Latin-American dictator who had been killed before he could take delivery.

In the grounds of the house, he set up a factory for his company Thanet Alloy Research, employing German ex-prisoners-of-war who did not want to go home and Koreans who did not speak any European language, so they would not be a security risk. He made one trip a year to India in the trawler and several trips to Switzerland. In 1954, his trawler went aground on the Goodwin Sands. He sold the wreck to a salvage company, which discovered gold dust in the timbers. It seems that Goldfinger had been melting down the old gold that he had been taking in at shops, chemically disguising it as fertilizer and sending it to India where it could be sold on the unregulated market at a huge mark-up, making Goldfinger one of the richest men in the world. When Bond first meets him, he is resident in the Bahamas, though visiting Miami at the time.

He has pale, china-blue eyes that Bond felt stared right through him. The lids droop. He has thin, chiselled lips and a big, bland face, usually devoid of expression unless he is talking about gold. He is obsessed with the metal. Jill Masterton reveals that Goldfinger always carries a million dollars in gold with him, except when he is going through Customs. He wears a belt with gold coins in it and his suitcases are made of gold and covered in leather. Bond even speculates that Goldfinger is married to the metal. Jill tells him that Goldfinger gets Oddjob to paint the bodies of young women with gold while he looks on, gloating. Normally, he left their spines uncovered so that the pore of the skin could breathe. But with Jill he did not do that and killed her.

The first time we meet Goldfinger, he is naked except for a yellow satin bikini slip, topping up his, presumably, golden tan. In the movie, he is played by German actor Gert Fröbe. However, in 1965 Fröbe revealed that he had been a member of the Nazi Party in Germany. As a result the film was banned in Israel. But the ban was lifted when Mario Blumenau, a Jew, informed the Israeli Embassy in Vienna that Fröbe had sheltered him and his mother during the war, saving their lives.

Oddjob

Goldfinger's chauffeur, factotum and occasional assassin, Oddjob, is a huge man. He has to be, to carry his employer's solid-gold luggage. He has a chunky, flat face and Bond guesses he is Korean, though stuffed into a black suit he looks like a sumo wrestler on his day off. He has a snout-like upper lip and a cleft palate. But this hardly matters as Oddjob never smiles and rarely speaks. He wears black patent-leather shoes that look like dancing pumps and, of course, his famous metal-brimmed bowler hat.

But that is not his only weapon. When he takes off his shiny black gloves, his hands are fat and muscular. All the fingers are the same length, with no fingernails and blunt at the tips, which look hard as if made of yellow bone. A hard ridge of bony substance also runs down the edge of the hands, which means that a blow from Oddjob could snap a man's neck like a daffodil. A blow from his foot could smash a heavy wood mantelpiece. And, of course, he eats cats.

In the movie, he is played by Harold Sakata, a native of Hawaii who won a silver medal for weight-lifting at the 1948 Olympics and wrestled under the name Tosh Togo. He doubles as Goldfinger's caddy, crushing a golf ball in his hand when Bond wins. He scarcely flinches when hit in the chest with a gold bar and demonstrates his lethal derby by decapitating a statue. In the film he is killed when his hat gets stuck between the bars in the vaults of Fort Knox and Bond adds an electric current. In the book, he dies when he is sucked out of the window of Goldfinger's private jet – a fate reserved for Goldfinger in the film. Bond strangles his boss in the book.

Max Zorin

The villains in the short story 'A View to a Kill' are faceless assassins, though the story started out as a backstory for Hugo Drax. In the film, Christopher Walken plays Max Zorin with cool charm and chilling menace. Zorin is the result of a Nazi experiment to boost intelligence at the foetal stage conducted by his father-figure Hans Glaub, aka Dr Carl Mortner, played by Willoughby Gray. A side-effect of the treatment has left Zorin a ruthless psychopath. Backed by the KGB, he takes over the microchip industry in France and England, making him a multimillionaire. But this is not enough. He plans to flood

Silicon Valley, to give him and his criminal associates a world monopoly. Bond naturally thwarts his plans and Zorin dies with a smile on his face as he falls to his death from the top of the Golden Gate Bridge.

Von Hammerstein, Major Gonazles, Aris Kristatos and friends

In 'For Your Eyes Only', M tells Bond about the ex-Gestapo man von Hammerstein, his henchman Gonzales and the two other Cuban hit men who killed his friends the Haverocks. In Vermont, Bond only sees them at a distance. Von Hammerstein is about five foot four with the physique of a boxer, though his stomach is going to fat and is barely concealed under a narrow strip of black fabric. Thick black hair covers his chest, shoulders, arms and legs, but there is no hair on his face or head – not even eyebrows. His eyes are piggish and close-set; his face is square like a Prussian officer's and his lips thick, wet and crimson. There is a deep dent at the back of his shiny whitish yellow skull – possibly a wound or the result of trepanning – and he wears a large gold wristwatch on a gold bracelet. Bond is relieved that von Hammerstein looks as unpleasant as he did in M's dossier.

The three Cubans are small and dark. Gonzales is neat and well dressed. The other two look like peasants and Bond concludes that the girls with them are cheap Cuban whores. Bond and Judy make short work of the four killers.

Only one of these villains appears in the movie. The Cuban hit man who murders the Havelocks is called Hector Gonzales, played by Stefan Kalipha. Bond finds himself up against two other hit men – Eric Kriegler, played by John Wyman, a KGB man who doubles as an East German skier, and Emile Leopold Locque, played by Michael Gothard, who kills Bond's contact in Cortina, Ferrara, and the Countess Lisl. Bond eventually pursues Locque's car on foot and, when it is balanced on the edge of a cliff, kicks it over.

But the real villain is Aris Kristatos, played by Julian Glover, who is borrowed from the short story 'Risico'. There he is a contact given to Bond by the CIA and has big hairy hands. It turns out he is a drug smuggler working for the KGB. In the movie, the British had awarded him the King's Medal for his resistance to the Nazis during their occupation of Greece. Again he is a drug smuggler and has stolen the ATAC machine to sell to the Soviets. He is killed by Colombo, his former comrade in the Resistance.

Dominic Greene and General Medrano

There is no discernible killer in the short story 'Quantum of Solace'. In the movie, however, there is Dominic Greene, played by French actor Mathieu Amalric, the businessman posing as an environmentalist who aims to take over the utilities in Bolivia. He said he based his performance on Tony Blair and Nicolas Sarkozy. As part of the plot, Greene plans to install General Medrano, played by Joaquin Cosio, as president. He is a rapist and murderer who killed the family of Camille Montes when she was a child.

Milton Krest

Although the villain of 'The Hildebrand Rarity' is not a power-mad megalomaniac, he is certainly unpleasant. Milton Krest regularly beats his wife with a stingray's tail he calls his 'Corrector' and boasts about it. He is also defrauding the IRS by claiming his round-the-world jaunts are research trips. So no one is at all concerned when he is murdered.

Emilio Largo

In the book *Thunderball*, Emilio Largo is number one in SPECTRE. Like other Bond villains he is a large man, but big-boned with no fat on him. He has fenced for Italy in the Olympic foils, but did not make the swimming team for the Australian crawl. Only weeks before he met Bond he had won the senior class in the Nassau water-ski championships and his muscles bulged under his sharkskin jacket. Even his hands are athletic, twice the normal size for a man of his stature.

He has the type of face you see on Roman coins, with a hooked nose and a lantern jaw. It is sunburnt mahogany brown and clean shaven, though he has long sideburns. His eyes are brown and slow-moving, like those of a furry animal. His hair glistens with pomade. His thick, curled lips are those of a satyr. Otherwise he is compared to a centurion, an adventurer, a pirate and a gentleman crook with an entrée into café society on four continents. He claims to be the last of a line of Roman grandees whose wealth he has inherited. In fact, he started out as a black-marketeer in post-war Naples and moved on to become a smuggler in Tangier and a jewel thief on the Riviera. Unmarried, he has a heart of ice, nerves of steel, a spotless police record and the ruthlessness of Himmler – the perfect man to run SPECTRE. He also has an animal quality that makes him irresistible to women. Consequently, this wealthy Nassau playboy is a great womanizer.

In the movie, Largo is played by Sicilian actor Adolfo Celi and retains much of the charm of the villain in the book. However, he has been demoted to SPECTRE number two under Blofeld. But he has lost none of the ruthlessness, ordering the murder of Count Lippe and Domino's brother, as well as torturing Domino herself.

In *Never Say Never Again*, the role is reprised by Austrian actor Klaus Maria Brandauer as Maximilian Largo. He has returned to SPECTRE number one as head of extortion, though Blofeld still appears in overall control. This Largo is not Italian and is said to have been born in Bucharest in 1945.

Francisco Scaramanga

In the book *The Man with the Golden Gun*, Francisco 'Pistols' Scaramanga is a Cuban assassin who is believed to have killed and maimed several British secret agents. Born to a Catalan family, Scaramanga had spent his childhood with a travelling circus where his father Enrico was manager. With little formal education, he trained as a trick shot. He was also a stand-in strongman for an acrobatic troupe, taking the place of the bottom man in the human pyramid. And he appeared as an elephant boy, riding the bull elephant named Max. One day, when Max was on heat, he threw the sixteen-year-old Scaramanga, trampled the crowd and made off down a railway line outside Trieste. The carabinieri caught up with him. Not realizing that the frenzy was now over, they opened fire, injuring the elephant and sending him into a fury again. Max fled back to the circus, where the young Scaramanga calmed him. At this point the police came storming in and the police captain emptied his revolver into the elephant's face. As Max lay dying, Scaramanga grabbed a pistol, shot the police captain through the heart and escaped into the night.

From Naples, he stowed away to the US. Entering the country illegally, he became a petty criminal before going to work as an enforcer for the Spangled Mob in Nevada. However, he got involved in a duel with Ramon 'The Rod' Rodriguez of the Detroit Purple Gang, putting two bullets in his heart at twenty paces before Rodriguez could loose one off in reply. Scaramanga was given $100,000 to leave the country. He worked for several Las Vegas interests in the Caribbean, as well as the dictators Rafael Trujillo in the Dominican Republic and Fulgencio Batista in Cuba. Though he was an assassin for Batista, he also worked undercover for Fidel Castro. After the revolution, Scaramanga settled in Havana as chief foreign enforcer for the Department of State Security and, through them, the KGB. He had killed two Secret Service agents in Havana and one each in Jamaica, Trinidad and Guyana. The Secret Service's area inspection officer had also been maimed by bullet wounds in both knees, forcing him to retire. Scaramanga had claimed victims in Panama, Haiti and Martinique too.

His trademark golden gun fires heavy, soft, bullets with a 24-carat gold core jacketed with silver, which Scaramanga makes himself. The tips are cross-cut, and so spread the bullet like a dum-dum to give the maximum wounding effect. With no police record he needs no disguises and the myth surrounding him gives him complete freedom of movement in the area of the

Caribbean he considers his territory. He travels on a number of passports, including Cuban diplomatic papers. He also has various credit cards and a numbered bank account in Zürich.

Now aged about thirty-five, he is six foot three inches tall, slim and fit. He has a gaunt face with light brown eyes, and ears that lie very flat to the side of his head. He has a pencil moustache, long sideburns and crew-cut reddish brown hair. His hands are large, his nails manicured. He is ambidextrous and his distinguishing mark is a third nipple about two inches below his left breast. Scaramanga's file notes that, in voodoo, this is considered a sign of invulnerability and great sexual prowess. He is an insatiable but indiscriminate womanizer, invariably having sexual intercourse before a killing in the belief that it will improve his aim – a common conviction among golfers, tennis players, marksmen and others.

However, a former Regius professor of history at Oxford who the Secret Service employs as an analyst does not believe that Scaramanga possesses a very high libido and *Time* magazine suggested that he was a homosexual because he could not whistle. The analyst concluded that the death of Max had traumatized the youthful Scaramanga and that, in his opinion, Scaramanga is a paranoiac in subconscious revolt against the father figure – that is, the figure of authority – and a sexual fetishist with homosexual tendencies.

In the movie, Scaramanga's biography is slightly different. He is the son of a Cuban ringmaster and a British snake charmer. By the age of ten, he was a trick shot and, after a bull elephant went berserk one day after a handler's mistreatment, it was the handler he shot. After becoming a paid gunman, he was recruited by the KGB, who trained him in Europe. He went freelance in the late 1950s and was currently charging a million dollars a hit. There are no known photographs, but somehow the British Secret Service knows about the supernumerary nipple. Again, he has sex with his mistress Andrea Anders before he kills, to improve his aim.

Scaramanga, played by Christopher Lee, wears casual sports

clothes and entertains himself in the 'fun house', killing victims laid on by his servant Nick-Nack – who hopes Scaramanga will die so he can inherit his empire. Scaramanga is an excellent shot, priding himself on needing only one bullet to do any job. He even removes the cork from a bottle of champagne at some distance when Bond arrives at his island home. Scaramanga is charming and witty, and feels some affinity with Bond – which Bond does not reciprocate. In the final shoot-out, it is, of course, Scaramanga who dies.

General Orlov and Kamal Khan

The villain in the short story 'Octopussy' is Major Dexter Smythe, who Bond is sent to arrest. No megalomaniac, he is not a true Bond villain and even gets a sympathetic mention in the film. The movie's top villain is General Orlov, played by Steven Berkoff. He believes that the nuclear incident he intends to manufacture in a US airbase in West Germany will force NATO to disarm, allowing the Soviet Union to invade Western Europe. He is aided in this by Kamal Khan, played by Louis Jordan, a corrupt Afghan prince who double-crosses Octopussy, his partner in a smuggling racket. Like other Bond villains, Khan can't help cheating when he is gambling – this time at backgammon. His loyal henchman is Gobinda, who tries to kill Bond several times. He and Khan die in the final sequence.

General Koskov, Necros and Brad Whitaker

'The Living Daylights' short story does not have a villain either. The movie has several. There is General Georgi Koskov, played by Dutch actor Jeroen Krabbé, who fakes his defection to the West to get MI6 to assassinate General Leonid Pushkin, who is about to arrest him for stealing government money. His henchman is Soviet assassin Necros, played by German actor Andreas Wisniewski, who springs Koskov from the MI6 safe house. After a fight in the back of a cargo plane with Bond, he falls to his death.

But the real Bond-style megalomaniac in the film is Brad

Whitaker, played by the Texas-born Joe Don Baker, who would return as Jack Wade, Bond's CIA contact in *GoldenEye* and *Tomorrow Never Dies*. Whitaker is an arms dealer and military fanatic who plays out war games in his home in Tangier. He surrounds himself with wax figures of his military heroes – Hitler, Napoleon, Attila the Hun, Julius Caesar – each with Whitaker's own face. It turns out that Whitaker was an army cadet who was expelled from West Point for cheating, but he continues to wear a uniform, insignia and medals which he is not entitled to. He is killed when Bond's exploding key chain tips over a cabinet commemorating the Battle of Waterloo and a bust of Wellington falls on him.

Franz Sanchez and associates

In *Licence to Kill*, the villain is drug lord Franz Sanchez, played by Robert Davi. He whips his girlfriend with a stingray's tail, borrowed from Milton Krest in 'The Hildebrand Rarity', and has her lover's heart cut out. But he is also cultured, polite and witty. He rewards loyalty and keeps his word, even when it costs him millions. Bond sets him on fire.

The name Milton Krest is also borrowed from the short story. However, the character played by Anthony Zerbe is not a tax-fiddling millionaire. He runs a small marine-engineering firm that is a front for drug running. He dies when Bond hides drugs money in a decompression chamber and Sanchez pushes him in afterwards. He inflates and explodes.

Then there is Ed Killifer, played by Everett McGill, the DEA man who springs Sanchez and has Felix Leiter thrown to the sharks. Bond arranges for him to suffer the same fate, but more permanently. The ex-Contra assassin Dario, played by Benicio Del Toro, recognizes Bond in the drugs laboratory and is pushed into the shredder. William Truman-Lodge, played by Anthony Starke, is the financial wizard behind Sanchez's operation. When Bond begins to destroy the operation, he panics and Sanchez machine-guns him. Professor Joe Butcher, played by singer Wayne Newton, is a televangelist who solicits donations for the retreat near Isthmus City that is a front for Sanchez's drugs laboratory. His broadcasts also signal the daily price of cocaine to international buyers.

Alex Trevelyan aka Janus

In *GoldenEye*, Bond pursues Russian Mafia boss Janus who, in reality, is his former double-O colleague Alec Trevelyan, played by Sean Bean. His motivation for betraying his country is that his parents were Lienz Cossacks who had collaborated with the Nazis during World War II. At the end of the war they had surrendered to the British, but were handed over to the Red Army, who massacred them. Trevelyan's parents survived, but his father could not live with the shame and killed Trevelyan's mother and himself.

Trevelyan is in league with General Ourumov, played by Berlin-born John Gottfried, who stages the fake execution of Trevelyan that Bond witnesses at the beginning of the film. A leading member of the Janus Crime Syndicate, he pretends to be making an inspection of the Severnaya tracking station that allows Xenia Onatopp to massacre the staff. Then he hands over the GoldenEye weapon to Trevelyan to exact his revenge on the City of London and make a fortune for all of them. They are aided by computer nerd Boris Grishenko, who is frozen solid by liquid nitrogen.

Elliot Carver

The villain of *Tomorrow Never Dies* is media-mogul Elliot Carver, played by Jonathan Pryce. He is another high-tech megalomaniac who somehow manages to recruit an army of uniformed men who are willing to give their life for him. He is intellectual, cultured, sarcastic and cold-blooded, sending professional assassin and amateur torturer Dr Kaufman, played by Vincent Schiavelli, to kill his wife Paris after Bond has slept with her. Carver is aided by his head of security, Aryan muscleman Stamper, played by German-born Götz Otto, and international techno-terrorist Henry Gupta, played by Ricky Jay.

Elektra King and Renard

Another terrorist is the villain of *The World is Not Enough*. He is
Renard aka Victor Zokas, played by Robert Carlyle. He carries
a bullet in his head from an assassination attempt. This will kill
him eventually, but in the meantime makes him impervious to
pain, or indeed any sensation. Considered too dangerous to
manage, he is cut loose by his KGB controllers. As a freelance
terrorist, he kidnaps Electra King, played by Sophie Marceau,
who suffers from Stockholm syndrome. She falls in love with
her captor and, as a result, ruthlessly murders her father. She
also wants to get her own back on M for advising her father not
to pay the ransom to free her. A highly sexed woman, she teases
Renard, who is in love with her but can do little about it as the
bullet has left him both impotent and doomed. Bond makes love
to her, then kills her.

Her devoted bodyguard Gabor, played by John Seru, is also
killed in the denouement. Her sinister head of security Sasha
Davidov, played by Ulrich Thomas, died earlier. Valentin
Zukovsky's amusing though treacherous bodyguard, Bullion,
played by Goldie, also dies – at the hands of his own boss. And
another would-be femme fatale also makes an appearance in the
pre-title sequence. Credited only as the 'Cigar Girl' and played
by Maria Grazia Cucinotta, she offers her boss, the Swiss
banker, a cigar before she kills him. She then tries to shoot
Bond. He chases her down the Thames in Q's mini-speedboat.
She then tries to make off in a hot-air balloon, but when it is
clear that she cannot escape, she shoots the balloon's gas tank
and blows herself up.

Colonel Moon aka Gustav Graves

In *Die Another Day*, Bond has seemingly disposed of villain
Colonel Tan-Sun Moon, played by Will Yun Lee, in the pre-title
sequence. The son of peace-loving North Korean General
Moon, he was educated at Oxford and Harvard. He had been
selling weapons for diamonds in order to enjoy the trappings of
Western life and indulge his passion for expensive sports cars.

However, Moon is not dead at all. After revolutionary gene therapy, he reappears in the guise of Sir Gustav Graves, who claims to be an orphan brought up in the diamond mines of Argentina. Arriving in Britain, he is immensely rich. Though it is said he has discovered a diamond mine in Iceland, his wealth comes from African blood diamonds. Nevertheless, he is naturalized and knighted. He is also insufferably arrogant and believes himself to be an unbeatable swordsman until challenged by Bond.

While excelling as a capitalist, Moon's objective is to reunite North and South Korea under Communist rule, holding the West at bay with orbiting super-laser Icarus. He is added by his diamond-studded henchman Zao, Rick Yune. But the villains Moon and Zao find themselves up again Bond. They are bound to fail.

10. Never Say Never Again

James Bond novels did not stop with Ian Fleming's death in 1964, or even with the posthumous publication of *The Man with the Golden Gun* in 1965 and *Octopussy* in 1966. Fleming himself left a scrapbook of ideas and the rudiments of unpublished short stories, which was sold at Sotheby's for £14,300 in 1992. It was bought by two nieces and a nephew who were determined to keep it in the family. However, most of the rights to Fleming's literal output had been assigned to Glidrose Productions, a company Fleming had bought after the completion of his first novel *Casino Royale*. It became Ian Fleming Publications in 1998.

In 1966, Glidrose commissioned South African novelist Geoffrey Jenkins to write a 'continuation' novel called *Per Fine Ounce*. Jenkins had been a friend of Fleming's at Kemsley where they both worked. According to Jenkins, in 1957 the two of them had discussed the idea of a Bond novel set in South Africa. John Pearson found a synopsis among Fleming's papers. The story concerned gold and featured gold bicycle chains, baobab tree coffins and the magical Lake Fundudzi. But when Jenkins finished the manuscript, it was rejected. Since then the manuscript has been lost, except for eighteen pages in the possession of Jenkins's son David. Apparently, the double-O section was closed down. Bond defies M and, on a matter of principle, resigns from MI6 to pursue his mission in South Africa alone.

The following year, *003½: The Adventures of James Bond Junior* was published in the UK by Jonathan Cape under the

Glidrose copyright and in the US by Random House. The author was said to be one R.D. Mascott and there is some speculation about who he may be. The protagonist is supposed to be James Bond's nephew, though Bond, according to *You Only Live Twice*, had no living relatives. Nevertheless, the child exhibits Bond's guile and audacity. He even has a girlfriend.

Author Kingsley Amis was a James Bond fan and had approached Fleming before he died to write an article about him. This turned into a book, *The James Bond Dossier*. Jonathan Cape also paid Amis for editorial work on *The Man with the Golden Gun* which seems to have amounted to little more than a literary critique. Then in 1968, he was commissioned by Glidrose to write *Colonel Sun* under the pseudonym Robert Markham. This was first of the proper continuation novels.

In it, M is kidnapped from Quarterdeck, while Hammond and his wife are killed. The trail leads Bond and the lovely Ariadne Alexandrou, a Greek agent working for the Soviets, to the Aegean island of Vrakonisi, where a Russian-backed peace conference is taking place. Colonel Sun Liang-tan of the China's People's Liberation Army plans to wreck the conference, torture Bond to death and dump his body, along with M's, so that the British get the blame. Bond and his sidekick Niko Litsas thwart Sun and his henchman, the German von Richter, and kill them. The book was well received, but Amis left it there.

In 1973, Glidrose allowed Fleming's biographer John Pearson to publish *James Bond: The Authorised Biography*. The premise of the book is that M is persuaded to let Fleming write books about Bond and his exploits to convince SMERSH that he is an invention of the Secret Service; consequently, they will cease their efforts to kill him. Bond then gets involved in an operation to foil the seemingly indestructible Irma Bunt's scheme to breed killer mutant desert rats in Australia.

Bond then makes an appearance in the 1977 *John Steed – An Authorised Biography (Volume One – Jealous in Honour)* about the hero of the classic British TV series *The Avengers*. According to the author Tim Heald, Steed met Bond at Eton in 1934. Since then their paths had crossed several times. They did not get on. There was no volume two.

The continuation series really got under way in 1981, when Glidrose approached John Gardner, author of the comic Boysie Oakes spy novels, to breathe new life into Bond. He began with *Licence Renewed* where physicist Anton Murik plans to blow up six nuclear power stations unless a ransom of $50 billion is paid, which he is going to use to build a truly safe reactor. Bond and Murik's attractive ward Lavender 'Dilly' Peacock put paid to his scheme. Bond kills Murik and his Scottish henchman Caber. In the Gardner books, Q Department is in the hands of Ann Reilly, Boothroyd's young assistant, who is dubbed Q'ute. Bond and Q'ute have a casual affair. And, with Gardner, Bond abandons the Walther PPK he has been using in the books since *Dr No* in favour of an ASP 9 mm.

The following year came *For Special Services* where Bond and Felix Leiter's daughter Cedar investigate millionaire Markus Bismaquer who is suspected of reviving SPECTRE. During their investigation, Bond beds Bismaquer's mono-mammaried wife Nena. The new SPECTRE is planning to take control of NORAD and America's military satellite network. But the plan goes awry when the bisexual Bismaquer fancies Bond. Nena kills Bismaquer. She then reveals that, as Blofeld's illegitimate daughter, she is the mastermind behind the operation, before falling into the grip of her own pet pythons. Leiter then turns up to rescue his daughter and deliver the *coup de grâce*. Bond and Cedar then head off on what Bond is determined will be a purely platonic vacation. Gardner already had Bond cut back to a low-tar brand of his Morland Specials. Now he switches to cigarettes from H. Simmons of Burlington Arcade.

Then came *Icebreaker* (1983) where Bond teams up with agents from the CIA, KGB and Israel's Mossad to take out Count Konrad von Glöda, who as head of the National Socialist Action Army fancies himself as the new Adolf Hitler. Everyone double-crosses everyone else on the way to the NSAA's supply base in the Arctic circle.

SPECTRE reappears in *Role of Honour* (1984). Having received an inheritance from his Uncle Bruce, Bond quits the service and joins a plot to free the world of nuclear weapons. However, SPECTRE's plan is really to destabilize the world so that their criminal organization can take advantage of the ensuing chaos. Bond stops them, but the new head of SPECTRE Tamil Rahani, though injured, escapes.

In *Nobody Lives Forever* (1986), the dying Tamil Rahani puts a price of ten million Swiss francs on Bond's head. To lure him to Key West, where Rahani plans to have Bond guillotined, Bond's housekeeper May and Moneypenny are kidnapped. Bond rescues them and rigs the bedhead that has to be raised so that the ailing Rahani can see the guillotining. Instead of Bond, the duplicitous bodyguard of Bond's new love, the Principessa Sukie Tempesta, gets the chop. Bond and Sukie then stay on Key West for 'remedial treatment'.

Five years before the beginning of the main story of *No Deals, Mr Bond* (1987), 007 helped extract a team of agents from East Germany after their cover was blown. Their mission had been to turn five enemy agents and get them to defect. Two of them have now been found murdered and mutilated. Bond has to track down the other three. The first is now called Heather Dare. Bond foils an attempt on her life. Together they fly to Eire to find another agent, Emile Nikolas alias Ebbie Heritage. They are captured by the operation's principal target Colonel Maxim Smolin of the GRU – the *Glavnoye Razvedyvatel'noye Upravleniye* or Soviet military intelligence – who is also holding Heritage. However, Smolin says that he was turned by Heather and is working for M now. The KGB is after him and is killing the agents. Along with the fifth agent in Hong Kong, they are all captured by General Konstantin Nikolaevich Chernov, head of what used to be SMERSH. Bond turns the tables by capturing Chernov, while he executes Heather Dare as a double agent.

In *Scorpius* (1988), Bond is pitted against arms dealer Vladimir Scorpius, who is masquerading as Father Valentine, head of the Society of Meek Ones. Using hypnotic powers and hallucinogenic drugs, he plans to get cult members to kill prominent politicians and causing a stock market crash. During the action, Bond marries IRS investigator Harriett Horner, albeit under the aegis of Father Valentine. She, of course, dies soon after while fleeing Scorpius's island headquarters, which is in the middle of a swamp in South Carolina. Though the authorities are about to swoop, Bond returns to the island to kill Scorpius in a similar fashion.

The Brotherhood for Anarchy and Secret Terrorism (BAST) aimed to disrupt a joint US–UK–Soviet naval exercise – itself a cover for a covet summit – in *Win, Lose or Die* (1989). Bond is reassigned to the Navy, where several attempts are made on his life. The BAST leader Bassam Baradj succeeds in capturing the summit leaders and demands $600 billion for their safe return. However, their governments refuse to pay up. It transpires that Baradj is con artist Robert Besavitsky, who has set up the fake terrorist organization to make money. He is killed by Bond's latest girlfriend Beatrice Maria da Ricci, a British agent who had earlier faked her own death to aid Bond's investigation.

Gardner followed that with a novelization of the movie *Licence to Kill* (1989). However, in *Brokenclaw* (1990), Bond expresses his frustration at his lack of action since returning from the Navy after *Win, Lose or Die*. He goes on vacation to British Columbia, where he comes across Lee Fu-Chu, a half-Blackfoot, half-Chinese known as 'Brokenclaw' because of his deformed hand. Bond is ordered to San Francisco where he and CIA agent Chi-Chi Sue go undercover and discover that Brokenclaw is behind a plot to steal the latest submarine deployment system for the Chinese while simultaneously hacking into the stock exchange computers. Bond and Chi-Chi catch up with Brokenclaw on an Indian reservation and are tortured in an initiation ceremony. In a duel with bows and arrows, Bond shoots Brokenclaw through the neck.

An elderly man kidnapped in New Jersey is *The Man from Barbarossa* (1991), a terrorist organization called the Scales of Justice claims. If he is not put on trial for his part in the massacre of Jews at Babi Yar in the Ukraine in 1941, they are going to assassinate high-level Soviet officials. In fact, the Scales of Justice has been set up by hardline Soviet General Yevgeny Yusovich to disrupt the Soviet Union after the *perestroika* thaw. The plan also involves nuking the US-led forces about to invade Iraq. Bond to the rescue. Averting nuclear catastrophe, he is awarded the Order of Lenin on behalf of President Gorbachev.

Gorbachev had fallen from power and Germany had been reunified by the time *Death is Forever* (1992) came out. Accompanied by CIA agent Elizabeth Zara 'Easy' St John, Bond is sent to find out why members of a network of former British agents in East Germany are being bumped off. The man responsible is former East German spymaster Wolfgang Weisen. It is part of a plot to blow up the Channel Tunnel while the inaugural train carrying political dignitaries is going through. With the help of a crack team of French soldiers, Bond electrocutes Weisen and saves the day.

Four seemingly random assassinations are linked to the death of Laura March, an MI5 agent, in Switzerland in *Never Send Flowers* (1993). A mysterious hybrid rose is sent to each funeral. Bond and Swiss agent Fredericka 'Flicka' von Grüsse – soon to be his lover – investigate. They discover that Laura had just broken off her engagement to former actor David Dragonpol, who is now a recluse living in a German schloss with his sister Maeve, creator of the rose. Dragonpol, it transpires, is a psychopathic killer who is planning to assassinate Princess Diana and the two princes when they visit EuroDisney. Lying in wait, Bond kills Dragonpol, while Flicka takes care of Maeve.

Bond must be getting old. In the next book *SeaFire* (1994), he is still with Flicka. He has been promoted head of the double-O section and is no longer answerable directly to M, who is ill, but to a watch committee called MicroGlobe One. Bond is on the trail of Sir Maxwell Tarn, an émigré millionaire with interests in publishing and shipping who thinks he's the new Hitler – a familiar formula for a Bond villain. During his pursuit around the world, Bond realizes that Tarn is always one jump ahead of him and exposes a junior minister who has been betraying him. Working with Felix Leiter, Bond discovers that Tarn plans to make his debut on the global stage by blowing up an oil tanker, then releasing marine organisms he has developed to clear up the slick. Bond thwarts him, but not before Felix and Flicka have been tortured. During the action, Bond proposes to Flicka, but nothing comes of it.

Gardner's next book is a novelization of *GoldenEye* (1995).

At the beginning of *COLD* (1996) – called *Cold Fall* in the US – the action has jumped back four years. Bond is assigned to investigate an air crash involving his old lover Principessa Sukie Tempesta. But she warns Bond against COLD – Children of the Last Days – before her remains are found in a burnt-out car. In Italy, the Tempesta brothers, themselves linked to the Calvinistic COLD and wanted by the FBI, try to persuade Bond that Sukie has been killed by retired US General Brutus Clay, who runs his own militia. Clay kidnaps M. While rescuing him, Bond shoots down Clay's helicopter. But as COLD's aim is to take over America, M decides that they pose no threat to the UK and takes Bond off the case.

The action flashes forward four years. Immediately after the end of *SeaFire*, the ailing Flicka – referred to in this book as Freddie – is taken to the Secret Service clinic in Surrey, where she dies. The FBI wants Bond back on the Tempestas' case. He rejoins Beatrice da Ricci from *Win, Lose or Die* and they infiltrate the Tempestas' lakeside villa. COLD is preparing a major briefing when Sukie – who is not dead – arrives. She and her giant henchman Kauffberger capture Bond and Beatrice. She then reveals that she downed the airliner because an opponent of COLD was on board. Sukie then marries Clay, who is not dead either. But on their wedding night, he kills Sukie and, as Italian Marines storm the villa, takes Bond and Beatrice hostage. Beatrice then shoots him in the arms; he falls in the lake and drowns. To cap it all M – who had recovered from his illness in *SeaFire* – decides to retire in favour of a woman, bringing the novels into line with the film series and the novelization of *GoldenEye* Gardner had already written.

After writing fourteen Bond books, Gardner gave up and the mantle was handed to the American Raymond Benson, author of *The James Bond Bedside Companion* (1988). Ignoring much of the development of the character under Gardner, Benson began his reign in 1997 with 'Blast from the Past', a short story for *Playboy* magazine. It follows on from *You Only Live Twice*, though many years have passed. Kissy Suzuki has died of ovarian cancer and Bond receives a message purporting to come from their son, James, who is in New York. But by the time Bond arrives, James is dead, poisoned. Finding a key to a safe-deposit box, Bond and MI6 agent Cheryl Haven go to the bank where James worked. When the maintenance man tries the key, a bomb goes off, killing him. Bond spots a bag lady outside the bank who had been outside his son's apartment earlier. He chases her into a warehouse, while Cheryl goes for help. Knocked out, Bond finds he is the prisoner of the imperishable Irma Bunt. She tries to force-feed him fugu, the poison she had used to kill his son. But Cheryl arrives and Bond shoots Bunt, killing her – for good this time?

Although Benson abandons Ann Reilly – Q'ute – and puts Q Department back in the hands of Major Boothroyd, he retains a female M with her new office in the MI6 building beside the Thames at Vauxhall. He also gives namechecks to Fredericka von Grüsse from *Never Send Flowers* and *SeaFire*, Harriet Horner from *Scorpius* and Easy St John from *Death is Forever*. Bond continues to smoke cigarettes from H. Simmons of Burlington Arcade, but he drops the ASP 9 mm in favour of his old PPK.

The action in *Zero Minus Ten* (1997) begins ten days before the British hand Hong Kong back to the Chinese. Bond is sent to investigate a series of murders that could disrupt the smooth handover. At the same time, there is an unexplained nuclear test in the Australian outback. In a casino in Macao, Bond spots shipping magnate Guy Thackeray, head of EurAsia Enterprises, cheating at mah-jong. As ever, Bond cheats the cheater and wins a large sum of money. But further investigation is stymied when Thackeray's car blows up, apparently killing him.

Bond's attentions turn to the Dragon Wing Tong. Its head, Li Xu Nan, gets Bond to go to China to recover an agreement signed by Thackeray and Li's grandfathers, returning the company to the Li family if the British ever left Hong Kong – otherwise, Bond and the hostess that helped him, Sunni Pei, will die. After Bond recovers the document he goes to Australia, where he finds another nuclear bomb and Thackeray, who is very much alive. He is planning to blow up Hong Kong and heads back there with Sunni and the bomb, leaving Bond to die. Bond escapes and heads back to Hong Kong. After a chase around Hong Kong harbour before the handover ceremony, Bond locates and disarms the bomb, kills Thackeray and rescues Sunni.

Benson then novelized *Tomorrow Never Dies* (1997) where, as in the movie, he exchanges his Walther PPK for an updated P99. The following year he wrote *The Facts of Death* (1998), which begins with a number of deaths from a mysterious syndrome known as Williams' Disease. Bond is in Cyprus investigating the murder of British troops and has to be rescued by Greek agent Niki Mirakos. M's fiancé and his son are also murdered. Suspecting a mathematical cult named Decada, Bond plays its head Konstantine Romanos at baccarat. At the casino, Bond is picked up by the voluptuous Hera Volopolous, who turns out to be number two in Decada. While Romanos aims to start a war between Greece and Turkey, Hera plans to make a fortune out of the vaccine for Williams' Disease she possesses. Bond puts paid to both plans. Sir Miles Messervy, the new M, Bill Tanner, Miss Moneypenny, May and Felix Leiter, now confined to a wheelchair, all make an appearance. The book was originally called *The World is Not Enough*, but neither Glidrose nor the publishers liked the title, saying it was not sufficiently 'Bondian'.

To celebrate the magazine's forty-fifth anniversary, *Playboy* commissioned Benson to write another short story, which was called 'Midsummer's Night Doom', in 1999. The action takes place at a party in the Playboy Mansion where, unbeknownst to Hugh Hefner, secrets from the Ministry of Defence are being passed to the Russian Mafia. Bond investigates and, along the way, has a dalliance with real-life centrefold Lisa Dergan.

Another Bond short story, 'Live at Five', was published in *TV Guide* the week *The World is Not Enough* appeared in the movie theatres across America in 1999. In it, Bond is on his way to a date with Chicago's Channel 7 news reporter Janet Davis – the second real-life person to become a Bond girl – when he recalls how he once helped a Russian figure-skating champion defect in front of the TV cameras.

The same year those two short stories appeared, Benson also completed the novelization of *The World is Not Enough* (1999) and the continuation novel *High Time to Kill* (1999). The formula for 'Skin 17' – a revolutionary coating for aircraft that lets them fly at five times the speed of sound – is stolen by a mysterious crime syndicate known as the Union. Reduced to a microdot, the formula is being transported to China inside the pacemaker in the chest of a retired Chinese agent. The plane transporting him is hijacked and crashes high in the Himalayas. Bond sets out to find it on an expedition led by RAF officer Roland Marquis, Bond's rival at school who organized the theft in the first place. Also part of the team are two Union killers, Bond's Gurkha Chandra and the high-altitude doctor Hope Kendal, who is destined to become a Bond girl. Meanwhile separate Russian and Chinese expeditions set out to retrieve the formula. Between them, Bond and Hope dispose of the opposition and return the formula to Britain. Bond then discovers that his personal assistant Helena Marksbury, who first turned up in *The Facts of Death* and has since become a Bond girl, has been blackmailed by the Union into betraying him. She turns up dead in Brighton. Such is the fate of Bond girls who get too close.

The year 2000 saw Benson's *DoubleShot*, the second in his Union Trilogy. After his exertions at high altitude in the Himalayas, Sir James Molony's assistant Dr Kimberly Feare diagnoses Bond with lesions on the brain that result in hallucinations, blackouts and other symptoms. Unable to return to work, he investigates the death of Helena Marksbury. After a session in bed with Bond, Feare is killed, slit ear to ear – a trademark of the Union, but Bond is suspected. The Marksbury investigation leads Bond to Tangier, where he uncovers a plan to assassinate the prime ministers of Britain and Spain and return Gibraltar to the Spanish. With the help of the Taunt twins, Heidi and Hedy, who are with the CIA, Bond foils the plot and assassinates the assassins.

In *Never Dream of Dying* (2001), Bond is given two weeks to track down the head of the Union, Le Gérant, before being assigned to the case of Japanese billionaire and suspected terrorist Goro Yoshida. The trail leads him to French film director Leon Essinger. Bond sleeps with his estranged wife, actress and model Tylyn Mignonne. After a chase through a film set, Bond is kidnapped by Draco and the Union Corse. Mathis has disappeared on Corsica. Bond goes after him and is captured by Le Gérant. During his torture, Bond discovers that the Union's plan, funded by Goro Yoshida, is to bomb the Cannes Film Festival. Draco prevents this. It then turns out that Le Gérant is Draco's nephew – Bond's cousin by marriage – and Draco has been part of the Union all along. He wants personal revenge on Bond, holding him responsible for the death of his second wife and child in a raid on the Union some months before. Bond then kills Draco and Le Gérant.

Finally, Benson came up with *The Man with the Red Tattoo* (2002), where a young woman on a flight from Japan to London dies of a mysterious disease. Bond is sent to Japan to investigate, and here he meets up with Tiger Tanaka, last seen in *You Only Live Twice*. It transpires that the family of the dead girl own a medical laboratory. Goro Yoshida and the Yakuza are planning to take over the lab so that they can spread a deadly disease. With the help of the dead girl's sister, Mayumi, Bond foils the Yazuka. Yoshida tries to kill Bond with a samurai sword. Failing, he commits hara-kiri. Benson survives to novelize *Die Another Day* (2002), but that is the end of his Bond output.

Meanwhile, Bond had been taking a parallel route via strip cartoons. They began in Britain in the *Daily Express* with the syndicated comic strip of *Casino Royale* in 1958 and ran until 1983. Forty-five adventures were syndicated in British newspapers and seven published abroad. Initially they were straightforward strip cartoon versions of Ian Fleming's books. Then stories were extended to novel length and weaker books had their plots invigorated with fresh material.

In 1966, in the comic strip of *The Man with the Golden Gun*, Bond is recuperating from his brainwashing at the hands of the Soviet Union. M sends another agent, a friend of Bond's named Philip Margesson who has been crippled by Scaramanga, to the same nursing home to motivate Bond for his next assignment. Bond discovers that the nurse attending Margesson is a Soviet agent.

In the comic strip of *Octopussy*, the characters of the two Chinese businessmen who handle Major Smythe's gold are built up and his daughter Trudi is introduced. This is seventeen years before Octopussy reveals that she is Smythe's daughter in the movie. Mary Goodnight also appears as she had been posted to Jamaica in *The Man with the Golden Gun*. Bond again poses as Mark Hazard.

The Hildebrand Rarity is given a proper James Bond spy story plot with an extended preface in which Milton Krest steals a top secret remote-controlled submarine code-named Sea Slave on its sea trials. Bond is sent to retrieve it and is invited to join Krest's specimen-hunting cover trip by a woman named Nyla Larsen.

The comic strip of *The Spy Who Loved Me* retains the central action of the book in the motel, but gives Bond a different reason for being in Vermont. He is investigating claims by a Canadian test pilot that he is being blackmailed by Horst Uhlmann, a member of SPECTRE, which has been newly reformed under a woman code-named Spectra. But Bond kills Uhlmann and is on his way to Washington, DC, to report to the FBI.

Then in October 1968, Jim Lawrence, who had scripted the previous five strip-cartoon adaptations of Ian Fleming's stories, wrote *The Harpies*, an entirely original piece. In it, scientist Dr John Phineus, inventor of the Q-ray, is kidnapped by an all-girl gang called the Harpies before he has handed his invention over to the government. Bond infiltrates Aerotech Security, which belongs to Phineus's rival Simon Nero, with the help of Nero's daughter Helen. He rescues Phineus, but Helen is killed – another Bond girl bites the dust. M, Moneypenny and Bill Tanner – who turns out to be a classics scholar – all make an appearance. SPECTRE gets a namecheck and Bond has moved downmarket to Earls Court, where he lives under the name Mark Hazard.

In *River of Death*, Bond is up against Dr Cat, the chief torturer of the Red Chinese, who is killing Secret Service agents. The plot involves the creation of a pan-American–Indian movement. Bond is helped in his assault on Dr Cat's Brazilian lair by Native American CIA agent Kitty Redwing. He also reverts to using his old Beretta.

The next strip cartoon in the *Express*'s series was Kingsley Amis's *Colonel Sun*. Then Madam Spectra reappears in *The Golden Ghost*, where the *Golden Ghost* – a nuclear-powered airship – is hijacked on its maiden voyage and its A-list inaugural passengers held to ransom. To get them to pay up, Bond is going to be fed to the sharks. But he escapes and kills the SPECTRE operative behind the plot.

SPECTRE is also behind a plot in the next cartoon: to substitute their own surgically altered agent for the US Secretary of Defense and ruin a peace conference in *Double Jeopardy*. True to his Scottish roots, Bond reveals that his favourite poet is Robert Louis Stevenson. He also reveals a renewed interest in birds – the feathered variety – dormant since *Dr No*, by posing as Jeremy Bland of the London Ornithological Society.

In *Starfire*, Bond tracks down rogue SPECTRE member Luke Quantrill, who eliminates enemies with balls of fire. Sadly, as Mark Hazard, Bond finds no love interest in the tale. Bond's search for 'the Box' in *Trouble Spot* takes him to a nudist colony in California. The love interest, Gretta, turns out to be after 'the

Box' too and dies. 'The Box' in question contains the head of a Russian double agent, proving he is dead. The strip was reprinted as *The Mystery of Box* by Diamond Comics in New Delhi.

A naked girl on horseback and black private detective Crystal Kelly – before the release of the movie *Live and Let Die*, Bond's first black love interest – lead him to a training school for female spies in *Isle of Condor*. Then in *The League of Vampires*, industrialist Xerxes Xerophane aims to nuke his father-in-law and have his wife murdered in the initiation ceremony of a vampire cult in order to inherit.

Bond battles the American Mafia, which is trying to get its hands on the sedative Nopane; this has become the latest recreational drug in *Die With My Boots On*. He gets to play with a wristwatch laser, a zip gun in his shoe and image-intensifying glasses. Bond gets involved in Middle Eastern politics to protect British oil interests with an un-Islamic apparatus that shows videos of women and dispenses drinks in *The Girl Machine*. Bond gets a lover and helpmate in *Beware of Butterflies*, where new double-O Suzi Kew helps him quash the Butterfly East European spy network.

SMERSH makes a reappearance in *The Nevsky Nude*. Bond thwarts Operation Nevsky, which involves the kidnapping of Secretary of State for Defence Lord Melrose, and SMERSH agent Ludmilla skydiving naked from the plane of renegade aristocrat Sir Ulric Herne, which is broadcasting a message purporting to come from King Arthur's ghost telling Britain to rise up.

The Phoenix Project takes Bond back to Turkey in a plot that involves the sabotaging of a suit of armour that is intended to make the wearer invulnerable to small arms, grenades and fire. Suzi Kew returns in *The Black Ruby Caper* to help Bond fight 'Mr Ruby', who aims to put a bomb inside a statue sculpted by African-American artist Roscoe Carver. Bond takes another black lover in the form of Carver's daughter Damara, a model. The love interest is white again in *Till Death Do Us Part* when the daughter of an MI6 agent is seduced by a married man who plans to sell her to the KGB.

Unfazed by his interest in other women, Suzi Kew helps Bond battle SMERSH in Acapulco over the Communist plan to subvert Latin America in *The Torch-Time Affair*. Fickle as always, Bond teams up with Palestinian freedom fighter Fatima Kalid and the PLO to prevent the resurrected Dr No downing a plane carrying US Secretary of State Henry Kissinger on his way to a Middle East peace conference in *Hot Shot*.

Suzi Kew is back on the scene in *Nightbird*, where Bond's old flame actress Lisa Farrar is one of a number of people kidnapped by what appears to be a Martian vessel. Lisa is found dead, but kidnap victims who return alive report they have been held on an artificial moon. The man responsible is Ferdinand Polgar, a movie producer who formerly, as a small-time crook, was hideously disfigured by acid in bungled raid on a laboratory.

The last strip to appear in the *Daily Express* was *Ape of Diamonds* where trained gorillas are used as assassins in a convoluted plot set in Egypt.

The baton was then handed to the *Daily Express*'s sister paper the *Sunday Express*, which began the strip *When the Wizard Wakes* in January 1977. The plot revolves around a traitor to the Hungarian Uprising, Hungary's Crown of St Stephen, SPECTRE, the CIA and the creator of a missile targeting system sought by the Russians.

Jim Lawrence and Yaroslav Horak, the artist for the bulk of the non-Fleming strips – or sometimes John McLusky, the artist in the original Fleming-story strips – began to find new outlets for Bond strips in Scandinavia. They produced *Sea Dragon*, *The Scent of Danger* and *Shark Bait*; in the last of these Bond teams up with alluring KGB agent Katya Orlova to foil a renegade Soviet Navy plot.

Suzi Kew makes another appearance in *Death Wing* where Bond is pitted against Matteo Mortellito, the inventor of a high-tech kamikaze. *The Xanadu Connection* takes Bond to Mongolia to rescue missing British archaeologist Ivor Bent. In *Snake Goddess*, Moneypenny's home is attacked by a giant snake and we find out that she sleeps in a single bed. However, Moneypenny

is assigned to work with Bond in *Double Eagle*, but is supplanted
as the love interest by turncoat agent Helga. You have to feel
sorry for the woman.

The Bond cartoon strip in the UK was then taken over by
another of the Express Newspapers stable, the *Daily Star*. It
began publishing *Doomcrack* in February 1981. Bond buys the
new sonic Doomcrack weapon for the British, but SPECTRE
seizes both the weapon and its inventor, and threatens to blow
up both the Eiffel Tower and the Statue of Liberty. Bond comes
face to face with Madam Spectra on board her submarine headquarters but is allowed to live because her Persian cat takes a
liking to him. The love interest, who has already betrayed him,
now realizes that she means nothing to Madam Spectra and
helps Bond escape. He turns the updated Doomcrack 2 on the
submarine and finishes off Madam Spectra.

Dependable Suzi Kew pops up again in *The Paradise Plot* to
help Bond thwart Father Star, the leader of a hippy cult who
also bristles with high-tech gadgetry. Ann Reilly – Q'ute – also
makes an appearance. She and Suki return in *Deathmask* where
megalomaniac Ivor Nyborg aims to spread a deadly virus from
his robotic plane.

The villain Dr Cat, who makes a remarkable recovery after
being shot at the end of *River of Death*, returns in *Flittermouse*.
Suzi Kew, Q'ute and Bond's housekeeper May all make an
appearance. But Bond teams up with another Native American,
the appealing Red Doe, in *Polestar* where he is pitted against
Robert Ayr, president of Polestar Petroleum in a plot that
involves runaway rocket scientist Jack Boyd.

After that, publication of the Bond strips ceased in the UK.
But the Scandinavians could not get enough of him and
continued their dedicated publication *Agent 007 James Bond*.
In *Codename: Nemesis* Bond survives being thrown off a train
in Eastern Europe and gets on the wrong side of Felix Leiter.
He teams up again with Leiter, a KGB agent and the mysterious 'Little' in *Operation: Little* to fight Wolff, a mad genetic
manipulator based at the South Pole. Although Bond is run

out of MI6 for gambling debts incurred while drugged, he takes on General Juan Diaz and his puppet Emperor Henry Christopher of Haiti, who plan to take over the Caribbean in revenge for the Falklands War.

Bond is kidnapped by aliens in *Operation: UFO*, then battles neo-Nazis in Norway in *Operation: Blücher*. He pursues assassin Walter Junghans in *Operation: Romeo* and tracks the hacker who has wiped the memory of bank computers in *Data Terror*. He is on the trail of Nazis in Brazil in *Experiment Z* and Russian agents in Greece in *Spy Traps*. Returning to the Amazon in *Deadly Double*, he comes up against a dinosaur, a tribe of beautiful bald women and a megalomaniac who wants to destroy New York. Bond is framed for murder in *Greek Idol* and helps CIA agent Melody Hopper track three rogue American soldiers on Cuba. In *The Amazons*, he has to work out which of the women protestors outsides a US Air Force base in Britain is a Soviet agent. Bond gets framed for murder again in *Lethal Dose* and tracks agent Z17 in *Deadly Desert*.

International art forgers turn terrorist in *Terror Times*, while judges vanish in *The Vanishing Judges*. Bond gets involved with boat people in *Flights from Vietnam*, while M plays battleships in the bath, and takes on mind control in *The Undead*. He goes back to Turkey in *Istanbul Intrigue*, while he is chased around Norway and the UK in *With Death in Sight*. He plays bodyguard to a ballerina in *Danse Macabre* and tackles the Leopard Women of the Ubokis in *Operation Uboki*. *The Living Dead* takes Bond to Thailand and in *Goodbye, Mr Bond* he thwarts a plan to replace the world's top agents with robots; then it is back to Japan for *Operation Yakuza*.

Dark Horse Comics published *Permission to Die* in three parts in 1989 and 1991. It pits Bond against mad rocket scientist Erik Wiziadio. Kerim Bey's daughter makes an appearance. Bond uses an ASP 9 mm as in the Gardner novels, and the alias Boldman from *Nobody Lives Forever*.

In 1991, James Bond Junior was resurrected as an animated series for American TV. Six episodes were novelized by

British writer John Peel under the name John Vincent. Marvel Comics issued a series of twelve comic books, and a video game was developed.

Dark Horse Comics continued their comic book series with *Serpent's Tooth* in 1992–93. In it, Bond is pitted against mega-lomaniac industrialist Indigo, who plans to wipe out most of humankind with a tidal wave then repopulate it with children sired by women he has kidnapped. If that was not enough, he is resurrecting dinosaurs, dodos and other extinct species using genetic engineering.

As bodyguard to a thirteen-year-old wheelchair-bound computer genius in *A Silent Armageddon*, Bond had to enter a virtual world to fight the crime syndicate Cerberus. His ward's avatar is a typical Bond girl, reflecting her crush on him. Bond is teamed up again with Tatiana Romanova, now with the KGB, to track down missing foreign aid in *Light of My Death*. In *Shattered Helix* – published in two parts as 'The Greenhouse Effect' and 'A Cold Day in Hell' – Bond comes up against Cerberus once more. This time they are involved in biological warfare. *Minute of Midnight* pits Bond against a cartel of terror-ists who aim to blow up nuclear power stations around the world. Then in *The Quasimodo Gambit* he returns to Jamaica before thwarting a plan by born-again Christian mercenary Maximilian 'Quasimodo' Steele to napalm Christmas shoppers in New York.

Sega's 1981 arcade game *005* clearly paid tribute to 007. Then in 1983 came the game *James Bond 007* where the player gets to be one of a series of double-O agents and the plots borrow heavily from the films made up to that point. Raymond Benson worked on the 1985 game *A View to a Kill*. Since then, James Bond computer games have come out based on individual films.

Then in 2005 the British Charlie Higson started the *Young Bond* series of books. The first book, *SilverFin*, begins with the thirteen-year-old Bond arriving at Eton in 1933. He meets an American bully and his arms-dealing father. The adventure continues in the Highlands during the Easter vacation. *SilverFin* also appeared as a graphic novel in 2008.

In *Blood Fever* in 2006, Bond is a member of the Danger Society, a secret club for risk-takers at Eton. In the summer holidays, he goes to Sardinia where he investigates the Millenaria, a secret society that aims to restore the Roman Empire.

Double or Die in 2007 has Bond poking round in the darker corners of London searching for a missing master. This spawned *The Young Bond Rough Guide to London* featuring the locations in the book. Later that year, *Hurricane Gold* takes Bond to the Caribbean where he foils a robbery. Then *By Royal Command* in 2008 deals with the incident with a maid mentioned in Bond's obituary in *You Only Live Twice* that led to his leaving Eton. The Royal Family and the Secret Service are also involved in the plot.

Higson wrote a Young Bond short story 'A Hard Man to Kill' which was published in *Danger Society: The Young Bond Dossier* in 2009.

The female point of view was supplied by Samantha Weiberg, under the nom de plume Kate Westbrook, in *The Moneypenny Diaries* where she pretends to be the editor of Moneypenny's work. The first book, *The Moneypenny Diaries: Guardian Angel,* was published in 2005. It fills in the entire backstory for Moneypenny and gives her, for the first time, a first name – Jane.

The short story 'For Your Eyes Only, James' was published in the November 2006 issue of *Tatler*: it tells the tale of a weekend that Bond and Moneypenny spent at Royale-les-Eaux in 1956.

The action in *Secret Servant: The Moneypenny Diaries,* published in 2006, takes place around the time of *The Man with the Golden Gun* when the Secret Service is in chaos, with one senior official on trial for treason, another having defected to Moscow and Bond having been brainwashed by the Soviets.

The Spectator published the short story 'Moneypenny's First Date with Bond' on 11 November 2006, telling the tale of Bond and Moneypenny's first meeting.

The Moneypenny Diaries: Final Fling, published in 2008, covers Moneypenny and Westbrook's efforts to get the diaries published in the face of official opposition.

In 2008, award-winning British author Sebastian Faulks – 'writing as Ian Fleming' – produced *Devil May Care* to mark the centenary of Fleming's birth. It is set in the 1960s with the Cold War at its height. Bond is assigned to investigate pharmaceutical magnate Dr Julius Gorner, who has a chip on his shoulder about his deformed hand, and his sinister bodyguard, Chagrin. Bond is warned that his performance is being monitored and a new double-O agent is waiting to take his place. It transpires that Gorner is flooding Europe with cheap drugs and plans to launch a two-pronged terrorist attack on the Soviet Union, whose retaliation will destroy the UK. The attack is to be made using both the stolen British airliner and an ekranoplan, a ground-effect plane. Bond is assisted by Scarlett Papava, who says her twin sister is under Gorner's thrall.

Bond is eventually captured by Gorner, who explains that Bond is to fly the captured airliner into the Russian heartland. However, with the aid of the pilot and Scarlett, who is hiding on board, Bond regains control of the airliner and crashes it into a mountainside after parachuting to safety. The second attack is foiled by an airstrike. Bond then disposes of Gorner. The new double O waiting in the wings to take over if things had gone wrong turns out to be Scarlett Papava herself. The story about her twin sister was only an excuse for her to accompany Bond. He would not have taken her if he had known she was a trainee double O. As it is, she is happy to become a Bond girl.

Then Ian Fleming Publications commissioned American thriller writer Jeffery Deaver to pen a new James Bond book, which was published on Fleming's birthday, 28 May, in 2011. Deaver is very definitely not 'writing as Ian Fleming'. Instead, he has been called in to give 007 a makeover. In *Carte Blanche*, Bond is still thirty-something, but a veteran of Afghanistan, not World War II.

He looks much the same: 'His black hair was parted on one

side and a comma of loose strands fell over one eye. A three-inch scar ran down his right cheek.' But Bond now lives in a world of BBC Radio 4, Boots, Waitrose, Asda and pubs in Canning Town where the Police, Jeff Beck and Depeche Mode used to play. Deaver, an American, has made Bond rather more parochial. He used to be transatlantic.

While he keeps his double-0 status, Bond now works for the Overseas Development Group – a new version of the wartime Special Operations Executive – not the SIS. After leaving the Royal Navy Reserve and a stint in Defence Intelligence, Bond was recruited into the ODG by a man known only as the 'Admiral' over lunch at the Travellers Club. This is M, whose first name we are later informed is Miles. He has a secretary named Moneypenny and a Chief of Staff named Bill Tanner. An updated René Mathis and Felix Leiter, now with all his limbs back, also put in an appearance.

Bond is still a conservative, though stylish, dresser with 'a navy-blue suit, a white sea island shirt and a burgundy Grenadine tie, the latter items from Turnbull & Asser'. He wears black slip-on shoes – 'he never wore laces, except for combat footwear or when tradecraft required him to send silent messages to a fellow agent via prearranged loopings'. On his wrist, as ever, is a Rolex Oyster Perpetual, and under his armpit a Walther. Otherwise, Bond lives in a land of laptops. He is surrounded by a bewildering array of new gadgets, including an iPhone – or rather, an iQPhone – with an app that does iris scans. These are supplied by the head of ODG's Q Branch, Sanu Hirani.

Bond 2011 no longer smokes, but he still drinks and has come up with a new cocktail that comprises a double shot of Crown Royal whisky, a half-measure of triple sec, two dashes of bitters and a twist of orange peel. He eats plain food in upmarket restaurants, washed down with copious amounts of wine – though his days of drinking 'significant quantities of Lillet and Louis Roederer' seem to be over. In England he drives a grey Bentley Continental GT, but develops a sneaking affection for the Subaru Impreza WRX – the STI model with a turbo-charged 305-horsepower engine, six gears and spoiler – which he is given when he goes undercover.

When it comes to women, Bond has obviously mended his ways. Mary Goodnight has reverted to being his secretary, but he no longer flirts with her. He manages to resist the blandishments of MI6 analysts Ophelia 'Philly' Maidenstone, who has temporarily broken up from her fiancé. Indeed, he manages to hold back until page 259, when he finally succumbs to charity fund-raiser Felicity Willing, though she had another agenda.

The villain, Severan Hydt, has a girlfriend named Jessica Barnes. A former beauty queen, she is now in her mid-sixties – and Hydt is into death and decay. Understandably, Bond does not even try to seduce her, while his contact in the South African Police Service Bheka Jordaan parries his every attempt at flirtation.

Hydt's aim is to take over the world by recycling – or a least, recycling the information he has gleaned from document shredders and the hard drives from decommissioned computers. He has a suitable lair in the midst of a huge garbage tip and a sociopathic sidekick called Niall Dunne. Bond beats them in the end, of course.

Deaver abandons what he calls Fleming's 'one-foot-in-front-of-the-other storytelling' for his own 'fast-paced, twisty-turny' style. But we do discover what really happened to Bond's parents. It wasn't a mountaineering accident or a suicide. They were killed by the Russians because Bond's mother was a spy.

Pre-production work was suspended on the twenty-third Bond film when MGM ran into financial difficulties. However shooting began in the autumn of 2011 with Daniel Craig as James Bond, Judi Dench as M and Bond girls Bérénice Marlohe. By the time you read this, *Skyfall* will be on a screen near you.

Further Reading

Alligator by I★n Fl★m★ng, The Harvard Lampoon, Cambridge, Massachusetts, 1962

The Blofeld Trilogy by Ian Fleming, Penguin Books, London, 2009

The Bluffer's Guide to Bond by Mark Mason, Oval, London, 2006

The Bond Affair edited by Oreste del Buono, Umberto Eco, MacDonald & Co., London, 1966

The Bond Files by Andy Lane and Paul Simpson, Virgin, London, 2002

Bond Girls are Forever by Maryam d'Abo, Boxtree, London, 2003

Casino Royale, Live and Let Die, Moonraker by Ian Fleming, Penguin Books, London, 2002

Colonel Sun by Robert Markham, Jonathan Cape, London, 1968

The Complete James Bond Movie Encyclopedia by Steven Jay Rubin, Contemporary Books, Chicago, Illinois, 2003

Danger Society: The Young Bond Dossier by Charlie Higson, Puffin, London, 2009

Death Rays, Jet Packs, Stunts and Supercars: The Fantastic Physics of Film's Most Celebrated Secret Agent by Barry R. Parker, Johns Hopkins University Press, Baltimore, Maryland, 2005

Devil May Care by Sebastian Faulks, Penguin Books, London, 2009

Diamonds are Forever by Ian Fleming, Penguin Books, London, 2004

The Diamond Smugglers by Ian Fleming, Jonathan Cape, London, 1957

Doctor John Dee or The Original 007 by Robin Brumby, Dacorum College, Hemel Hempstead, Hertfordshire, 1977

The Essential Bond by Lee Pfeiffer and Dave Worrall, Boxtree, London, 2000

The Facts of Death by Raymond Benson, Hodder & Stoughton, London, 1998

For Special Services by John Gardner, Hodder & Stoughton, London, 1982

For Your Eyes Only: Ian Fleming and James Bond by Ben Macintyre, Bloomsbury, London, 2008

From Russia with Love; Dr No & Goldfinger by Ian Fleming, Penguin Books, London, 2002

Goldfinger by Ian Fleming, Penguin Books, London, 2002

High Time to Kill by Raymond Benson, Hodder & Stoughton, London, 1999

Ian Fleming by Andrew Lycett, Weidenfeld & Nicolson, London, 1995

Ian Fleming and James Bond: The Cultural Politics of 007 edited by Edward P. Comentale, *et al.*, Indiana University Press, Bloomington, 2005

Ian Fleming Introduces Jamaica edited by Morris Cargill, André Deutsch, London, 1965

Ian Fleming: The Man with the Golden Pen by Richard Grant, Mayflower Books, London, 1966

The James Bond Bedside Companion by Raymond Benson, Boxtree, London, 1988

The James Bond Dossier by Kingsley Amis, Jonathan Cape, London, 1965

James Bond: The Authorised Biography by John Pearson, Century, London, 2006

James Bond: The Man and His World by Henry Chancellor, John Murray, London, 2005

John Dee: Scientist, Geographer, Astrologer and Secret Agent to Elizabeth I by Richard Deacon, Frederick Muller, London, 1968

Licence Renewed by John Gardner, Jonathan Cape, London, 1982

The Life Line by Phyllis Bottome, Little, Brown & Co., Boston, 1946

The Life of Ian Fleming by John Pearson, Jonathan Cape, London, 1966

The Man Who Saved Britain by Simon Winder, Picador, London, 2006

The Man Who Was 'Q': The Life of Charles Fraser-Smith by David Porter, Paternoster Press, Exeter, 1989

The Man with the Golden Gun by Ian Fleming, Penguin Books, London, 2002

The Man with the Golden Gun by Ian Fleming, Jim Lawrence and Yaroslav Horak, Titan Books, London, 2004

Martinis, Girls and Guns by Martin Sterling, Robson, London, 2003

No Deals, Mr Bond by John Gardner, G.P. Putnam's Sons, New York, 1987

Octopussy by Ian Fleming, Jim Lawrence and Yaroslav Horak, Titan Books, London, 2004

One Girl's War by Joan Miller, Brandon Book Publishers, Dingle, Co. Kerry, 1986

On Her Majesty's Secret Service by Ian Fleming, Henry Gammidge and John McLusky, Titan Books, London, 2004

The Paradise Plot by Ian Fleming, Jim Lawrence, John McLusky and Yaroslav Horak, Titan Books, London, 2008

Polestar by Ian Fleming, Jim Lawrence and John McLusky, Titan Books, London, 2008

Public Faces by Harold Nicolson, Constable, London, 1932

Q, The Biography of Desmond Llewelyn by Sandy Hernu, S.B. Publications, Seaford, East Sussex, 2000

Quantum of Solace: The Complete James Bond Short Stories by Ian Fleming, London 2002

The Science of James Bond by Lois H. Gresh, Wiley, Hoboken, New Jersey, 2006

Secret Agents edited by Jeremy Packer, Peter Lang, Oxford, 2009

The Secret War of Charles Fraser-Smith by Charles Fraser-Smith with Gerald McKnight and Sandy Lesberg, Michael Joseph, London, 1981

Secret Warriors: Hidden Heroes of MI6, OSS, MI9, SOE and SAS by Charles Fraser-Smith with Kevin Logan, Paternoster, Exeter, 1984

Shark Bait by Ian Fleming, Jim Lawrence, Yaroslav Horak and Harry North, Titan Books, London, 2008

SilverFin by Charlie Higson, Puffin, London, 2005

The Sixth Column by Peter Fleming, Hart-Davis, London, 1951

The Spy Who Loved Me by Ian Fleming, Penguin Books, London, 2002

The Spy Who Loved Me by Ian Fleming, Jim Lawrence and Yaroslav Horak, Titan Books, London, 2005

The Third Hour by Geoffrey House, Chatto & Windus, London, 1937

Three Weeks by Elinor Glyn, Duckworth & Co., London, 1907

Thrilling Cities by Ian Fleming, Jonathan Cape, London, 1963

Tomorrow Never Dies by Raymond Benson, Hodder & Stoughton, London, 1997

The Traveller's Tree: A Journey through the Caribbean Islands by Patrick Leigh Fermor, John Murray, London, 1950

Win, Lose or Die by John Gardner, Hodder & Stoughton, London, 1989

You Only Live Once: Memories of Ian Fleming by Ivar Bryce, Weidenfeld & Nicolson, London, 1984

17F: The Life of Ian Fleming by Donald McCormick, Peter Owen, London, 1993

Index

Initials JB refer to James Bond; initials IF refer to Ian Fleming

Aki 106–7, 222
Amasova, Major Anya 118, 119, 120, 121, 224
Ambler, Eric 25, 35, 59
Amis, Kingsley 54, 165
    Colonel Sun 166, 167, 177, 264, 275
Anders, Andrea 224
Andress, Ursula viii, 42, 98, 218, 221
anti-Semitism 163, 234
Arterton, Gemma 232
Aston Martin 102, 182, 184–5, 187, 194, 196, 199, 200
Atkins, Vera 170
Aubergine, Achille 133–4, 193

Bambi 223
Baron Samedi 72, 115, 236
Beam, Gregg 157, 175
Bennett, Victoire 170
Benson, Raymond
    'Blast from the Past' 270
    DoubleShot 272–3
    High Time to Kill 172, 272
    'Live at Five' 272
    'Midsummer's Night Doom' 271–2
    Never Dream of Dying 175, 273
    The Facts of Death 167, 168, 271
    The Man with the Red Tattoo 273
    Zero Minus Ten 270–1
Berry, Halle 229–30
Bianca 225
Big, Mr 71–2, 73, 113, 114, 204, 235–6
    see also Kananga, Dr
Blackman, Honor 220
Blackwell, Blanche 35, 37, 39, 43, 45
Blackwell, Chris 41, 45
Blofeld, Ernst 89, 90, 91, 92–3, 107–8, 109–10, 112, 124–5, 131–2, 186, 187, 192, 240–3
Blush, Fatima 131, 132, 193, 226, 227
Bond, Andrew (JB's father) 47, 48, 55–6, 57, 58
Bond, Henry (JB's brother) 56, 57, 59

Bond, James
    007 code name 16, 22, 50, 63, 65, 67–8
    athleticism 49, 51, 59
    attitude to women 54
    awards and honours 50
    biography 47–68
    character vii–viii, 55
    drinking and smoking 52–4
    family background 47–9, 55–6
    family motto 42, 147
    gambling 15, 55, 58, 61, 63, 70, 154, 155
    linguistic skills 49, 51
    marriage 50, 91, 110, 215
    obituary 43–4, 49, 50, 165
    physical description 51
    prototype Bonds 12, 15–17, 66–7
    quipster Bond 102, 187, 191, 192, 194, 199
    wardrobe and accessories vii, 52
Bond, James (ornithologist) 24, 45, 66–7
Bond, Monique (JB's mother) 47–8, 55–6, 57–8
Boothroyd, Major 14, 37, 181–2, 183
Bouvar, Colonel Jacques 104
Bouvier, Pam 139, 140, 141, 195, 228
Brand, Gala 74–5, 177, 205
Brandt, Helga 106, 107, 187
Bright, Joan 19, 170–1
Broccoli, Albert R. ('Cubby') 41, 98, 108, 247
Brosnan, Pierce 67, 141, 150, 225
Bryce, Ivar 18, 22, 26, 33, 36, 39, 53, 173
Buckmaster, Maurice 165
Bullion 261
Bunt, Irma 90, 92, 93, 109, 110, 241–2
Burgess, Guy 27, 34, 35
Butcher, Professor Jo 259–60

Caplan, Paula 105, 220
cars 102, 182–5, 184–5, 187, 188, 189, 191, 193, 194, 196, 197, 198, 199, 200, 283–4

Caruso, Miss 188, 223
Carver, Elliot 144–6, 147, 198, 260–1
Carver, Paris 144, 145, 229
Carver, Rosie 113–14, 223
Case, Tiffany 75–6, 77, 111, 112, 113, 206–7, 223
Casino Royale
　film (1967 32, 33, 97–8, 169, 176, 193, 220–1, 234–5
　film (2006) 153–6, 168, 171, 174, 176, 200, 231, 235
　novel 15, 16, 28, 29–31, 34, 35, 45, 51, 53, 54, 62, 63, 65, 69–71, 81, 169, 173, 175, 180, 182, 202–3, 209, 233–4
　strip cartoon 37, 274
Chandler, Raymond 33, 35, 36, 38, 59
Chang 121, 122, 238
Chitty Chitty Bang Bang 41
Christie, Agatha 66
Churchill, Winston 2, 8, 11, 13, 19, 23, 170
CIA 14, 37, 44, 63, 103, 122, 155, 157, 158, 173, 174
Cigar Girl 261
Cleese, John 198
Colombo, Enrico 85
Colombo, Milos 126, 127, 225
computer games 280
Connery, Sean vii–viii, 41, 98, 108, 110, 130, 192, 220
Connolly, Cyril 24, 29, 44
continuation novels and short stories 166–7, 172, 173, 175, 263–74, 281–4
Cotton, Sydney 11
Coward, Noël 24, 25, 26, 28, 35
Craig, Daniel 153, 200, 231, 284
Crowley, Aleister 68, 163
Cumming, Commander Mansfield 161
Cuneo, Ernie 33, 39, 40
Cureo, Ernie 33, 76

Dahl, Bibi 126, 225
Dahl, Roald 25, 105
Dalton, Timothy 136
Dalzel-Job, Patrick 66
Dansey, Lieutenant-Colonel Sir Claude 164
Dario 139, 140, 141, 259
Davidov, Sasha 148–9, 261
Day, May 134, 135, 193, 227
Deaver, Jeffrey, *Carte Blanche* 282–4
Dee, Dr John 68
Delmer, Sefton 12, 17, 21
Dench, Judi 141, 168, 284
Dent, Professor 98, 99, 244
Derval, Domino 104, 105, 220

Derval, François 104, 105
Di Vicenzo, Comtesse Teresa (Tracy) 50, 89, 90, 91, 109, 110, 214–15, 222
Diamonds are Forever
　film 110–13, 174, 177, 187–8, 222–3, 239, 240, 242–3
　novel 9, 14, 32, 33, 35, 36, 37, 62, 75–7, 173, 176, 177, 180, 182, 203, 206–7, 239
Die Another Day 67, 150–3, 168, 169, 171, 173, 199–200, 229–31, 261–2, 273
　novelization 273
Dimitrios, Alex 154
Dolly 123, 124
Donovan, William 14, 15, 17, 18, 23, 63
Dr No
　film 41, 42, 98–100, 174, 176, 183, 218–19, 244, 250
　novel 9, 36, 37, 38, 51, 52, 54, 63, 67, 79–81, 171, 175, 176, 181, 182, 205, 208–9, 248–50
Draco, Marc-Ange 90, 109, 215
Drax, Hugo 74, 75, 121–2, 123, 124, 190, 191, 236–8
Dryden 153
Du Pont, Junius 81, 250
Dufour, Corinne 121, 122, 224, 238
Dunderdale, Commander Wilfred 12

Eden, Anthony 34, 37

Faulks, Sebastian, *Devil May Care* 175, 282
Fearing, Patricia 86, 211, 220, 226
Fekkesh 118–19
Fields, Strawberry 232
Fleming, Amaryllis (IF's half-sister) 3, 42
Fleming, Ann (née Charteris: IF's wife) 10, 17, 20, 22, 23–4, 25, 26, 27, 28, 29, 30, 32, 33, 34, 36, 37, 38–9
Fleming, Caspar (IF's son) 29, 30, 41
Fleming, Evelyn (IF's mother) 2, 3, 4, 5, 6, 7, 8–9, 10, 26, 56, 165–6
Fleming, Ian
　as a character in others' novels 5
　background research for novels 30, 31, 32, 33–4, 39–40
　in banking and stockbroking 6–8
　birth and early life 2–5
　book collection 4, 8, 55
　character and temperament 2, 3, 5, 7, 9
　death 45
　education 2, 4–5
　family background 1–2
　fatherhood 29, 41
　health and illnesses 6, 10, 25, 36, 39, 41, 45

interest in gadgetry 14, 23, 180–1
juvenilia 4
linguistic skills 4–5, 49
marriage 28
naval commission 11, 26
parallels with Bond viii, 49, 51, 56, 66
passion for fast cars 4, 33
political views 8, 10
publishing director 29
Reuters journalist 5–6
smoking and drinking 7, 17, 23, 25, 39, 45
starts writing Bond books 27, 28
Sunday Times foreign manager 23, 25–6, 31, 32, 35, 37, 39, 40, 41, 45
Swiss fiancée 5, 6, 56
wartime intelligence work viii, 10–11, 12, 13–21, 67
womanizing 2–3, 4, 6, 8, 9, 10, 11, 19, 23, 24, 38
writing routine 27, 32
Fleming, Michael (IF's brother) 15
Fleming, Peter (IF's brother) 2, 4, 7, 8, 10, 12–13, 19, 23, 26, 28, 29, 66, 170
Fleming, Robert (IF's grandfather) 1, 6
Fleming, Valentine (IF's father) 2
For Your Eyes Only
 film 124–7, 167, 172, 191–2, 225, 243, 253–4
 short story collection 26, 39, 83–6, 165, 178, 209, 211, 253
Frampton, Jean 171
Fraser-Smith, Charles 14, 181
From Russia With Love
 film 44, 100–1, 178, 184, 219, 242, 244, 247
 novel 33, 36, 37, 40, 49, 59, 66, 77–9, 164, 171, 175, 176, 178, 180, 207–8, 209, 243–7
Frost, Miranda 151–2, 153, 230

Gabor 261
gadgetry and guns 14, 23, 37, 54, 64, 180–201
Galore, Pussy 82, 83, 102, 103, 210, 220
Gardner, John 166, 172, 270
 Brokenclaw 267
 COLD 269–70
 Death is Forever 268
 For Special Services 173, 242, 265
 Icebreaker 265
 Licence Renewed 265
 Never Send Flowers 268
 No Deals, Mr Bond 266

Nobody Lives Forever 266
Role of Honour 266
Scorpius 266–7
SeaFire 268–9
The Man from Barbarossa 267–8
Win, Lose or Die 166, 267
geishas 216
Gettler, Adolph 71
Glaub, Hans 134, 135, 136, 252
Glidrose Productions 30, 48, 263, 264, 265
Gobinda 128, 130, 258
Godfrey, Admiral John 11, 15, 17, 18, 163, 164–5
Gogol, General 118, 119, 125, 127, 130, 134, 136, 138, 167, 178
GoldenEye 141–3, 168, 172–3, 175, 179, 195–6, 228–9, 260
 novelization 269–70
Goldeneye (IF's house) 22, 24, 35, 37, 45, 172
Goldfinger
 film 101–3, 168, 174, 184–5, 203, 219–20, 251, 252
 novel 17, 38, 39, 52, 81–3, 173, 180, 209–10, 250–2
Goldfinger, Auric 38, 81–3, 102–3, 108, 185, 250–1
Goldfinger, Erno 38
Gonzales, Hector 84, 125, 253
Goodhead, Dr Holly 121, 122, 123–4, 190, 224, 225
Goodnight, Mary 50, 94, 95, 117, 172, 180, 217–18, 223–4
Grant, Donald ('Red') 34, 77, 78–9, 100, 101, 180, 184, 244–7
Graves, Gustav 151, 152, 153, 200, 262
 see also Moon, Colonel Tan-Sun
Greene, Dominic 157, 158–9, 201, 231, 232, 254
Greene, Graham 30, 161
Grishenko, Boris 142, 143, 260
guns *see* gadgetry and guns
Gupta, Henry 144, 145, 146, 260

Hai Fat 116, 117
Hammond 166
Hargreaves, Admiral 167, 168
Havelock, Judy 84, 209, 211
Havelock, Melina 125, 126, 127, 191, 225
Henderson, Dikko 40, 106, 177
Higson, Charlie, *Young Bond* books 48, 280–1
'Hildebrand Rarity, The'
 short story 38, 64, 85–6, 139
 strip cartoon 274

Horak, Yaroslav 277
Horowitz, Sol 88
Hughes, Richard 40, 43, 177

Ian Fleming Publications 48, 263, 282
Ivanova, Pola 135, 224, 227

Janus *see* Trevelyan, Alec
Jaws 118–19, 120, 121, 122, 123, 124, 189,
  191, 238, 239
Jenkins, Geoffrey 263
John, Augustus 2, 3
Johnson, Celia 4, 8
Johnson, Giacinta 'Jinx' 151, 152, 153, 199,
  229–31
Jonathan Cape 29, 71, 89, 263, 264
Jones, Dr Christmas 149, 150, 229
Jones, Grace 227
Jordan, John 186

Kabira, Yusef 156, 159
Kalba, Max 119
Kananga, Dr 113, 114, 115, 188, 235–6
  see also Big, Mr
Kaufman, Dr 145, 260
Kemsley, Lord 11, 22, 25, 29, 30, 42
Kennedy, John F vii, 40, 59
Kerim Bey, Ali 100, 101, 184, 219, 247
Kerim, Darko 34, 77, 78, 164, 176
KGB 23, 93, 134, 136, 178, 180
Khan, Kamal 128, 129, 130, 258
Kidd, Mr 76, 110–11, 112, 113, 188, 239,
  240
Kil, Mr 152
Killifer, Ed 259
King, Elektra 148, 149, 150, 179, 198, 199,
  229, 261
King, Sir Robert 147, 148, 168
Klebb, Rosa 36, 77, 79, 100, 101, 175, 184,
  207, 243–4
Knight, Maxwell 162–3
Koskov, Georgi 136, 137, 138, 194, 258
Krebs 74
Krest, Elizabeth 85, 86, 211
Krest, Milton 85–6, 139, 140, 254, 259
Kriegler, Eric 126, 253
Krilencu 247
Kristatos, Aris 85, 126, 127, 253–4
Kronsteen 100, 101

Lamora, Lupe 138–9, 140, 141, 228
Largo, Emilio 87, 104, 105, 212, 254–5
Largo, Maximilian 132–3, 255
Lawrence, Jim 274–5, 277
Lazenby, George 108

Le Chiffre 69–70, 98, 153, 154, 155, 200,
  233–5
Lee, Bernard 167, 168
Lehmann, Rosamond 24, 26
Leigh Fermor, Patrick 30, 72
Leiter, Felix 36, 72, 73, 76, 83, 87, 94, 95,
  98, 102, 103, 104, 105, 111, 112, 113,
  114, 132, 133, 138, 139, 141, 155, 157,
  158, 173–5, 188, 228
Licence to Kill 138–41, 171, 173, 174, 195,
  228, 259–60
  novelization 267
Lippe, Count 86, 87, 104, 105
Live and Let Die
  film 113–15, 174, 175, 176, 188, 223,
    235–6
  novel 9, 18, 24, 30, 31–2, 33, 37, 55,
    71–4, 160, 165, 173, 176, 180, 204–5,
    235, 258
Living Daylights, The
  film 136–8, 168, 171, 174, 194–5,
    227–8, 258–9
  short story 42, 46, 95–6, 136, 183, 218,
    258
Llewelyn, Desmond 181, 184, 185, 188,
  189, 192, 194
Locque, Emile Leopold 125–6, 127, 191,
  253
Lorre, Peter 97, 234
Loti 228
Lynd, Vesper 51, 53, 70, 71, 98, 154,
  155–6, 159, 202–4, 209, 221, 231, 232

M 17, 63, 64, 66, 74, 84, 93, 109, 119, 136,
  139, 141, 144, 147, 148, 149, 150, 151,
  154, 156, 157, 158, 161, 162–9, 180, 487
McClory, Kevin 39, 41, 45, 98, 103
Maclean, Donald 27, 34, 35
McLusky, John 277
McVean Gubbins, Major-General Sir
  Colin 162
Magda 128, 226
Man with the Golden Gun, The
  film 115–17, 172, 175, 188–9, 223–4,
    257–8
  novel 9, 45, 50, 53, 59, 64, 93–5, 164,
    165, 166, 172, 173, 176, 209, 217–18,
    239, 255–7, 263, 264
  strip cartoon 274
Manuela 122, 225
martinis 16, 17, 53
Masterton, Jill 81, 82, 102, 209–10, 219,
  251
Masterton, Tilly 82, 83, 102, 203, 209, 210,
  219–20

Mathis, René 61, 70, 79, 154, 155, 156, 157, 158, 175–6
Maxwell, Robert 34, 147
Medrano, General 157, 158, 231, 232, 254
Melville, William 163–4
Messervy, Sir Miles 63, 164, 167, 168
Metro-Vickers spy trial viii, 6, 49, 57
MI5 37, 160, 164
MI6 viii, 160, 161
Michel, Vivienne 87–9, 212–14
Milovy, Kara 137, 138, 178, 227
Mitchell 156–7
Molony, Sir James 79, 91, 94, 178
Moneypenny, Miss 109, 119, 169–71, 200, 209, 227, 230
Montes, Camille 157, 158, 159, 231, 232
Moon, Colonel Tan-Sun 151, 152, 153, 261–2
see also Graves, Gustav
Moonraker
film 34, 121–4, 190–1, 224–5, 238
novel 31, 32, 51, 64, 74–5, 164, 171, 177, 182, 205, 236–7
Moore, Roger 41, 113, 133, 191
Morant, Sluggsy 88, 89, 239
Morzeny 178, 247
Mr Big *see* Big, Mr

Naomi 119, 224
Necros 137, 138, 258
Never Say Never Again 130–3, 169, 171, 174, 192–3, 226–7, 243, 255
Nick Nack 115, 116, 117, 258
Nicole 132, 227
Niven, David 41, 97, 169, 216, 220
No, Dr Julius 35, 79, 80, 98–9, 248–50

Obanno, Steven 153, 154
Oberhauser, Hans 62, 95
O'Brien-Ffrench, Conrad 66
Octopussy
film 127–30, 167, 171, 192, 218, 225–6, 258
short story collection 43, 46, 62, 95, 95–6, 178, 258, 263
strip cartoon 274
Oddjob 82, 83, 102, 103, 108, 251–2
On Her Majesty's Secret Service
film 108–10, 167, 186, 222, 242
novel 36, 42, 44, 47, 50, 52, 54, 59, 62, 64, 89–91, 165, 166, 172, 180, 203, 214–15, 241, 242
Onatopp, Xenia 141–2, 143, 196, 228
Orlov, General 128, 129, 130, 178, 258
O'Toole, Plenty 111–12, 222–3

Ourumov, Colonel Arkady 141, 142, 196, 260

Pearson, John 28, 48, 49, 54, 55, 56, 58, 60, 61, 62, 65, 66, 165–6, 263, 264
Pepper, Sheriff J.W. 114, 117, 175, 189
Petachi, Domino 132, 133, 226, 227
Petachi, Giuseppe 86–7
Petachi, Captain Jack 131
Pettigrew, Kathleen 169–70
Philby, Kim 40, 44
Pleasence, Donald 242
Ponsonby, Loelia 171–2
Popov, Dusko 15–16
Priestley, Margaret 170
Profumo, John 44
'Property of a Lady, The' 44, 46, 96, 128, 177
Pushkin, General Leonid 137–8, 195

Q 14, 123, 140, 180, 181, 184, 185, 187, 188, 190, 191, 192–3, 194, 195, 196–7, 198, 199, 200
see also gadgetry and guns
Quantum of Solace
film 156–9, 160, 168, 173, 174–5, 200–1, 231–2, 254
short story 36, 84–5, 254
Quarrel 71, 73, 80, 98, 99, 176
Quarrel Jr. 114, 176, 188

racism 74
Reilly, Sidney 163
Renard 148, 149, 150, 261
Richard, Marthe 34–5
Rider, Honeychile 36, 80, 81, 208–9
see also Ryder, Honey
Rimington, Stella 141, 168
'Risico' 38, 85, 124, 177, 253
Robinson, Charles 173
Romanova, Tatiana 77–8, 79, 100, 101, 207–8, 209, 219, 243
Roper, Barrington 36, 176
Russell, Mary Ann 83, 211
Ryder, Honey 99, 100, 218
see also Rider, Honeychile

Saito, Torao 40, 43, 177
Saltzman, Harry 41, 98, 100, 108
Sanchez, Franz 138–9, 140, 141, 228, 259
Scaramanga, Francisco 45, 94, 95, 115, 116, 117, 189, 224, 239, 255–8
Secret Intelligence Service (SIS) 12, 13, 19, 23, 26, 63, 160, 161–2
Sellers, Peter 98, 221

Shatterhand, Dr Guntram 92, 242
Simonova, Natalya 142–3, 196, 228–9
Skarbek, Krystyna 202
Skyfall 284
Slate 157
Smallbone, Penelope 171, 226
SMERSH 39, 51, 52, 54, 64, 65, 66, 69, 70, 71, 77, 78, 81, 100, 235
Smythe, Major Dexter 62, 95, 129, 258
Solitaire 72–4, 113, 114, 115, 204–5, 223
Spang, Jack 76–7, 239
Spang, Seraffimo 76, 239
Special Operations Executive viii, 13, 19, 66, 162, 170
SPECTRE 39, 86, 88, 89, 99, 100, 101, 104, 107–8, 131, 178, 186, 187, 240, 247
spoofs 44, 108
   see also *Casino Royale* film (1967)
Spy Who Loved Me, The
   film 118–21, 167, 168, 178, 189–90, 224, 239
   novel 3, 26, 40–1, 43, 52, 87–9, 183, 212–14, 239
   strip cartoon 274
Stamper 144, 145, 146, 147, 260
Steed, John 264–5
Stephenson, William 16–17, 18, 23, 43, 105, 165
Strangways, John 73, 79, 98, 176
Strap, Jack 239
strip cartoons 37, 274–9
Stromberg, Karl 118, 120, 190, 239
Sutton, Stacey 135, 136, 194, 227
Suzuki, Kissy 92, 93, 107, 108, 216–17, 222

Tanaka, Tiger 40, 91–2, 106, 107, 108, 177, 186, 187
Tanner, Bill 64, 168, 172–3
Taro, Miss 99, 218–19
Tee Hee 72, 114, 115, 188, 235, 236
30 Assault Unit viii, 20, 21, 66, 170
Thumper 223
Thunderball
   film 39, 45, 103–5, 174, 185, 220, 242, 255
   novel 19, 40, 41, 45, 52–4, 86–7, 169, 171, 173, 175, 182–3, 209, 211, 212, 241, 254–5
Tibbett, Sir Godfrey 133, 134, 194
Tiffy 217
Tomorrow Never Dies 143–7, 171, 173, 175, 196–8, 229, 260, 271
   novelization 271

Trench, Sylvia 218, 219
Trevelyan, Alec (Janus) 141, 142, 143, 196, 260
Troop, Captain 178
Trueblood, Mary 79, 171
Trueblood, Una 171
Truman-Lodge, William 259
TV series 32, 36–7, 39, 171, 279–80

Vallance, Ronnie 177
View to a Kill, A
   computer game 280
   film 133–6, 193–4, 227, 252
   short story 83, 133, 211, 252–3
villains 233–62
Vitali, Domino 87, 212
Volpe, Fiona 105, 220
Von Hammerstein 83, 84, 253
Von Schlaf, Countess Lisle 126, 225

Wade, Jack 142, 143, 145, 175, 196
Wai Lin 144–5, 146–7, 197, 229
Walken, Christopher 252
Warmflash, Dr Molly 229
Waugh, Evelyn 29, 33, 45
Welles, Orson 98, 234–5
Westbrook, Kate (Samantha Weinberg) 171, 281
Whisper 188
Whitaker, Brad 137, 138, 195, 258–9
White, Mr 153, 155, 156, 157
Whyte, Willard 111, 112, 187
Wint, Mr 76, 110–11, 112, 113, 188, 239, 240
women, Bond's 202–32
World is Not Enough, The 42, 147–50, 162, 168, 169, 171, 173, 179, 198–9, 229, 261
   novelization 271, 272
World War II vii, viii, 11–21, 161, 162, 164, 181

You Only Live Twice
   film 105–8, 167, 169, 186–7, 222
   novel 40, 43, 47, 62, 91–3, 177, 216–17, 241

Zao 151, 152, 199, 262
Zorin, Max 133, 134, 135, 136, 178, 193, 252–3
Zukovsky, Valentin 142, 148, 149–50, 168, 179